The Vegetable Lover's Cookbook

The Vegetable Lover's Cookbook

Shauna Cooney Brenner
Deborah Shields Smoot

Contemporary Books, Inc.
Chicago

Library of Congress Cataloging in Publication Data

Brenner, Shauna Cooney.
The vegetable lover's cookbook.

Includes index.
1. Cookery (Vegetables). I. Smoot, Deborah Shields.
II. Title.
TX801.B7 1983 641.6′5 83-1831
ISBN 0-8092-5642-8

Illustrations by Shauna Cooney Brenner

Published by Contemporary Books, Inc.
180 North Michigan Avenue, Chicago, Illinois 60601
Manufactured in the United States of America
Library of Congress Catalog Card Number: 83-1831
International Standard Book Number: 0-8092-5642-8

Published simultaneously in Canada by
Beaverbooks, Ltd.
150 Lesmill Road
Don Mills, Ontario M3B 2T5
Canada

To our mothers, Betty Cooney and Shirlee Shields, who fed us for all those years. To Ina Parkinson, Ellie Dombrowski, and Vera Cooney—the best cooks we know. And to Grandpa Wendell Smoot, whose green thumb and abundant harvest served as the inspiration for this book.

Contents

Preface

This cookbook began as an answer to Grandpa Smoot's green thumb and ended four years later as a collection of the best fresh vegetable recipes we could find from Washington, D.C., to Los Angeles. They range from the simple to the exotic. We've included some real surprises and hope you will be delighted to find new ways for old favorites. Thanks to all dear friends and relations who parted with secret sauces and family favorites to make our book unique. Thanks also go to husbands and children for eating all that zucchini while we tried things out. We've had a ball writing this book. Hope you and yours enjoy cooking from it.

Information for the Cook

TABLE OF EQUIVALENTS

16 ounces = 1 pound
16 fluid ounces = 1 pint
16 tablespoons = 1 cup
3 teaspoons = 1 tablespoon
4 cups = 1 quart
4 quarts = 1 gallon
8 quarts = 1 peck
4 pecks = 1 bushel
cream = half-and-half or coffee cream
double cream = whipping cream

CONTENTS OF CANS (common sizes— approximate contents)

8 ounces = 1 cup
picnic = 1¼ cups
no. 300 = 1¾ cups
no. 1 tall = 2 cups
no. 303 = 2 cups
no. 2 = 2½ cups
no. 2½ = 3½ cups
no. 3 = 4 cups
no. 10 = 12–13 cups

SUBSTITUTIONS

1 cup sugar = 1 cup honey and ½ teaspoon soda (reduce liquid in recipe by ¼ cup)
1 cup maple syrup and ¼ cup corn syrup (reduce liquid by ¼ cup)
1 cup sour milk = 1 tablespoon lemon juice or vinegar plus sweet milk to make 1 cup (let sit about 15 minutes before using)
1 cup butter = ⅞ cup corn, nut, or cottonseed oil
1 cup canned tomatoes = 1⅓ cups chopped tomatoes simmered 10 minutes

See each category for pound to cup equivalents of each vegetable.

Our vegetables tasted fresh after freezing in airtight, heavyweight plastic bags. They are easy to store and stack and you can see the contents.

Nutritive values of vegetables are from *Nutritive Value of American Foods in Common Units* by Catherine F. Adams, Agriculture Handbook No. 456, Agriculture Research Service, USDA.

SPECIAL MICROWAVE INSTRUCTIONS

To microwave frozen vegetables: the water inside the food does the cooking. Don't add more water when defrosting. Use 50 percent power to defrost. Drain and arrange in a serving dish covered with a lid or plastic wrap. Cook on high or 100 percent power 6 minutes or less per pound.

Don't add extra salt and remember to cook only 80 percent in the microwave because there is 20 percent residual cooking of the vegetables during standing time.

Thick-bottomed vegetables like broccoli need to be placed with the tips toward the center for best results. Remember, porous vegetables and those with high water content take less time to cook than dense ones. See any good microwave cookbook for detailed instructions for specific vegetables.

Asparagus

1 pound = 12 to 18 spears = 3 to 4 servings
4 spears = 12 calories, 1.3 grams protein, 2.2 grams carbohydrates, 110 milligrams potassium, vitamins A and C

It is best to eat this delectable plant within 24 hours after it is picked or it may get woody and tough. Store with the ends in water as you would cut flowers.

Asparagus is always best steamed. Use a tall, slender pan with boiling water in the bottom. Cover and steam for approximately 7 minutes.

To freeze: Remove any scales from the stems and cut off the dry, dirty ends. Scald in boiling water 3 to 4 minutes. Chill in cold water. Drain. Package in airtight containers. Freeze.

Soups

COLD ASPARAGUS SOUP

You can easily freeze this soup.

1 pound asparagus (cut off tough ends)
1½ tablespoons butter or margarine
½ cup sliced onion (can use green onions)
1½ tablespoons flour
1½ cups chicken broth
1½ cups milk (can use 2 percent low-fat)
1 cup half-and-half
2 tablespoons lemon juice
2 tablespoons dry sherry (optional)
Onion salt and pepper to taste
1 cup sour cream (optional) for garnish

Either microwave asparagus about 6 minutes or until tender in ¼ cup water, or cook on stove in a small amount of water until tender. Reserve cooking water.

Melt butter in large pot. Sauté onions until tender. Stir in flour and cook 1 to 2 minutes. Add asparagus water, chicken broth. Heat to boiling and simmer 5 minutes. Add asparagus and puree in blender.

To mixture in blender add milk, half-and-half, lemon juice, and sherry. Season to taste with onion salt and pepper. Chill overnight or longer.

Serve with sour cream garnish, if desired. Freezes well. More milk or water can be added if the soup is too rich for your taste.

SERVES 6 to 8

ICED CREAM OF ASPARAGUS SOUP

A quick version of the more complicated cold asparagus soup.

2 pounds fresh asparagus
Bunch scallions
¼ cup water
¼ cup flour
2 cups chicken stock or chicken bouillon (strong)
Salt and pepper
1 cup heavy cream

Cut the tips off 2 pounds fresh asparagus and set them aside. Snap off the tough white ends and discard them. Wash the stalks, slice them into 2-inch pieces, and put them in a saucepan with the scallions, thinly sliced, and ¼ cup water.

Cover the pan and cook the vegetables very slowly until they are tender. Add flour and blend well. Pour in chicken stock and stir the mixture until it reaches the boiling point. Remove the pan from the heat and strain. Add salt and pepper to taste and set the soup aside to cool.

Add cream and blend well. Garnish the soup with the reserved asparagus tips, cooked until tender and chilled, and serve it very cold.

SERVES 4 to 6

CURRIED ASPARAGUS SOUP

Interesting and different—a good introduction to a fish entree.

1 pound fresh asparagus
5 cups chicken stock
4 tablespoons butter
4 tablespoons flour
1½ teaspoons curry powder
3 egg yolks
¾ cup light cream
½ teaspoon lemon juice
Salt and freshly ground pepper

Remove the woody ends of the asparagus. Peel and coarsely chop the stalks, reserving the tips. Simmer the chopped asparagus in chicken stock, covered, for 45 minutes. Cool slightly and puree in the blender. In another pan, melt the butter, add flour, and cook for 2 minutes. Stir in curry powder. Add the pureed stock and bring to a boil, stirring frequently, until it has thickened slightly. At this point, the soup can be set aside.

Cook the reserved tips in boiling, salted water for 4 minutes; drain and set aside for garnish.

While the soup reheats, beat the egg yolks into the cream. Stir them into the soup and heat to a point just under the boil, so that the soup has thickened and is slightly glossy. Remove from heat, add lemon juice, and season to taste. Garnish with the reserved tips.

SERVES 4 to 6

Salads

ASPARAGUS VINAIGRETTE

A cold vegetable to use instead of salad, a great way to use leftover asparagus.

6 servings asparagus (8 to 10 spears per serving)
½ dill pickle, finely chopped
1 tablespoon onion, finely chopped
1 teaspoon capers, finely chopped
¼ teaspoon dry mustard (optional)
1 teaspoon salt
2 tablespoons wine vinegar
1 teaspoon lemon juice (optional)
½ cup olive oil
1 tablespoon parsley, finely chopped
1 tablespoon pimiento, finely chopped
1 teaspoon hard-cooked egg white, finely chopped

Cook asparagus. Although you can use leftover asparagus very nicely, the vegetable is firmer if you have boiled and chilled it especially for this dish. Allow 8 to 10 spears of asparagus per serving, with about 2 tablespoons of sauce.

To make vinaigrette sauce, place in a screw-top jar the dill pickle, onion, capers, dry mustard (optional), salt, wine vinegar, lemon juice (optional), and olive oil. Put top on jar and shake vigorously for about ½ minute, or until all ingredients are well blended.

Remove top and add parsley, pimiento, and hard-cooked egg white. Stir well and pour over asparagus. Makes about ¾ cup.

SERVES 6

ARTICHOKE, ASPARAGUS, AND TRUFFLE SALAD

This green salad looks beautiful in a glass bowl.

On a nest of lettuce leaves, arrange equal amounts of cold cooked artichoke bottoms, cooked asparagus tips, and truffles cut in julienne or thinly sliced raw mushrooms. Serve with vinaigrette French dressing.

SERVES 4 to 6

MARINATED ASPARAGUS SPEARS

So quick and easy—marinated in Wishbone Italian dressing.

1 pound thin asparagus spears, cooked 5 to 7 minutes in boiling water and drained, *or* 1 can extra-long green asparagus spears
5 small pieces pimiento

Marinate asparagus spears in Wishbone Italian dressing for at least 24 hours. Serve 4 or 5 spears per serving. Handle spears carefully as they are very fragile. Serve with a small piece of pimiento.

SERVES 5

HONEY-ASPARAGUS SALAD

Honey and vinegar dressing over fresh vegetables, marinated artichoke hearts, and hard-cooked eggs.

1 cup asparagus, sliced diagonally into 2-inch pieces
1 cup green beans, sliced diagonally into 2-inch pieces
1 cup fresh or thawed frozen peas
2 tablespoons cider vinegar
2 teaspoons honey
1 teaspoon garlic salt
¼ teaspoon pepper
1 cup sliced radishes
1 6-ounce jar marinated artichoke hearts
2 hard-cooked eggs, quartered

Arrange asparagus, beans, and fresh peas (do not cook thawed peas) in a vegetable steamer and steam over boiling water just until barely tender when pierced, about 2 to 4 minutes. Plunge vegetables in cold water to cool quickly; drain well. Cover and refrigerate if cooked ahead.

In a bowl or jar, combine vinegar, honey, garlic salt, and pepper. Drain marinade from artichoke hearts into vinegar mixture; stir or shake together. Pour dressing over vegetables. Add radishes and marinated artichoke hearts to vegetables, then toss together; cover and chill about 30 minutes. Garnish with eggs.

SERVES 4

Side Dishes

ASPERGES MIMOSA

2 pounds fresh asparagus, woody ends cut off, *or* 2 1-pound packages full-length frozen asparagus spears
2 hard-cooked egg yolks
Salt and pepper
¼ pound butter
½ cup dry fine bread crumbs

Cook asparagus just until tender. Sieve the egg yolks and add salt and pepper. Heat butter until bubbly. Stir in bread crumbs. Place hot asparagus on plate. Sprinkle bread crumbs in a wide band down middle of asparagus. Spoon egg yolks down middle of bread crumbs.

SERVES 8

FRESH ASPARAGUS WITH HERB BUTTER

A simple, beautiful way to show off the season's best asparagus—for people who like to taste their vegetables.

1½ pounds fresh asparagus
6 tablespoons butter, softened
¼ teaspoon dried thyme, *or* 2 teaspoons fresh
¼ teaspoon paprika
½ teaspoon salt
2 tablespoons lemon juice

Snap the woody ends of the asparagus and run a vegetable peeler lightly over the stalks; this way they will be fork-tender. Store them until cooking time in the refrigerator, with the ends of their stems in water. Cream the butter with the remaining ingredients; set aside at room temperature.

Just before serving, cook the asparagus in boiling, salted water for about 7 minutes, until just tender. Drain well, lay in a warmed serving dish, and spread on the herb butter so that it melts evenly over the hot asparagus.

SERVES 4 to 6

Main Dishes

ASPARAGUS-MUSHROOM-CHEESE BAKE

A good brunch dish—the sauce can be made ahead of time and refrigerated.

1 cup sliced fresh mushrooms
2 teaspoons butter
1 teaspoon lemon juice
1 egg, beaten
1 cup milk
1 teaspoon dry mustard
½ teaspoon salt
1 cup American cheese, diced
2½ pounds asparagus, cooked
Parsley
6 mushroom caps, sautéed in butter

Sauté mushrooms in butter and lemon juice until tender. In top of double boiler combine egg, milk, mustard, and salt. Stir and cook over hot water until hot and slightly thickened (do not overcook). Blend in cheese. Heat until sauce has thickened. Add sautéed mushrooms and heat. Serve over hot cooked asparagus. Garnish with parsley and mushroom caps.

SERVES 6

SPRINGTIME ASPARAGUS QUICHE

A simple vegetable quiche made with Swiss cheese.

1½ pounds fresh asparagus, *or* 2 10-ounce packages frozen asparagus spears
1 quart water
1 teaspoon salt
1 package commercial piecrust mix
1 egg white, beaten slightly
8 bacon slices, sautéed until crisp, drained and crumbled
½ pound natural Swiss cheese, grated
4 eggs
1½ cups half-and-half
⅛ teaspoon nutmeg
⅛ teaspoon salt
Dash pepper
6 cherry tomatoes, halved

Wash asparagus; break off and discard tough portion. Scrape ends of asparagus with vegetable parer. Set aside 16 of the best spears for decoration. They should be 5 inches long. Cut rest of asparagus into ½-inch pieces.

In a large saucepan, bring 1 quart water to boiling; add 1 teaspoon salt and the asparagus. Bring back to boiling; reduce heat; simmer, covered, 5 minutes. Drain; rinse asparagus under cold water.

Prepare piecrust as package label directs. Roll pastry to form a 12-inch circle. Flute edge if using pie plate. Brush bottom surface with egg white.

Preheat oven to 400°F.

Sprinkle bottom of pie shell with bacon and cheese, then cut-up asparagus. In a medium bowl, beat eggs with half-and-half, nutmeg, salt, and pepper until mixture is combined. Pour egg mixture into pie shell. Arrange tomato halves and reserved asparagus spears, spoke fashion, on pie. Bake 35 minutes, or just until puffy and golden. Serve warm.

SERVES 12

ASPARAGUS–SWISS CHEESE CUSTARD

A light entree especially nice with ham.

1¼ to 1½ pounds asparagus, tough ends removed
1 small onion, finely chopped
2 tablespoons butter or margarine
2 tablespoons all-purpose flour
¼ teaspoon salt
⅛ teaspoon each ground nutmeg and white pepper

1½ teaspoons chicken bouillon granules, dissolved in 1 cup hot water
½ cup whipping cream
2 teaspoons lemon juice
4 ounces Swiss cheese, *or* 1 cup shredded Swiss cheese
4 eggs

In a frying pan with enough boiling water to cover, cook the asparagus 8 minutes, or until fork tender. Drain, dash with cold water, then pat dry with paper towels. Cut into ½-inch pieces; you should have 1¾ cups.

In a 3-quart pan over medium heat, sauté the onion in the butter until limp. Blend in the flour, salt, nutmeg, and pepper; then gradually stir in the bouillon and the cream. Cook, stirring, until mixture boils and thickens. Remove from heat. Stir in the lemon juice and the cheese.

In a large bowl, beat the eggs. Slowly stir cheese mixture into eggs, blending well; then stir in the asparagus. Pour custard into a buttered 5- or 6-cup ring mold. Bake in a 325° F. oven for 40 minutes, or until a knife inserted in the center comes out clean. Let stand 10 minutes, then invert on a platter.

SERVES 6

ASPARAGUS SOUFFLÉ ROLL

Courage is required to attempt this soufflé, but if all goes well the results are spectacular!

6 tablespoons butter or margarine
¾ cup all-purpose flour (unsifted)
1 teaspoon dry mustard, or more
½ teaspoon salt, or more
3½ cups milk
4 eggs, separated
1 to 1¼ pounds fresh asparagus, *or* 1 pound package frozen asparagus spears
1 cup (about ¼ pound) shredded Swiss cheese

Line the bottom of a greased 10″ × 15″ × 1″ jelly-roll baking pan with foil; grease and flour foil and set pan aside.

In a saucepan, melt butter over medium heat. Stir in flour, 1 teaspoon mustard, and ½ teaspoon salt; then very gradually stir in 3 cups milk. Cook, stirring until thickened, 8 to 10 minutes, then remove from heat. Measure out 1 cup of this white sauce and set aside.

Slightly beat egg yolks and gradually beat in all but the 1 cup white sauce. Beat egg whites until they form firm, moist peaks and fold into egg yolk mixture. Pour into the prepared pan and bake in a 325° F. oven for 35 to 40 minutes, or until center springs back when lightly touched.

While soufflé bakes, snap off tough ends of the fresh asparagus and place spears in a vegetable steamer; cook, covered, over boiling water until tender (about 7 minutes). Or, cook frozen spears according to package instructions; drain. Keep spears warm.

In the saucepan, combine the reserved 1 cup white sauce and remaining ½ cup milk; set over medium heat. Stir in the Swiss cheese and cook, stirring, until cheese melts. Taste and add more mustard and salt if desired. Keep warm.

When soufflé is done, immediately invert it onto a clean towel. Spoon about ¼ cup of the cheese sauce across one of the narrow ends; arrange asparagus over sauce. Using the towel for support, roll up the soufflé to enclose asparagus; place, seam side down, on a serving platter.

To serve, pour cheese sauce into a separate dish to pass at the table.

SERVES 6

ASPARAGUS DUTCH STYLE

The Dutch usually eat white asparagus, but fat green asparagus tastes fine too. Include ham or chicken and this makes a good light meal.

3 pounds asparagus
Water
1½ teaspoons salt
4 eggs
12–16 thin slices cooked ham or chicken
1½ cups chicken stock
½ pound butter
Salt
Nutmeg

Clean and cut tough ends from asparagus. Tie in large loose bunch. In a deep pan bring to a boil 1 quart water and 1½ teaspoons salt. Stand asparagus bunch in boiling water, keeping tips up. Cover and let boil from 7 to 15 minutes. Asparagus should be tender but not overcooked. Drain asparagus on rack and keep warm.

Hard-cook eggs for 10 minutes. Peel and mash them. Poach slices of ham or chicken in chicken stock over moderate heat for 20 minutes. Keep warm. Melt butter.

Put some mashed egg on each plate. Add 2 or 3 tablespoons of the melted butter, a little salt, and a sprinkle of nutmeg. Each person mixes this with a fork, making a thick sauce. Put slices of ham or chicken and some asparagus beside the sauce.

SERVES 4

Beans

1 pound = 3 cups sliced = 4 servings
1 cup cooked = 31 calories, 6.8 grams carbohydrates, 2 grams protein, vitamins A, B, C

Get your beans to the refrigerator immediately. Store them in an airtight plastic bag—and it helps to sprinkle a little water in the bag. They will only keep 4 to 5 days before they start to wilt. To cook, cut on a slant, French style, in long, thin pieces or leave whole. Snap off tips. Boil in salted water for 7 minutes. Adding a little lemon helps green beans stay green.

To freeze: Rinse, snap off tips, scald in boiling water, chill in ice water, drain, freeze.

Soups

GERMAN GREEN BEAN AND SAUSAGE SOUP

Well worth the effort and time it takes.

4 slices bacon, cut crosswise into ½-inch strips
2 medium-sized onions, chopped
1 large (50 ounce) can chicken broth, regular strength
4 medium-sized thin-skinned potatoes, peeled and chopped into ½-inch cubes (about 2 pounds)
2 medium-sized carrots, thinly sliced
¼ cup chopped parsley
1 teaspoon dill weed
½ teaspoon marjoram leaves
¼ teaspoon white pepper
1 pound Polish sausage, bratwurst, or frankfurters, thinly sliced
1 pound green beans, cut into 1-inch lengths

Place a 5- to 6-quart kettle over medium heat. Cook bacon until lightly browned. Spoon off about 1 tablespoon of drippings. Add onions and cook until limp. Add all remaining ingredients except sausage and green beans; bring to a boil, reduce heat and simmer until potatoes are tender when pierced with a fork (approximately 45 minutes).

With a slotted spoon lift out about half the vegetables and set aside. Using the same spoon, slightly mash remaining vegetables into broth to thicken soup. Return reserved vegetables to kettle, adding sausage and green beans. Bring to a boil and cook uncovered, stirring occasionally, until beans are tender (about 15 minutes).

MAKES 3½ QUARTS

Salads

MONETTA'S MARINATED BEAN SALAD

Great and keeps a long time in the refrigerator. We always have this salad at our Fourth of July picnic. This is a flexible salad; use what you have on hand, and it will still taste good.

1 16-ounce can green beans, drained, *or* 1 pound fresh beans cooked and drained
1 16-ounce can wax beans, drained
1 16-ounce can kidney beans, drained and rinsed
1 onion, chopped
1 cup cauliflower flowerets, cut small
1 cup each sliced carrots and celery, boiled 5 minutes
1 cup sliced, fresh mushrooms

MARINADE

½ cup oil
⅔ cup vinegar
½ cup sugar
Little salt and pepper

Combine vegetables and marinate overnight in the above dressing.

SERVES 8 to 12

CHILI-SPICED BEAN SALAD

A must at a cookout—good with hamburgers.

1 pound fresh green beans, french cut
1 3-ounce can *each* red kidney beans, pinto beans, and garbanzos
1 3-ounce can whole kernel corn
½ cup thinly sliced green onion
¼ cup chopped parsley
1 cup sliced celery
1 4-ounce can diced green chilies

Lettuce (optional)

CHILI DRESSING

¾ cup olive oil or salad oil
¼ cup wine vinegar
1 clove garlic, minced or pressed
1½ teaspoons salt
1 teaspoon *each* chili powder and oregano leaves
¼ teaspoon liquid hot pepper seasoning

Place the beans, garbanzos, and corn in a large colander. Rinse with water; drain well. In a salad bowl (about 4-quart size) combine the bean mixture, green onion, parsley, celery, and chilies.

To make chili dressing, combine in a small bowl or jar with a cover the oil, vinegar, garlic, salt, chili powder, oregano leaves, and liquid hot pepper seasoning. Stir or shake to blend thoroughly.

Pour the chili dressing on the vegetable mixture, stirring to coat all ingredients. Cover and chill, stirring several times, for 6 hours or overnight. Transfer salad to a serving container or lettuce-lined platter.

SERVES 8 to 10

CHRISTMAS MARINATED BEAN SALAD

The most colorful of the marinated salads.

½ bell pepper, minced
3 cups french-cut green beans
1 3-ounce can petite pois peas
1 2-ounce jar pimiento
½ cup diced celery
1 onion, minced
½ teaspoon garlic salt
Salt and pepper to taste
1 cup vinegar
½ cup vegetable oil
½ cup sugar
Any two of the following:
1 16-ounce can garbanzos
1 16-ounce can kidney beans
1 16-ounce can wax beans
1 16-ounce can whole-kernel corn

Mix pepper, green beans, peas, pimiento, celery, onion, and seasonings. Drain all the canned vegetables. Combine salad with the vinegar, oil, and sugar.

This is the basic recipe. To this you can add any two from the list of garbanzos, kidney beans, wax beans, and corn. Let the salad marinate for several hours or overnight.

SERVES 8 to 12

Main/Side Dishes

GREEN BEANS BISCAY

1 tablespoon butter or margarine
2 onions, chopped fine
2 garlic cloves, chopped fine
1 small green pepper, chopped fine
1 cup tomato puree
1½ pounds green beans, snapped or cut
½ pound ham, cut in ½-inch cubes
½ cup dry white wine (optional—may use water)
Salt, thyme, cayenne

Melt butter in a large saucepan and sauté onions, garlic cloves, and green pepper over very low heat. When the onions turn slightly golden, add tomato puree and let the mixture simmer for 5 minutes. Add green beans, ham, and dry white wine. Season to taste with salt, thyme, and cayenne.

Cover the saucepan and let the mixture simmer for 25 to 35 minutes, or until the beans are tender. Add small amounts of wine or water if the sauce reduces too much during cooking. There should be about ¼ cup liquid remaining when the beans are cooked.

SERVES 6 to 8

STRING BEANS MEXICAN

½ cup minced onion
6 tablespoons salad oil
2 8-ounce cans string beans, drained, *or* 1 pound fresh beans, cut and cooked
2 8-ounce cans tomato sauce
2 tablespoons sugar
1 teaspoon salt
2 teaspoons lemon juice

Combine ingredients in baking dish. Bake for 20 minutes in a 350°F. oven. May be prepared ahead of time and frozen or refrigerated.

SERVES 6 to 8

GREEN BEANS DAL BOLOGNESE

Green beans, simple and beautiful.

1½ pounds fresh green beans
2 tablespoons olive oil
1 clove garlic, mashed
1 tablespoon snipped fresh rosemary *or* ½ teaspoon dried
Salt and pepper

Snip the beans on the diagonal into 2-inch pieces and set them aside in cold water until dinner time. Then cook them in boiling, salted water for 10 minutes; drain. Toss them in a saucepan over low heat with the oil, garlic, rosemary, salt, and pepper. Serve at once.

SERVES 6

GOURMET VEGETABLE CASSEROLE

A creamed vegetable side dish.

1 medium white onion
2 pounds green beans, raw fresh or frozen French-sliced
1 cup water chestnuts, sliced
1 cup bamboo shoots, sliced and well drained
Salt and pepper
2 10½-ounce cans undiluted mushroom or celery soup
2 ounces grated Parmesan cheese
French-fried onions, crushed

Chop onion and sauté until tender. Layer all ingredients in a buttered baking dish, starting with 1 pound green beans, then half the water chestnuts, bamboo shoots, salt, pepper, and soup which has been mixed with sautéed onion. Sprinkle with 1 ounce cheese and repeat another layer.

Bake for 25 minutes at 400°F. Remove from oven and cover with topping of crushed french-fried onions. Return to oven for 5 to 10 minutes until topping is golden brown.

SERVES 6 to 8

GREEN BEAN CASSEROLE WITH SOUR CREAM

This recipe can be made a day ahead if necessary.

½ cup onion, sliced thin
1 tablespoon minced parsley
2 tablespoons butter or margarine
2 tablespoons flour
1 teaspoon salt
¼ teaspoon pepper
½ teaspoon grated lemon peel
1 cup sour cream
5 cups fresh green beans, *or* 3 3-ounce cans, *or* 9 ounces frozen
½ cup grated yellow cheese
2 tablespoons melted butter
½ cup bread crumbs or cracker crumbs

Cook onion and parsley in 2 tablespoons butter or margarine until tender, not brown. Add flour, salt, pepper, and lemon peel. Add sour cream and mix well. Stir in beans. (If using canned beans, drain. If using frozen beans, cook first, then drain.) Put in a casserole dish; top with grated cheese. Combine butter and bread crumbs or cracker crumbs, and put on top of casserole. Bake at 350°F. for 30 minutes.

SERVES 4 to 6

Cooney '82

Beets

1 pound = 4 medium beets = 2 cups cooked and diced
1 cup cooked = 54 calories, 1.9 grams protein, 12.2 grams carbohydrates, 354 milligrams potassium, vitamins A and C

Beets are really a "two-crop" crop. You can eat not only the bottom red roots, but the leafy tops also. Beets seem to grow everywhere and don't pick up many of the common garden diseases.

Cut the tops off 2 inches above the crown and wash. Be careful. If you cut the taproot the beet will bleed when cooked. For mature beets you will have to cover with salted water and boil 30 minutes to an hour. When they cool, scrape the skin off and serve.

To freeze: Cut off tops 2 inches above the crown. Boil for 30 minutes in salted water completely covering the beets. Slide the skin off and dice or slice. Package in bags and freeze.

Soups

ICED CUCUMBER AND BEET SOUP

Serve this soup with a few slices unpeeled cucumber and an ice cube in the soup plate.

1 clove garlic
½ teaspoon salt
2 cups finely chopped cucumber
1 cup chopped cooked beets
4 cups sour cream
1 cup milk
2 teaspoons chopped parsley
2 teaspoons chopped chives
Salt and pepper

Finely chop garlic clove with salt, and mix thoroughly with cucumber and beets. Add sour cream, milk, parsley, and chives, and salt and pepper to taste. Chill.

SERVES 12 to 16

FRESH BEET BORSCH

An old-fashioned method.

1 bunch beets
1 quart water
Juice of 1 lemon
¼ cup sugar
½ teaspoon salt
Dash pepper
2 eggs
6 tablespoons sour cream
6 scallions, sliced thinly

Bring water to boil. Add beets and cook slowly for 1 hour. Remove beets and peel. Add lemon juice and sugar to the water. Simmer slowly 5 minutes. Add salt and pepper. Grate the beets into the soup stock. Simmer 20 minutes. Remove from heat and allow to cool to room temperature or colder.

Beat the eggs. Slowly add the borsch to the eggs, mixing as you pour. Strain and serve chilled. Top each bowl with a tablespoon of sour cream and float on it 1 scallion sliced thinly.

The amounts of sugar and lemon juice are purely arbitrary, depending on the cook's taste and the sweetness of the beets. The suggested quantities are a starting point.

SERVES 6

SWEET-AND-SOUR BORSCH

Plain yogurt dabbled over each individual portion dresses this sweet-tart soup.

3 medium-sized beets with leafy tops
1 tablespoon salad oil
1 small onion, chopped
1 pound lean ground pork or beef (optional)
2 large carrots, diced
2 cups coarsely shredded red or green cabbage
¼ cup lemon juice
2½ tablespoons sugar
¼ teaspoon dill weed
2 tablespoons chicken bouillon granules dissolved in 6 cups water
Salt and pepper
Plain yogurt

Trim the fresh, tender-looking leaves from beet stems; discard stems and coarse leaves. Rinse tender leaves and chop. Peel beets and shred coarsely; set aside.

Heat the oil in a 5-quart pan over medium heat. Add the onion and meat (if used) and cook, stirring, until onion is limp and meat is browned. Add the beets and tops, carrots, cabbage, lemon juice, sugar, dill, and bouillon. Cover and simmer over low heat for 45 minutes, or until beets and cabbage are tender. Season with salt and pepper to taste. Serve with yogurt.

SERVES 4 to 6

Salads

BEETS IN WHIPPED CREAM

1 3-ounce can whole beets
Vinegar (enough to cover beets)
6 to 12 whole cloves, depending on taste
½ cup cream, whipped, or sour cream
Horseradish to taste
Salt to taste
Garlic to taste
Whole cloves to garnish

Marinate beets in vinegar with cloves, then remove cloves. With a teaspoon, hollow out a deep well in top of each beet. Fill with whipped cream which has been beaten with horseradish. Strengthen to your liking with salt and a faint bit of garlic. Stick cloves in each beet. Use 2 to 3 beets per person. Serve ice cold.

SERVES 4

SWEET-AND-SOUR BEETS

6 medium beets
1 tablespoon sugar
¼ cup vinegar
2 teaspoons butter
1 tablespoon cornstarch
Salt and pepper to taste

Cut off beet tops, leaving 2 inches of the stems. Clean well; place in pot and cover with boiling water. Cook until tender. Slip off outer skins and dice. You should have 3 cups. Strain and save one cup of water in which beets were cooked. Add sugar, vinegar, and butter. Thicken with cornstarch and cook to consistency of cream. Add diced beets, salt, and pepper, and heat.

SERVES 4 to 6

BEETS IN MUSTARD DRESSING

Served on a bed of lettuce.

6 cups fresh or canned cooked beets, cut in julienne strips
Lettuce
Chopped hard-cooked eggs

MUSTARD DRESSING

1 tablespoon white wine vinegar
2 tablespoons lemon juice
2 teaspoons sugar

¼ cup Dijon mustard
⅓ cup olive oil
1 tablespoon finely chopped parsley
3 tablespoons snipped fresh dill, *or* 1 teaspoon dried
Salt and pepper

Combine the vinegar, lemon juice, and sugar; stir until the sugar has dissolved. Add the mustard and olive oil and whisk until the dressing is creamy. Stir in the parsley and dill, and add salt and pepper to taste. Combine the beets and dressing and chill at least 4 hours or overnight. Serve on salad greens with a chopped egg garnish.

SERVES 12

MOLDED BEET SALAD

This salad is especially good with cold beef, turkey, or shellfish.

1 3-ounce package lemon gelatin
1¾ cups hot liquid (water and beet juice)
3 tablespoons vinegar
2 teaspoons minced onion
¼ cup horseradish
1 teaspoon salt
½ cup diced cucumber
1 cup diced cooked beets or canned beets
Mayonnaise

Dissolve gelatin in hot liquid. Add vinegar, onion, horseradish, and salt. Chill until slightly thickened; fold in cucumbers and beets. Turn into mold. Double recipe for more than six. Serve with mayonnaise.

SERVES 6

WATERCRESS AND BEET SALAD

Fresh beets
Watercress
French dressing

Use whatever quantities you desire.

Wash and trim beets, leaving an inch of the stem, and bake them in a moderate oven (350° F.) until they are tender. Cool, peel, and slice them thinly; combine them with an equal amount of young watercress. Serve with French dressing.

BEET AND ORANGE SALAD

Orange slices
Cooked beets
Endive hearts
French dressing

Put alternate slices of oranges and cold cooked beets on halved hearts of endive. Chill the salad and serve with vinaigrette French dressing.

Side Dishes

BEETS WITH GREENS

4 beets, 2 inches in diameter, with tops
Water to cover
½ teaspoon salt
2 tablespoons margarine
Lemon wedges or slices

Wash beets carefully. Cut tops from beets, leaving about 1½ inches of stem. Put beets in boiling water and boil gently until tender. Wash greens well and cut into 2-inch lengths with kitchen shears or with sharp knife on chopping board. Remove beets from kettle when tender and slip off skins. Cook greens in small amount of beet liquid 5 to 7 minutes. Add peeled beets to greens in kettle to keep hot. When greens are tender, all juice should be absorbed. Add salt and margarine, stirring in lightly.

Arrange greens in mound in vegetable dish.

Cut beets in slices or wedges and place around the outside of the greens. Garnish with slices of lemon if the beets are cut in wedges or with wedges of lemon if beets are cut in slices.

SERVES 4

HARVARD BEETS WITH HONEY

3 cups beets, cooked and sliced
⅓ cup beet liquid
2 tablespoons raw honey or brown sugar
¾ teaspoon salt
1 tablespoon flour or cornstarch
¼ cup water
3 tablespoons lemon juice

Follow method in above recipe for preparing and cooking beets. Remove skins and slice. Mix beet liquid, honey, and salt. Heat in saucepan.

Combine flour and water and stir until smooth. Stir into boiling liquid and continue stirring until thickened and clear. Add lemon juice and sliced beets. Heat briefly and serve.

SERVES 6

PIQUANT BEETS

Cloves give this recipe its flavor.

⅓ cup butter or margarine
1 teaspoon onion salt
1 tablespoon sugar
1 teaspoon cloves
3 tablespoons vinegar
4 cups beets, diced and cooked until tender

Melt butter. Stir in onion salt, sugar, cloves, and vinegar. Cook 3 minutes over low heat. Add hot beets; toss lightly.

SERVES 6 to 8

BEETS WITH ORANGE

Delightful with ham or beef.

½ cup sugar
1 teaspoon salt
1 tablespoon cornstarch
½ cup vinegar
2 tablespoons beet juice
Juice and grated rind of 1 orange
3½ cups fresh or canned small beets, cooled and drained
3 tablespoons butter
Dash nutmeg

In a saucepan mix sugar, salt, cornstarch, vinegar, beet juice, and orange juice. Bring to a boil and stir until clear. Stir in orange rind and beets. Heat gently, and before serving add butter and nutmeg.

SERVES 6 to 8

Pickles and Relishes

THE BEST PICKLED BEETS

8 to 12 large whole beets, uncooked
2 cups sugar
2 cups water
2 cups vinegar
1 teaspoon whole cloves
1 teaspoon whole allspice
1 tablespoon cinnamon (or 1 3-inch stick)
1 lemon, thinly sliced
Hard-cooked eggs (optional)

Cook beets until tender crisp (or use canned whole beets). Slice crosswise. Cook all remaining ingredients until just boiling. Cool slightly and pour over beets.

Hard-cooked eggs may also be added. In 24 to 48 hours, they will be beet-colored through the whites—hence "beet eggs."

MAKES 20 cups

QUICK PICKLED BEETS

Quick and easy, but so good.

3 cups sliced beets, cooked and drained, *or* 2 #3 cans sliced or whole beets
½ cup sugar
½ cup beet juice
½ cup vinegar
¾ teaspoon cinnamon
¼ teaspoon cloves
¼ teaspoon allspice

Cook and drain beets. Combine sugar, beet juice, vinegar, and spices in a saucepan. Add beets and heat to boiling. Put in a glass jar; cover and put in refrigerator. Will keep for several weeks.

MAKES 2 pints

BEETS IN SOUR CREAM

This is a treat—almost like a borsch!

1½ pounds small beets
1 10½-ounce can consommé soup
¼ cup butter, melted
1 tablespoon flour
1¼ cups sour cream
2 tablespoons Madeira red wine or wine vinegar
¼ teaspoon allspice
Salt and pepper to taste

Scrub beets. Simmer in concentrated consommé 45 minutes, until tender. Drain. Set aside. Melt butter. Blend in flour, stirring constantly. Gradually add sour cream, wine, allspice, salt, and pepper. Add beets. Stir and simmer until hot and well coated.

SERVES 8

ORANGE-GLAZED BEET RELISH

Don't serve ham without it! Always at our Easter dinner.

¼ cup honey
½ to 1 teaspoon grated orange peel
¼ cup orange juice
¼ cup lemon juice
½ teaspoon salt
1 16-ounce can (2 cups) julienne-style beets, well drained

Combine honey, orange peel, and juices with salt. Add beets and mix gently. Refrigerate several hours, turning occasionally. Drain and serve as a relish.

MAKES 4 cups

Cooney

Broccoli

1 pound = 2 3-inch heads = 4 cups flowerets
1 cup cooked = 40 calories, 4.8 grams protein, 7.0 grams carbohydrates, 414 milligrams potassium, large amounts of vitamin A (3,880 units), and vitamin C

Broccoli is a member of the Brassica family which includes cabbage, cauliflower, and brussels sprouts. They are all cool-weather crops that can be planted early in the season for a summertime harvest.

Broccoli will stay tender up to 5 days, so don't ever peel garden-fresh stems. Before cooking, soak broccoli 30 minutes in cold, salty water to crisp it and drive out insects. Steam 5 to 10 minutes depending on size.

To freeze: Trim bottom stalks, remove leaves. Slice into equal-sized pieces. Soak 30 minutes in cold salty water, steam 5 minutes, plunge into ice water, drain, package, freeze.

Dip

HOT BROCCOLI DIP

1 1-pound package frozen chopped broccoli
2 ribs celery, chopped
1 medium white onion, chopped
¾ stick margarine
1 5-ounce can mushroom pieces
1 5-ounce roll garlic cheese
1 10¾-ounce can cream of mushroom soup
1 5-ounce can water chestnuts, sliced
1 teaspoon Worcestershire sauce

Cook broccoli as directed and drain well. Sauté celery and onion in margarine until tender. Add mushrooms, cheese, cream of mushroom soup, and broccoli. Stir well and heat until cheese is melted. Add water chestnuts and Worcestershire sauce. Serve in chafing dish.

Use as dip for fresh vegetables.

SERVES 20 to 24

Soups

FRESH BROCCOLI SOUP

The basic soup base can be used with a variety of fresh vegetables.

BASIC SOUP BASE

2 large baking potatoes, peeled
1 bunch celery
1 onion, minced
1 10¾-ounce can chicken broth

MAKES 3 CUPS

Wash and chop vegetables. Put into a large pot with chicken broth. Cover and cook until soft. Put through blender. Add more broth if necessary to make blend possible. Store in refrigerator or freeze for future use.

2 bunches broccoli
1 clove garlic, crushed
2 carrots, cut up
1 10¾-ounce can chicken broth
3 cups Basic Soup Base
2 tablespoons butter
2 tablespoons sour cream or low-calorie imitation sour cream
Rosemary
Salt and pepper
Lemon juice

Cover and cook broccoli, garlic, and carrots in chicken broth until soft. Blend. Add more broth if necessary. Heat together broccoli–chicken broth mixture, 3 cups Basic Soup Base, butter, and Imo or sour cream. Add seasonings to taste and more chicken broth for desired consistency.

SERVES 4 to 6

BROCCOLI-CHEESE SOUP

3 tablespoons butter
2 tablespoons minced onion
3 tablespoons flour
4 cups milk
1 pound broccoli, fresh or frozen. Cook and drain to make 1½ cups.
Salt to taste
1 teaspoon Worcestershire sauce
1 cup grated Cheddar cheese (sharp)

Melt butter and add onion. Blend in flour and add milk. Cook until smooth and fairly thick. Add broccoli, salt, and Worcestershire sauce. Add grated cheese just before serving.

SERVES 4

Salads

LAYERED VEGETABLE-HERB SALAD

We make this in a deep glass dish—and get 20 requests for the recipe every time we take it to a luncheon.

4 cups shredded iceberg lettuce
⅔ cup chopped parsley
1 green or red bell pepper, coarsely chopped
2 cups coarsely chopped broccoli or cauliflower
3 stalks celery, thinly sliced
2 large carrots, shredded
2 zucchini, shredded
1 10-ounce package frozen peas, thawed
1 cup mayonnaise
1 cup sour cream
2 tablespoons Dijon mustard
1 tablespoon fresh rosemary leaves, minced, *or* 1 teaspoon dried rosemary, crumbled
1 tablespoon fresh basil leaves, minced, *or* 1 teaspoon dried
1 tablespoon fresh oregano leaves, minced, *or* 1 teaspoon dried
2 teaspoons garlic salt
½ teaspoon pepper
2½ cups shredded Cheddar cheese
½ cup thinly sliced green onion
½ pound bacon, crisply browned and crumbled

In a shallow 4-quart serving dish, place lettuce in an even layer. Distribute parsley, pepper, broccoli, celery, carrots, zucchini, and peas in even layers over lettuce. Mix together mayonnaise, sour cream, mustard, rosemary, basil, oregano, garlic salt, and pepper. Spread evenly over top. Sprinkle cheese and green onion over top. Cover and chill up to 24 hours. Just before serving, sprinkle bacon over top.

SERVES 10 to 12

MARINATED BROCCOLI AND GRAPEFRUIT SALAD

This is an interesting combination that works!

1 grapefruit
2 pounds fresh broccoli
1 cup Italian style dressing
¼ cup fresh squeezed lemon or grapefruit juice
¼ cup sliced black pitted olives
2 tablespoons pimiento strips, *or* 1 small chopped tomato

Peel and section grapefruit over bowl to reserve juice. Drain and refrigerate sections. Clean and trim fresh broccoli; cook until tender but still crisp (about 5 minutes). Drain carefully and place in a shallow glass dish. Combine dressing and lemon or grapefruit juice. Pour over hot broccoli. Cover and chill until very cold, at least 2 hours. Chill remaining ingredients. When ready to serve, arrange on serving dish and add grapefruit sections. Garnish with black olives and pimiento strips or tomatoes.

SERVES 6 to 8

MOLDED BROCCOLI SALAD

For a summer luncheon side dish.

1½ cups consommé or beef stock, heated
1 envelope gelatin, unflavored
1 to 1½ large bunches broccoli, cooked and chopped
½ cup mayonnaise
½ cup sour cream
6 hard-cooked eggs, chopped

Dissolve gelatin in heated consommé. Put into mixer with broccoli. Add the mayonnaise and sour cream and mix. Fold in eggs. Pour into molds, refrigerate, and let stand about 3 hours.

SERVES 8

Side Dishes

CASSEROLE SUPREME OF BROCCOLI AND CARROTS

You can easily use other combinations of vegetables if you like.

8 thin slices of bread
½ pound sliced processed American cheese
2 tablespoons flour
½ stick butter
2 cups sweet milk
Dash pepper
2¼ to 3 cups half-cooked cut broccoli and cooked, diced carrots
Paprika

Trim crusts from bread and make 4 sandwiches using a slice of cheese, trimmed to fit bread, in each. Cut each sandwich in half diagonally. Make a cream sauce with the flour, butter, milk, and pepper. Add pieces of cheese cut from sandwich slices and other slices of cheese to cream sauce, stirring until melted.

Add well-drained vegetables; pour mixture into a rather large, shallow casserole. Stand sandwiches in it with their points up. Sprinkle freely with paprika. Cook in a 350°F. oven about 30 minutes, or until sandwiches are lightly browned.

SERVES 8

ELLIE'S BROCCOLI CASSEROLE

Colorful side dish of broccoli and white rice.

2 pounds chopped fresh broccoli, steamed 7 minutes, *or* 2 10-ounce packages frozen chopped broccoli, thawed and drained
2 cups cooked white rice, drained
2 10¾-ounce cans cream of mushroom soup
1 small can Cheese Whiz
½ medium onion, chopped

Put broccoli and rice together in a casserole. Heat soup, cheese, onion; pour over rice and broccoli and mix. Heat in a 350°F. oven for 45 minutes.

SERVES 8

BROCCOLI BAKE

You can freeze this one and it is a perfect side dish with beef or chicken.

2 10-ounce packages frozen chopped broccoli, *or* 5 cups fresh broccoli, chopped, cooked, and drained
½ package dry herb stuffing
Water
Butter
1 10¾-ounce can cream of celery soup
⅓ can sweetened condensed milk

Cook broccoli until tender. Drain. While cooking, mix stuffing with water and butter per package directions.

Mix broccoli and stuffing. Place in a buttered baking dish. Mix soup and milk together, both undiluted, and pour on top. Bake at 350°F. for 1 hour.

SERVES 6 to 8

SOUPED-UP BROCCOLI

Quick, and children like it.

1 large bunch fresh broccoli cut into 1-inch pieces
2 cups diced carrots
1 10¾-ounce can cream of mushroom soup
½ cup grated Cheddar cheese
½ cup toasted bread crumbs

Cook the broccoli for 5 minutes, placing the stems underneath and the flowerets on top. Drain. Cook the carrots for 10 minutes. Drain.

In a buttered 2-quart casserole, arrange a layer of half the broccoli, then a layer of half the carrots. Repeat. Cover the vegetables with the undiluted mushroom soup. Top with the grated cheese and bread crumbs. Bake 35 to 45 minutes at 350°F.

SERVES 6 to 8

Main Dishes

BROCCOLI AND CHEESE CASSEROLE

Serve with fruit salad and rolls for a tasty autumn meal.

3 cups farmer style cottage cheese
1 10-ounce package chopped frozen broccoli, thawed but not cooked
3 eggs, beaten
¼ cup vegetable oil
¼ pound yellow cheese, diced
3 tablespoons flour
1 teaspoon salt
Minced onion or onion salt

Combine all ingredients and pour into an oiled 9″ × 13″ pan. Cover pan and place in another pan of hot water. Bake in a 350°F. oven for 1 hour or until set.

SERVES 8

BROCCOLI GARDEN SCRAMBLE

A wok dish.

2 tablespoons salad oil
1 large clove garlic, minced
1 cup broccoli flowerets, cut in ½-inch slices
1 cup cauliflower flowerets, cut in ½-inch slices
3 tablespoons water
½ cup carrots, cut diagonally in ½-inch slices
½ red bell pepper, cut in ½-inch strips
Salt and pepper
Whole roasted cashews

Place wok over high heat. When wok is hot, add 1 tablespoon of the oil. When oil is hot, add garlic; stir-fry for 30 seconds. Add broccoli and cauliflower and stir-fry for 1 minute. Add 2 tablespoons of the water; cover and cook, stirring frequently, for about 3 minutes. Remove vegetables from wok and set them aside.

Add remaining 1 tablespoon oil to wok. When oil is hot, add carrots and red pepper. Stir-fry for 1 minute. Add remaining 1 tablespoon water; cover and cook, stirring occasionally, for about 2 minutes or until vegetables are tender-crisp. Return broccoli and cauliflower to wok and stir-fry to heat through. Add salt and pepper to taste and garnish with cashews.

SERVES 2 to 3

BROCCOLI SOUFFLÉ

3 tablespoons butter
3 tablespoons flour
1 cup milk
1 teaspoon salt
Few grains nutmeg
1 teaspoon lemon juice
1 cup cooked broccoli
4 eggs, separated
1 cup grated Cheddar cheese (optional)
1 tablespoon grated onion (optional)

Melt butter in a saucepan; blend in flour. Gradually add milk, stirring constantly, and cook until smooth and thick. Add salt, nutmeg, and lemon juice. Measure 1 cup of the cooked chopped broccoli. Beat egg yolks; add cream sauce to them and let cool. If you are assembling the soufflé hours before serving time, keep it in a cool place; then before cooking, beat egg whites until stiff but not dry, and fold into broccoli mixture.

Bake in a 300°F. oven for 1½ hours, or for a quicker method, bake soufflé at 425°F. for 25 minutes. Serve with Hollandaise or cheese sauce.

SERVES 6 to 8

ELLEN'S GARDEN-PATCH CASSEROLE

Good, and can be a meatless main dish.

1½ cups cottage cheese
½ cup sour cream
1 tablespoon flour
3 eggs
2 tablespoons minced onion
1½ teaspoons salt
¼ teaspoon pepper
2 10-ounce packages chopped broccoli, cooked and drained
1 17-ounce can whole kernel corn
¼ cup grated Parmesan cheese

Beat or blend cottage cheese, sour cream, flour, eggs, onion, salt, and pepper together. Fold in vegetables. Pour into a 2-quart casserole; top with Parmesan cheese. Bake at 325°F. for 45 minutes.

SERVES 6 to 8

BROCCOLI-SUNFLOWER SEED SOUFFLÉ

Broccoli is the base for many great vegetarian delights.

1 pound fresh broccoli, chopped, *or* 1 10-ounce package frozen chopped broccoli
3 tablespoons butter or margarine
3 tablespoons flour
1 cup milk
1 teaspoon salt
¼ teaspoon nutmeg
⅛ teaspoon pepper
¼ cup sunflower seeds
5 eggs, separated
Grated Parmesan cheese

CHEESE SAUCE

2 tablespoons butter or margarine
2 tablespoons flour
1 cup milk
½ teaspoon dry mustard
½ teaspoon salt
Dash cayenne
1¼ cups shredded Cheddar cheese

Cook broccoli just until tender; drain in a colander, pressing with a spoon to remove liquid. In a 2-quart pan, melt butter over medium heat. Blend in flour, stirring until mixture bubbles. Remove from heat and gradually stir in milk until smooth; cook, stirring constantly, until it boils and thickens. Add salt, nutmeg, pepper, sunflower seeds, and the drained broccoli. Remove from heat; add 5 egg yolks and beat vigorously with a wooden spoon.

Beat egg whites until moist, soft peaks form; carefully fold into broccoli mixture. Pour into a 1- to 1½-quart soufflé dish that has been well greased and dusted with grated Parmesan cheese. If desired, top with about 1 tablespoon sunflower seeds. Bake in a 375°F. oven for 30 minutes or until a wooden pick inserted comes out clean.

While soufflé bakes, prepare Cheese Sauce.

In a small pan over medium heat, melt butter. Add flour and cook until mixture bubbles. Remove from heat and gradually stir in milk; cook, stirring until it boils and thickens. Stir in mustard, salt, cayenne, and cheese. Stir until cheese is melted. Pass at the table.

SERVES 4

EASY CHICKEN DIVAN

Tastes as good as the time-consuming divan.

2 10-ounce packages frozen broccoli, *or* 2 bunches fresh
2 cups sliced cooked chicken, *or* 3 chicken breasts, cooked and boned
2 cans condensed cream of chicken soup
1 cup mayonnaise
1 teaspoon lemon juice
½ cup shredded sharp processed cheese
½ cup soft bread crumbs
1 tablespoon butter or margarine, melted
Pimiento strips

Cook broccoli in boiling, salted water until tender. Drain and arrange stalks in a greased baking dish. Place chicken on top. Combine soup, mayonnaise, and lemon juice and pour over chicken. Sprinkle with cheese. Combine bread crumbs and butter; sprinkle over all. Bake at 350°F. for 25 to 30 minutes, or until thoroughly heated. Trim with pimiento strips.

SERVES 6 to 8

CHICKEN-BROCCOLI BAKE

The best of the chicken-broccoli bunch.

8 chicken breasts, with skins
3 cups water
2 bay leaves
1 teaspoon celery salt
2 bunches broccoli spears, *or* 2 10-ounce packages frozen broccoli spears
⅔ cup grated Parmesan cheese

SAUCE

2 cups milk
2 8-ounce packages cream cheese, softened
1 teaspoon salt
½ teaspoon garlic salt
½ cup grated Parmesan cheese

Put chicken breasts, water, bay leaves, and celery salt in a large pot. Simmer 1 hour; cool. Discard liquid. Skin and bone chicken. Cook broccoli spears until just tender and cool. Drain. Set aside.

In a saucepan mix milk, cream cheese, salt, garlic salt, and ½ cup Parmesan cheese. Stir and cook until thick. Put broccoli in bottom of greased 9″ × 9″ baking dish. Pour in 1 cup sauce. Put in chicken breasts. Pour in remaining sauce. Sprinkle ⅔ cup Parmesan cheese on top. Bake at 350°F. for 25 minutes.

SERVES 6 to 8

BEEF-BROCCOLI PIE

A whole meal in itself made with crescent refrigerator rolls.

1 10-ounce package frozen broccoli, *or* 3 cups fresh broccoli, chopped
1 pound ground beef
¼ cup onion, chopped
2 tablespoons flour
¾ teaspoon salt
¼ teaspoon garlic salt
1¼ cups milk
1 3-ounce package cream cheese, softened
1 egg, beaten
2 packages refrigerator crescent rolls
4 ounces Monterey Jack cheese, sliced

Cook frozen broccoli according to package directions, or steam fresh broccoli until just tender; drain well. set aside. Brown beef and onion. Pour off fat. Stir in flour, salt, and garlic salt; add milk and cream cheese. Cook and stir until thick and smooth. Slowly add a cup of hot mixture to beaten egg. Mix well. Gradually stir this back into skillet. Cook and stir over medium heat until thick (2 minutes). Stir in drained broccoli.

Unroll one package of rolls. On a floured surface, press 4 opened sections together, forming a 12″ × 7″ rectangle. Seal perforations. Roll to a 12-inch square. Repeat with other package of rolls. Set one 12-inch square aside. Fit other into bottom of a 9″ × 9″ pan; trim. Put in meat mixture. Top with sliced cheese. Cover with remaining dough square. Trim; seal edges with fork, and cut a few slits on crust. Brush crust with milk. Bake at 350°F. for 30 minutes. Cover with foil and bake 10 minutes more. Let stand 10 minutes before serving.

SERVES 6

HAM, CHEESE, AND BROCCOLI STRATA

12 slices bread, crusts trimmed
¼ pound sharp American cheese, sliced
1 10-ounce package frozen chopped broccoli, cooked and drained, *or* 1 bunch fresh broccoli, cooked and drained
2 cups ham, chopped fine
6 eggs, slightly beaten
3½ cups milk
2 tablespoons instant minced onion
½ teaspoon salt
¼ teaspoon dry mustard
Cheddar cheese, grated

Cut 12 circles from bread; set aside. Fit remaining scraps of bread in a 9″ × 13″ × 2″ buttered pan. Place American cheese in a layer over the bread; add layer of broccoli, then ham. Put circles of bread on top.

Combine eggs, milk, onion, salt, and mustard; pour over bread. Refrigerate 6 hours or overnight. Bake, uncovered, 55 minutes at 325°F. Sprinkle with Cheddar cheese 5 minutes before done. Let stand 10 minutes before cutting into squares.

SERVES 6

TURKEY BUFFET CASSEROLE

4 ounces (2 cups) medium-wide noodles
1 10-ounce package frozen broccoli spears, *or* 1 bunch fresh broccoli
3 tablespoons margarine
3 tablespoons flour
1 teaspoon salt
¼ teaspoon pepper
¼ teaspoon prepared mustard
2 cups milk
1 cup (¼ pound) grated American cheese
2 cups diced turkey
⅛ cups slivered almonds

Cook noodles as directed. Cook frozen broccoli as directed, or steam fresh broccoli until just tender; drain well. Dice broccoli stems but leave flowerets whole.

In a saucepan, melt margarine over low heat; stir in flour, salt, pepper, mustard, and milk. Cook, stirring constantly, until thick and smooth. Remove from heat; stir in cheese until melted.

In a greased shallow casserole, arrange noodles, broccoli stems, and turkey; pour cheese sauce over all. Arrange flowerets on top, pressing lightly into sauce. Sprinkle with almonds. Bake uncovered at 350°F. for 15 minutes or until bubbling hot.

SERVES 4 to 6

Brussels Sprouts

1 pound = 40 sprouts = 3½ cups
1 cup cooked = 56 calories, 6.5 grams protein, 9.9 grams carbohydrates, 425 milligrams potassium, vitamins A and C

One hearty plant can give you 100 sprouts! They should appear compact and bright green when you pick them. Soak 30 minutes, then cook in water, or sauté. Always parboil sprouts before using them in a casserole. You'll need to peel the outer leaves of the larger ones and cut a shallow X in the bottom to even the cooking. Cook in 2 inches of boiling water for 7 minutes.

To freeze: Peel outer leaves. Soak in salted water 30 minutes to drive out insects. Scald 4 minutes. Plunge in cold water. Drain, package, freeze.

Soup

BRUSSELS SPROUTS BISQUE

A brussels sprouts soup.

1½ pounds brussels sprouts
1 large bay leaf
1 thin slice garlic
1 whole clove
6 thin slices onion
3 sprigs parsley
Salt, pepper, nutmeg, marjoram to taste
1½ quarts beef stock
½ cup sweet cream
3 egg yolks, well beaten

Wash and trim brussels sprouts and put them in boiling salted water with bay leaf, garlic, clove, onion, and parsley. Cook the sprouts, uncovered, until they are tender. Drain the vegetables well and rub them through a fine sieve into a large saucepan. Season to taste with salt, pepper, nutmeg, and marjoram. Stir in beef stock and bring the liquid to a boil. Remove the saucepan from the heat and beat in cream mixed with egg yolks, beating briskly to prevent curdling. Return the saucepan to the heat and bring the soup almost to a boil, stirring constantly. Serve the soup at once.

SERVES 12

Salads

DILLY BRUSSELS SPROUTS

2 pounds fresh or frozen brussels sprouts
Salt and pepper to taste
1 cup Italian dressing
1 teaspoon dill weed
2 tablespoons shredded green onions or dehydrated chives

In salted boiling water, cook brussels sprouts until just tender. Drain. Add remaining ingredients and chill in covered container overnight. Serve with crackers as hors d'oeuvres. Fresh mushrooms may be added.

SERVES 10 to 12

MARINATED BRUSSELS SPROUTS

Will keep in refrigerator up to 10 days.

2 10-ounce packages frozen baby brussels sprouts, *or* 1¼ pounds fresh sprouts, outside leaves removed
½ cup tarragon vinegar
½ cup salad oil
1 small fresh garlic, crushed
1 tablespoon sugar
1 teaspoon salt
1 medium white onion, cut in ¼-inch rings

Cook frozen sprouts according to directions, or steam-cook fresh sprouts until done, but still green and firm. Combine vinegar, oil, garlic, sugar, and salt. Beat with fork. Add drained sprouts and onion rings.

Refrigerate 24 hours or more. Drain and serve.

SERVES 6

ZUCCHINI AND BRUSSELS SPROUTS SALAD

A wonderful new way to serve vegetables.

1 teaspoon salt
Water
2 cups fresh brussels sprouts
2 zucchini, unpared and sliced
¼ cup green onions, sliced
1 cup vegetable oil
¼ cup fresh lemon juice
¼ cup vinegar
2 cloves garlic, crushed
2 teaspoons seasoned salt
1 teaspoon sugar
½ teaspoon dry mustard
½ teaspoon salt
¼ teaspoon red chilies, crushed
Salad greens
10 tomato slices or cherry tomatoes

Bring 2-inch-deep salted water to a boil. Add brussels sprouts. Cover and return to a boil. Reduce heat; simmer until just crisp tender, about 4 or 5 minutes. Plunge immediately into cold water.

Cut brussels sprouts into thin wedges. Toss with zucchini and onions. Set aside. Shake oil, lemon juice, vinegar, garlic, seasoned salt, sugar, dry mustard, salt, and chilies in covered jar to blend. Pour over vegetable mixture. Cover. Refrigerate 4 to 24 hours, stirring occasionally. Serve on salad greens. Garnish with tomatoes.

SERVES 10

Side Dishes

BRUSSELS SPROUTS LOUISIANA

Sweet potatoes, pineapple, maple syrup make brussels sprouts a vegetable everyone will eat!

3 cups sliced, cooked sweet potatoes
2 cups pineapple, cut into small pieces
1 cup maple syrup
1 pound cooked brussels sprouts
3 tablespoons butter
1 cup cooked chestnuts (optional)

Make a ring of overlapping rounds of sliced cooked sweet potatoes, alternating them with small pieces of pineapple. Sprinkle potatoes and pineapple with maple syrup and glaze them in the oven, basting frequently with syrup. Fill the center of the ring with cooked brussels sprouts sautéed in butter and mixed with cooked chestnuts (optional) sautéed in butter.

SERVES 8 to 12

SAUTÉED BRUSSELS SPROUTS

Cloves give this an interesting flavor—good with ham.

1½ pounds brussels sprouts
1 medium-sized onion, chopped
2 whole cloves
1 bay leaf
¼ cup butter

Pick over brussels sprouts and discard wilted leaves; soak sprouts for 15 minutes in lightly salted tepid water and drain. Cook the sprouts with onion, cloves, and bay leaf in enough boiling salted water to cover for 10 to 15 minutes, or until sprouts are tender. Drain well. Heat butter, add drained sprouts, and sauté over low heat, shaking the pan frequently, until they are delicately browned. Serve very hot.

SERVES 3 to 4

BRUSSELS SPROUTS IN CELERY SAUCE

The celery sauce is like a white sauce.

1½ pounds brussels sprouts
1 cup chopped celery
3 tablespoons butter
2 tablespoons flour
Light cream
Celery salt, white pepper, nutmeg
½ cup grated cheese

Pick over brussels sprouts and discard wilted leaves; soak sprouts for 15 minutes in lightly salted tepid water and drain. Cook sprouts in boiling salted water to cover for 10 to 15 minutes, or until tender. Drain and keep hot. Cook celery in boiling salted water until tender. Drain celery, reserving stock.

In the top of a double boiler heat butter and blend in flour. Stirring constantly, gradually add enough hot celery stock and light cream to make 2 cups sauce. Season to taste with celery salt, white pepper, and freshly grated nutmeg. Add celery to sauce and pour over the brussels sprouts. Sprinkle the top with grated cheese and brown cheese under the broiler.

SERVES 6

SOUTHERN SPROUTS

1 pound brussels sprouts
Boiling water
3 slices bacon
1 tablespoon butter or margarine
1 medium-sized onion, chopped
2 small tomatoes, seeded and diced
Salt and freshly ground pepper
Sour cream

Trim brussels sprouts, cut in half, and rinse. Arrange sprouts in a vegetable steamer and cook, covered, over boiling water for 8 to 10 minutes or until just tender when pierced. Drain well.

Meanwhile, cook bacon in a wide frying pan over medium heat until crisp. Drain and crumble. Discard all but 2 tablespoons of the drippings. Add butter and onion to drippings and cook until onion is limp. Stir in the tomatoes and bacon, and add salt and pepper to taste. Heat through. Transfer sprouts to the onion mixture and mix well. Turn into a serving dish and pass sour cream to spoon over individual servings.

SERVES 4

BRUSSELS SPROUTS AND PECANS

Made with stuffing mix—a complete side dish.

2 10-ounce packages frozen brussels sprouts, thawed, *or* 2 pounds fresh sprouts, washed and drained
1 cup packaged stuffing mix

SAUCE

3 tablespoons margarine
4 tablespoons flour
¾ cup nonfat dry milk
1¾ cups boiling chicken broth
¼ teaspoon nutmeg
¼ cup chopped pecans

Preheat oven to 400° F. Cook brussels sprouts uncovered in small amount of salted boiling water until tender.

To prepare sauce, melt margarine over low heat and blend in flour. Cook 1 minute, stirring. Add dry milk, then boiling broth at once, beating with wire whisk to blend. Cook and stir until sauce comes to boil and thickens. Remove from heat; stir in nutmeg and pecans.

Place cooked brussels sprouts in an oiled 1½-quart casserole. Pour in cream sauce and top with stuffing mix. Bake until topping is lightly browned (about 10 minutes).

SERVES 8

Cabbage

1 pound = 4 cups shredded
1 cooked cup = 29 calories, 1.6 grams protein, 6.2 grams carbohydrates, 236 milligrams potassium, vitamin A, and some vitamin C

Cabbage needs attention or it will attract several types of pests. However, it has been cultivated for 4,000 years, so that should encourage you! There are three kinds of cabbage: green, smooth-leaved; red, smooth-leaved; and green, curly-leaved, "Savoy."

You may need to soak cabbage in salted water if insects are evident. You can refrigerate and store for up to two months. To cook, cut stem and core from center, take off outer leaves. You can cook cabbage whole, steaming approximately 10 minutes. Red cabbage takes longer to cook and will discolor unless vinegar or wine is added to the cooking water.

To freeze: We don't recommend it! It loses its texture.

Soups

CABBAGE SOUP

Smooth and rich.

3 medium potatoes, diced
3 medium carrots, diced
3 medium onions, diced
2 cloves garlic
4 to 6 cups chicken stock or broth
¼ teaspoon white pepper
1 small head cabbage, cut fine
Croutons (optional)

Place the potatoes, carrots, onions, and garlic in a saucepan. Add chicken stock or broth and bring to a boil. Simmer for 30 minutes. Add pepper. Salt should not be added until you taste the soup because as a general rule, the broth or stock will have enough salt in it.

Add finely chopped cabbage to the soup, but reserve 1 to 2 cups to be added later. Simmer for an additional 15 minutes. Remove from heat and transfer soup to a blender and blend until smooth. Return to the soup pot. At this point, add the cabbage which was reserved, and keep hot. May be served with croutons.

SERVES 4 to 6

CABBAGE ALMOND SOUP

2 cups finely chopped cabbage
½ cup chopped blanched almonds
2 tablespoons margarine
1 teaspoon caraway seed
2 teaspoons salt
¼ teaspoon paprika
½ cup water
1 egg, well beaten
1 quart milk
¼ cup grated sharp Cheddar cheese

Stew cabbage, almonds, margarine, caraway seed, salt, and paprika in water for 10 minutes. Combine egg with milk and add to cabbage mixture. Heat to just boiling. Top with grated cheese and serve.

SERVES 4

LOW-CALORIE TOMATO-CABBAGE SOUP

1 46-ounce can tomato juice
7 tablespoons lemon juice
2 tablespoons instant minced onion
½ cup water
2 envelopes instant beef broth
½ teaspoon leaf oregano, crumbled
½ teaspoon leaf basil, crumbled
2 cups shredded cabbage (¼ medium-sized head)
1 tablespoon sugar

Combine tomato juice, lemon juice, onion, water, beef broth, oregano, and basil in a large saucepan and bring to boiling. Add cabbage; cover and simmer 20 minutes (cabbage will be crisp-tender), or until cabbage is done as you like it. Stir in sugar.

SERVES 6

Salads

APPLE-GRAPE-CABBAGE SALAD WITH HONEY AND SOUR CREAM DRESSING

Honey and sour cream make a delightful fruit dressing.

1 large red apple, unpeeled, diced
2 teaspoons lemon juice
1 cup purple or red grapes, halved and seeded, or green seedless grapes halved
2 cups packed shredded green cabbage
¼ cup soup cream
1 tablespoon honey
¼ teaspoon crushed aniseed or celery seed
½ teaspoon salt
⅛ teaspoon pepper
Romaine or other lettuce leaves (optional)

In a large bowl toss apple with lemon juice to prevent darkening. Add grapes and cabbage. Mix to blend sour cream, honey, aniseed, salt, and pepper; spoon over salad and toss lightly; chill ½ hour. Serve on lettuce leaves (optional). Especially good with ham or pork.

SERVES 4

SWEET-AND-SOUR CABBAGE SALAD

You can make this the night before and serve with any kind of meat.

½ medium onion, chopped
½ green pepper, minced
1 small jar pimientos, chopped
1 small cabbage, chopped

MARINADE

½ cup sugar
⅓ cup vinegar
Salt to taste
¼ cup salad oil
¼ cup water

Combine the onion, green pepper, and pimientos with the cabbage. Mix together the marinade ingredients, and pour over the cabbage mixture. Place in a covered container in the refrigerator, and let stand overnight. Drain off liquid before serving.

SERVES 6

CURRIED CABBAGE-CARROT-PINEAPPLE SALAD

2 teaspoons curry powder
1 tablespoon hot water
⅓ cup mayonnaise
2 tablespoons milk
½ teaspoon salt
3 cups shredded green or red cabbage
2 carrots, coarsely shredded
1 8-ounce can pineapple chunks in own juice, drained
¼ cup chopped nuts

In a salad bowl blend curry powder with water; blend in mayonnaise, milk, and salt. Add cabbage, carrots, and pineapple; toss to mix. Chill ½ hour before serving. Sprinkle with nuts.

SERVES 4

CABBAGE AND DRIED FRUIT SALAD WITH TANGY MAYONNAISE DRESSING

Dried fruits make this chewy and good.

¼ cup mayonnaise
¼ cup milk

2 teaspoons lemon or lime juice
½ teaspoon salt
⅛ teaspoon pepper
4 cups shredded green or red cabbage
1 cup pitted dates or prunes, cut in quarters, *or* ⅔ cup raisins, plumped
¼ cup toasted slivered almonds

In a salad bowl blend mayonnaise, milk, lemon juice, salt, and pepper. Add cabbage and dates; toss to mix. Chill ½ hour before serving. Sprinkle with almonds. Especially good with broiled chicken.

SERVES 4

WALNUT-CABBAGE SALAD

A colorful, crunchy touch to any meal—not sweet.

1 red cabbage
¾ tablespoon salt
½ cup chopped walnuts or pecans
2 tablespoons chopped fresh mint
Juice of ½ lemon

VINAIGRETTE DRESSING

1 teaspoon Dijon-style mustard
½ teaspoon salt
3 tablespoons red wine vinegar
Ground pepper
½ cup oil

Cut cabbage in half, wash thoroughly, and dry. Cut in fine strips; place in a bowl and sprinkle with the salt. Mix well and let stand 2 hours. Then wash off all the salt and pat dry.

To make Vinaigrette Dressing, place mustard, salt, vinegar, and pepper in blender. Turn blender on medium speed and add oil slowly until well blended.

Toss cabbage with Vinaigrette Dressing and stir in nuts and chopped mint. Sprinkle with the lemon juice and chill 2 hours before serving. If you are going to serve any later than 2 hours after mixing with dressing, add the nuts at serving time or they will become soggy. Keep in the refrigerator several days.

SERVES 8 to 10

SUMMERTIME CABBAGE ASPIC

The Roquefort cheese makes this aspic rich and unusual.

2 tablespoons unflavored gelatin
½ cup cold water
1 cup boiling water
1 teaspoon salt
¼ cup tarragon vinegar
¼ cup cider vinegar
⅓ cup sugar
2½ cups grated cabbage
1 stalk celery, chopped
2 pimientos, chopped
1 green pepper, chopped
1 cup pecans, chopped
2 3-ounce packages cream cheese
1 3-ounce package Roquefort cheese
Cream to soften

Soften gelatin in cold water. Dissolve in boiling water. Add salt, vinegars, and sugar. Allow this mixture to cool. Then add cabbage, celery, pimientos, green pepper, and pecans. Pour into oiled mold and chill until firm. Serve with cream cheese and Roquefort cheese which have been mixed together and softened with cream.

SERVES 8

LIME, PINEAPPLE, AND CABBAGE SALAD

Green, green, green—sweet molded salad!

1 3-ounce package lime gelatin
1 cup hot water

10 marshmallows, quartered
1 cup finely cut cabbage
1 cup crushed pineapple, drained
½ cup chopped walnuts
¾ cup mayonnaise
1 6-ounce can evaporated milk, chilled and whipped

Dissolve gelatin in hot water. Stir in marshmallows. Cover with plate to speed melting. Add cabbage, pineapple, walnuts, and mayonnaise. Chill until almost set and fold in whipped evaporated milk. Chill until firm.

SERVES 10

WEDDING CAKE SALAD

A beautiful main dish, molded shrimp salad. Perfect luncheon fare—you'll get rave reviews from friends.

10 3-ounce packages fruit-flavored gelatin (your choice of flavors)
1 head Chinese cabbage, slivered
1 head red cabbage, slivered
2 14-ounce cans crushed pineapple
2 bunches green onions, finely chopped
1 bunch carrots, grated
1 bunch celery, finely chopped
2 pounds Bay shrimp, or crab meat, or combination of both
Lettuce
Watercress
Can of whipped cream
Fruit garnish of your choice

To each 3-ounce package of gelatin, add ¾ cup boiling water, ¾ cup cold water. The gelatin will be divided into four layers, as follows:

Bottom layer: 4 packages gelatin, molded in 10-inch round cake pan
Second layer: 3 packages gelatin, molded in 8-inch round cake pan
Third layer: 2 packages gelatin, molded in 6-inch round cake pan
Top layer: 1 package gelatin, molded in 4-inch round cake pan

Add cabbage, pineapple, onions, carrots, celery, and shrimp to each gelatin layer, dividing proportionately. Fill each mold until they are all solid. Set in refrigerator.

When firm, place on large lettuce bed, one on top of the other like a wedding cake. Decorate edges with watercress and whipped cream. Garnish with fruit. Use wedding centerpiece on top.

SERVES 8

PANTRY COLESLAW

The best of the coleslaws.

1½ cups + 2 tablespoons mayonnaise
6 tablespoons + 1 teaspoon sugar
3 tablespoons + ½ teaspoon wine vinegar
¾ cup + 1 tablespoon oil
⅛ teaspoon *each* garlic, onion, mustard, and celery powders
Dash black pepper
1 tablespoon + 2 teaspoons lemon juice
¾ cup + 1 tablespoon half-and-half
½ teaspoon salt
2 heads cabbage, very finely shredded

Blend together mayonnaise, sugar, vinegar, and oil. Add spice powders, pepper, lemon juice, half-and-half, and salt. Stir until smooth. Pour over shredded cabbage in a large bowl and toss until cabbage is well coated.

If wished, use only half the dressing to a head of cabbage and save remaining to dress fruit salad or other salads. The dressing, covered tightly, keeps well in the refrigerator for several days. Makes about 1 quart dressing.

SERVES 12

QUICK SLAW

1 small head cabbage
1 small sweet onion
Bottled Italian dressing

Shred cabbage to make 6 cups. Thinly slice onion and combine with cabbage. Mix in enough Italian or other oil-and-vinegar-type dressing to moisten (about ½ cup).

SERVES 6 to 8

OVERNIGHT CABBAGE SLAW

1 medium head cabbage (about 2½ pounds)
2 small mild red onions, thinly sliced into rings
1 green pepper, seeded and chopped
½ cup sliced pimiento-stuffed green olives
1 teaspoon salt
1 teaspoon celery seed
½ teaspoon pepper
½ cup cider vinegar
¼ cup sugar
2 tablespoons salad oil
2 teaspoons Dijon mustard

With a knife, shred cabbage; you should have 10 cups. In a bowl, combine cabbage, onion, green pepper, and olives. Sprinkle with salt, celery seed, and pepper.

In a small pan, combine vinegar, sugar, oil, and mustard. Bring to a boil, stirring, then boil 1 minute. Remove from heat and let cool to warm. Pour over cabbage mixture and mix gently; cover and chill 24 hours.

To serve, stir slaw well, then lift from bowl, draining briefly. Spoon into serving bowl. If desired, moisten slaw with 1 to 2 tablespoons of the drained dressing.

SERVES 8

SOUR CREAM COLESLAW

1 teaspoon minced onion
1 teaspoon salt
¼ teaspoon sugar
½ cup sour cream
3½ cups shredded cabbage
1 tablespoon minced onion
⅓ cup chopped celery
⅓ cup green pepper strips
⅓ cup coarsely grated carrots
¼ cup sliced radishes
Salad greens

Combine 1 teaspoon onion, salt, and sugar; fold in sour cream. Cover and chill.

In a large bowl, combine cabbage, 1 tablespoon onion, celery, green pepper, carrots, and radishes; chill. Just before serving toss the dressing with the cabbage mixture. Line a salad bowl with greens, place cabbage mixture in center, and garnish with sliced radishes.

SERVES 6

Side Dishes

HOT SWEET-SOUR CABBAGE

Uses red cabbage—a colorful side dish with beef or pork.

1 large red cabbage (about 2 pounds)
2 tablespoons chopped onion
3 tablespoons butter
⅓ cup brown sugar
⅓ cup lemon juice
1 teaspoon caraway seeds
½ teaspoon salt

Shred cabbage and set aside. Brown onions in melted butter and add sugar, lemon juice, caraway seeds, and salt. Add shredded cabbage. Cook and stir for 18 minutes; serve immediately.

SERVES 8

BRAISED CABBAGE

Wedges of hot cabbage sprinkled with bread crumbs.

2 large onions, sliced
¼ cup margarine
½ head cabbage, cut in 6 wedges
½ teaspoon salt
½ teaspoon sugar
2 tablespoons water
⅛ cup bread crumbs
2 tablespoons melted butter

Brown onion slices in margarine. Remove onions and keep warm. Add cabbage to butter and cook over low heat until lightly browned. Turn carefully to preserve shape. Sprinkle with salt and sugar during browning. Place onions at side of skillet. Add water, then cook and simmer 10 minutes, turning cabbage once. Toss onions over cabbage. Mix bread crumbs and butter together and sprinkle over cabbage.

SERVES 6

STEAMED CABBAGE WITH APPLES AND ONIONS

Wonderful with corned beef!

2 tablespoons salad oil, butter, or margarine
1 large onion, sliced
2 tart green apples, sliced thin
Salt and pepper
1 large cabbage (about 2 pounds)

In a large frying pan, heat oil over medium heat. When hot, add onion; cook, stirring, for about 10 minutes, or until limp. Add apples (peeled if desired) and reduce heat; cover and cook, stirring occasionally, for about 20 minutes, or until apples are tender. Add salt and pepper to taste.

Meanwhile, cut cabbage into 1½- to 2-inch-thick wedges and place in a vegetable steamer. Cook, covered, for about 15 minutes, or until tender. Arrange cabbage on platter, then spoon apple-onion mixture over or alongside the wedges.

SERVES 6 to 8

SCALLOPED CABBAGE

Good dish with ham or chicken.

1 small head cabbage
4 tablespoons margarine
6 tablespoons flour
1½ cups milk
1 teaspoon seasoned salt
½ teaspoon pepper
1 teaspoon powdered onion
2 cups grated Cheddar cheese

Cut cabbage into bite-sized pieces. Cook in salted boiling water about 15 minutes or until transparent. Drain. Prepare white sauce with the margarine, flour, milk, salt, pepper, and onion. Combine cabbage and sauce in greased casserole and top with cheese. Bake for 45 minutes at 350° F. May be made ahead of time, and baked when ready to serve.

SERVES 6 to 8

Main Dishes

CABBAGE CASSEROLE

A quick main dish.

1 medium head cabbage
1 pound hamburger
1 large onion, chopped
1 10½-ounce can undiluted cream of tomato soup

Shred cabbage; set aside. Brown meat and onion together; drain. Layer meat mixture and cabbage in casserole. Dilute tomato soup with 1 can water and pour over. Bake 30 minutes at 350° F.

SERVES 3 or 4

CABBAGE ROLLS

It's the cottage cheese that makes these so good.

½ pound pork sausage
½ cup rice, uncooked
1 tablespoon diced onions
½ teaspoon salt
2 teaspoons paprika
½ teaspoon sage
1 cup cottage cheese
6 large cabbage leaves
1 cup cream of tomato soup
½ cup milk
1 cup sour cream

Sauté sausage, rice, and onions together in a skillet, stirring constantly, for 5 minutes. Add salt, paprika, and sage. Remove from heat; cool and add cottage cheese.

Place cabbage leaves in boiling water and let stand until limp. Remove and drain leaves. Pile meat mixture on cabbage leaves, roll, and fasten with toothpicks. Arrange in casserole. Blend soup, milk, and sour cream. Pour over cabbage rolls. Bake in moderate oven (350°F.) for 1 to 1½ hours.

SERVES 3 or 4

CORNED BEEF AND CABBAGE IN A CROCK

3 to 4 pounds corned beef (one piece)
2 cups water
½ cup brown sugar
¼ teaspoon ground cloves
1 teaspoon pickling spice
1 teaspoon dry mustard
1 teaspoon horseradish
1 onion, chopped
1 bay leaf
1 head cabbage

Place corned beef in crock cooker. Mix together the water and all other ingredients except cabbage. Pour mixture over meat. Cover and cook at low heat for 10 to 12 hours. Remove corned beef and keep it warm. Strain juice, and return it to the cooker along with the cabbage which has been cut into wedges. Cover and cook on high for 20 to 30 minutes, or until the cabbage is done.

SERVES 6

Relishes

LINDBERG CABBAGE RELISH

A must with your Easter ham.

2 medium heads cabbage
8 medium carrots
4 red peppers
4 green peppers
12 medium onions
½ teaspoon salt
3 pints vinegar
6 cups sugar
1 teaspoon mustard seed
1 teaspoon celery seed

Put vegetables through food chopper; add salt and stir well. Let stand 2 hours; drain. Mix together vinegar, sugar, mustard seed, and celery seed until sugar dissolves. Stir well; pour over vegetables. Needs no cooking. Keep refrigerated, unsealed.

MAKES APPROXIMATELY 12 PINTS

UNCOOKED CABBAGE RELISH

Easy, but good.

2 cups chopped green pepper
2 cups chopped sweet red pepper
4 cups chopped cabbage
2 cups chopped onion
2 or 3 hot peppers
5 tablespoons salt
2 teaspoons celery seed
4 cups sugar
1 quart vinegar

Put each vegetable through food chopper, using coarse blade. If vegetables are covered with liquid, drain off and discard liquid. Measure each vegetable after chopping. Mix vegetables with salt and let stand overnight. Drain off as much liquid as possible and discard. Stir celery seed, sugar, and vinegar into vegetables. Pack into sterilized jars and seal.

MAKES ABOUT 3 PINTS

RED CABBAGE FOR HORS D'OEUVRE

1 red cabbage, shredded
1 tablespoon salt
1 clove garlic
1 bay leaf
8 peppercorns
2 tablespoons vinegar

Clean a red cabbage, quarter it, and remove the hard core. Shred the quarters and put the shreds in a bowl with salt. Leave the cabbage in a cold place for 24 hours, turning it over from time to time. Squeeze out all the water. Add garlic clove, bay leaf, peppercorns, and vinegar and let the cabbage stand for a few hours to pickle.

MAKES ABOUT 3 CUPS

Carrots

1 pound = 7 to 8 medium carrots = 4 cups diced
1 cup cooked = 48 calories, 1.4 grams protein, 11 grams carbohydrates, 344 milligrams potassium, loads of vitamin A (your mom was right!)

Carrots are another crop that give you a lot for your space and money. Carrots store better left in the ground than in your refrigerator, so only pick when you are ready to use them. They can store in the refrigerator up to two weeks. You'll need to peel older carrots, but simply scrub the young ones with a brush.

You can cook carrots in a variety of ways. Boil whole carrots for 20 minutes, small ones 8 to 10 minutes; sauté shredded carrots 4 to 6 minutes; slice carrots, dot with butter, and bake for 30 minutes (be sure to cover with a lid or foil).

To freeze: Scald carrots 3 to 5 minutes depending on size. Plunge in ice water. Drain. Freeze.

Soups

CARROT SOUP

A thick carrot and rice soup.

1½ cups (2 medium) sliced onions
Butter
2 cups chopped carrots
1 14-ounce can chicken broth
1 teaspoon salt
½ cup uncooked instant white rice
2 cups milk
⅛ teaspoon white pepper
Chopped parsley or chives

Sauté onions in butter. Place in a pan with carrots, chicken broth, and salt. Cook until carrots are tender. Add rice and let stand 10 minutes. Place soup, half at a time, in blender and blend on high speed for 30 seconds. Add milk and pepper; reheat over boiling water. Soup will be very thick. Garnish with chopped parsley or chives.

SERVES 6 to 8

CANADIAN CHEESE-CARROT SOUP

This silky soup is tasty hot or cold.

1 medium-sized carrot, finely diced (⅔ cup)
½ cup water
1 medium-sized onion, finely chopped (½ cup)
5 tablespoons butter or margarine
½ cup sifted all-purpose flour
2 tablespoons cornstarch
4½ cups milk
4⅔ cups chicken broth (homemade, *or* 3 13¾-ounce cans)
⅛ teaspoon baking soda
⅛ teaspoon paprika
1 pound sharp American or Cheddar cheese, cut in small cubes or coarsely shredded
2 teaspoons salt
½ teaspoon pepper

Cook carrot in water in a small covered saucepan about 15 minutes until tender; drain and reserve.

Stir-fry onion in butter in a large saucepan 5 minutes until limp and golden. Combine flour and cornstarch and blend in; cook, stirring constantly, 3 minutes or until no raw starchy taste remains. Stir in milk; cook, stirring constantly, until thickened and smooth. Stir in broth, reserved carrot, baking soda, and paprika. (At this point you may hold the soup over low heat as long as 1 hour, stirring occasionally.)

Add cheese gradually, stirring all the while. Keep the heat low and do not allow soup to boil or it will curdle. Season with salt and pepper. Serve hot.

SERVES 10

CARROT VICHYSSOISE

Serve in chilled bowls with grated carrot on top.

2 cups potatoes
1½ cups carrots
1 leek
3 cups chicken stock
Pinch white pepper
Salt
1 cup cream
Shredded raw carrot

Into a saucepan put peeled, diced potatoes; sliced carrots; sliced leek, white part only; and chicken stock. Bring to a boil and simmer for 25 minutes, or until vegetables are tender.

In an electric blender puree half the vegetables and liquid at a time for 30 seconds at high speed (or you can puree with a food mill). Empty into mixing bowl or pitcher.

Stir in white pepper, salt, and cream. Serve in chilled bowls, icy cold, with a topping of shredded raw carrot.

SERVES 4 to 6

Salads

MARINATED CARROT SALAD

This can be used as an appetizer by adding other vegetables and serving on toothpicks.

1 10½-ounce can tomato soup
¾ cup vinegar
⅝ cup sugar
⅝ cup vegetable oil
1 teaspoon prepared mustard
1 teaspoon Worcestershire sauce
Salt to taste
2 bunches carrots, sliced
2 medium onions, sliced in rings
Lettuce

Thoroughly heat condensed tomato soup, vinegar, sugar, vegetable oil, mustard, Worcestershire sauce, and salt. Set aside. Cook carrots 10 minutes in salted water. Drain. Stir hot carrots and raw onion rings into tomato soup mixture. Cover and refrigerate overnight. Serve on lettuce.

SERVES 6 to 8

CARROT-RAISIN SLAW

¼ cup lemon juice, preferably fresh squeezed
1 tablespoon vegetable oil
1 tablespoon milk
¼ teaspoon salt
1 pound carrots, peeled and coarsely grated (4 cups)
½ cup raisins

Mix lemon juice, oil, milk, and salt. Pour over carrots and toss well. Cover and chill up to 24 hours. Just before serving add raisins and toss again.

SERVES 4 to 5

PINEAPPLE-CARROT SALAD

Sour cream and walnuts in a molded salad.

1 3-ounce package orange gelatin
2 cups boiling water
1 cup sour cream
1 13½-ounce can crushed pineapple
2 cups carrots, grated
½ cup walnuts or pecans, chopped

Dissolve gelatin in boiling water. Gradually add mixture to sour cream until well blended. Chill until mixture begins to set. Stir in pineapple, grated carrots, and chopped nuts. Pour into a lightly oiled 2-quart mold and chill about 4 hours.

SERVES 10 to 12

CARROT PARTY SALAD

Rich and good—a molded party salad.

1 3-ounce package lemon or lime gelatin
1 cup hot water
1 8-ounce package cream cheese
1 cup chopped celery
1 cup grated carrots
1 cup crushed pineapple, drained
1 cup whipping cream, whipped
1 cup chopped pecans

Dissolve gelatin in 1 cup hot water. Add cheese while gelatin is hot. When cool, but before it sets, add rest of ingredients. Pour into a mold and chill.

SERVES 16

CARROT-ORANGE CUP

A molded cream cheese salad—with a bright orange color.

1 3-ounce package orange gelatin
¼ cup sugar
1½ cups boiling water
1 4-ounce package cream cheese
½ cup orange juice
½ teaspoon shredded lemon peel
2 tablespoons lemon juice
1 cup shredded carrot
1 cup chopped apples

Dissolve gelatin and sugar in boiling water. Add cream cheese and beat until smooth. Stir in orange juice, lemon peel, and lemon juice; chill until partially set. Add carrot and apples. Double everything to make a large salad.

SERVES 4 to 6

Side Dishes

CARROT AND ZUCCHINI SAUTÉ

If you sauté vegetables right they remain crunchy.

5 medium-sized carrots
3 small zucchini
2 tablespoons butter or margarine
2 cloves garlic, minced or pressed
Pinch fresh or dry rosemary
Salt and pepper to taste
Water
1 tablespoon capers (optional)

Slice the carrots and zucchini about ¼ inch thick. Melt the butter in a frying pan over medium heat; stir in carrots and cook 2 minutes, then stir in the zucchini, garlic, rosemary, salt, and pepper. Stir until zucchini is heated through, then add 1 or 2 tablespoons water and cover pan. Cook over medium heat until carrots are barely fork tender, shaking pan and stirring occasionally. Don't overcook; a little crunch won't hurt. Stir in capers, if desired, and serve.

SERVES 4

HOT-WEATHER CARROTS WITH MINT

3 medium-sized carrots
½ cup butter
½ cup sugar
1 tablespoon chopped, fresh mint leaves
Butter, salt, and pepper to taste

Wash and scrape carrots; cut into ¼-inch slices, then into strips or fancy shapes. Cook 15 minutes in boiling salted water. Drain. Cook slowly with ½ cup butter, sugar, and mint until soft and glazed. Season with butter, salt, and pepper.

SERVES 8

SWEET-AND-SOUR CARROTS

A summer carrot side dish—served cold.

2 pounds carrots, peeled
1 onion, thinly sliced
1 green pepper, slivered
1 10½-ounce can condensed tomato soup
½ cup sugar
¾ cup oil
½ cup white vinegar
1 tablespoon grated horseradish

Cut the carrots in whatever way you find most attractive and cook them in unsalted water until they are barely tender. Drain and cool. Arrange the carrots in a serving dish with the onion and green pepper.

Heat the last 5 ingredients together to form a dressing. Pour the dressing over the vegetables and let stand overnight in the refrigerator. Serve chilled.

SERVES 6 to 8

CARROTS AND CAULIFLOWER AU GRATIN

We always make this recipe when in a hurry and use a can of white sauce from our pantry—but you can make your own.

1 head cauliflower
1½ cups diced carrots
1 cup medium white sauce
½ cup grated cheese

Separate cauliflower into large flowerets. Cook carrots and cauliflower together in salted water for about 15 minutes or until both are barely tender. Drain and place in a baking dish. Season white sauce with salt and pepper to taste and pour over top of vegetables. Sprinkle with cheese and bake in a 400°F. oven for 20 minutes until nicely browned.

SERVES 4 to 6

CARROT BALLS

Crunchy—kids like these!

2 cups cooked carrots
1½ cups soft bread crumbs
1 cup grated sharp cheese
Salt
Pepper
1 egg white
Crushed corn flakes
Parsley

Sieve the carrots and combine with crumbs and cheese. Season to taste with salt and pepper. Beat egg white and fold in. Form mixture into 12 to 14 balls and roll in corn flake crumbs. Place on a baking sheet and bake at 375°F. for 30 minutes, or until brown. Garnish with parsley.

SERVES 6

FRENCH-FRIED CARROTS

Batter can also be used for fried cauliflower, zucchini, tomatoes, onion, and eggplant.

Carrots

BATTER FOR FRENCH-FRIED VEGETABLES

1 egg yolk, well beaten
6 tablespoons milk
1 tablespoon melted butter
½ cup sifted flour
1¼ teaspoons baking powder
Salt and pepper to taste

Use whatever quantity of carrots you desire. Scrape or peel carrots, and wash. Cut into strips lengthwise, as for french-fried potatoes, but slightly smaller. Drop into boiling salted water and boil until tender. Drain and cool.

To prepare batter, add well-beaten egg yolk to milk and melted butter, and mix. Sift in flour and baking powder. Beat until thoroughly mixed, and if not smooth beat with egg beater until it is. Stir in salt and pepper.

Dip carrots in Batter for French-Fried Vegetables. Drop into deep hot fat, and fry until a golden brown. Remove from fat and drain. Serve hot.

CANDIED CARROTS

A favorite with the younger set.

1 bunch carrots, sliced diagonally
¼ cup butter or margarine
¼ cup cranberry sauce
1 tablespoon orange juice
2 tablespoons brown sugar
½ teaspoon salt

Cook carrots in boiling salted water until tender. Put in shallow flameproof casserole. Put remaining ingredients in a bowl and blend thoroughly. Spoon mixture over carrots. Place under broiler and broil 4 to 5 minutes or until glazed.

SERVES 6

GLOSSY CARROTS IN ORANGE SAUCE

Perfect for small, young carrots from the garden.

¼ cup butter
¼ cup thawed orange juice concentrate
2 teaspoons honey
½ teaspoon ground ginger
½ teaspoon salt
1 pound small whole carrots, cooked and drained

In a skillet blend butter, orange juice concentrate, honey, ginger, and salt. Add carrots; set over low heat, turning carrots until well glazed. Serve at once.

SERVES 4 to 6

CARROT LOAF

2 cups grated raw carrots
1½ cups grated cheese
1 cup dry bread crumbs
2 eggs, slightly beaten
1½ cups milk
½ teaspoon salt
⅛ teaspoon pepper
Creamed peas (optional)
Chopped parsley (optional)

Mix carrots, cheese, and bread crumbs; then add slightly beaten eggs, milk, salt, and pepper. Pour into a buttered casserole, set in a pan of hot water, and bake at 350°F. for 1 hour. Serve with creamed peas and chopped parsley.

SERVES 6

CARROT SOUFFLÉ

2½ cups riced or grated carrots
1 teaspoon salt
1 tablespoon grated onion
2 tablespoons butter
3 eggs, slightly beaten
1 cup milk

Combine ingredients and mix well. Put in casserole, set in pan of water, and bake at 325°F. for 40 minutes.

SERVES 6

Main Dishes

LENTIL AND CARROT ROAST

High protein, meatless main dish.

2 cups cooked lentils
1 14½-ounce can evaporated or condensed milk
½ cup cooking oil

1½ cups fine dry bread crumbs
1 egg, beaten
1 cup chopped nuts
1 teaspoon salt, or to taste
½ teaspoon sage
1 teaspoon grated onion
1 cup grated fresh carrots
1 cup grated celery
Gravy (optional)

Combine all ingredients and mix thoroughly. Add more bread crumbs if a drier loaf is desired. Spoon into a greased 1½-quart casserole and bake in a 350° F. oven for 1 hour. Serve with gravy if desired.

SERVES 8 to 10

GOLDEN CHEESE AND CARROT BAKE

Vegetarian main dish.

2 cups cooked rice
3 cups finely grated raw carrots
½ cup milk
2 eggs, beaten
2 teaspoons minced onion
1½ teaspoons salt
2 cups grated American cheese

Toss together all ingredients except ½ cup of cheese. Pour into a 1½-quart baking dish. Sprinkle remaining cheese on top. Cover and bake in a 350° F. oven for 30 minutes. Remove cover and bake for 30 minutes longer.

SERVES 6 to 8

LAZY OVEN CARROT AND POTATO STEW

2 pounds stew beef
¼ cup flour
2 teaspoons salt
¼ teaspoon pepper
2 tablespoons oil
2 8-ounce cans tomato sauce
1 cup water
4 onions
4 carrots
4 potatoes, if desired
3 celery stalks

Cut meat into bite-sized pieces. Coat meat with mixture of flour, salt, and pepper. In a 3-quart casserole, toss meat with oil. Bake uncovered at 400° F. for 30 minutes, stirring once. Add remaining ingredients, mixing well. Bake covered at 350° F. for 1¾ hours or until meat and vegetables are tender. Hint: For a time-saver, cut up vegetables while meat is browning.

SERVES 4 to 6

Breads

OLD-FASHIONED CARROT BREAD

Carrot bread characteristically has a spicy flavor, a fine texture, and a crisp crust.

4 eggs
2 cups sugar
1¼ cups salad oil
3 cups unsifted all-purpose flour
2 teaspoons baking powder
1½ teaspoons soda
¼ teaspoon salt
2 teaspoons cinnamon
2 cups finely shredded raw carrots

Beat the eggs; add the sugar gradually, beating until thick. Add the oil gradually and continue beating until thoroughly combined. Stir in the flour, baking powder, soda, salt, and cinnamon until mixture is smooth. Stir in the carrots until blended well. Turn into 2 well-greased 5″ × 9″ loaf pans or 4 well-greased 1-pound cans, filling them no more than ⅔ full. Bake the bread in a moderate oven (350° F.) for 1 hour for large loaves or 45 minutes for small loaves, or until a cake tester comes out clean.

MAKES 2 LARGE LOAVES or 4 SMALL

CARROT-COCONUT BREAD

The moist quality of this loaf is due to the carrots although you won't taste them.

3 eggs
½ cup salad oil
1 teaspoon vanilla
2 cups finely shredded carrots
2 cups packaged grated coconut
1 cup raisins
1 cup chopped walnuts
2 cups unsifted all-purpose flour
½ teaspoon salt
1 teaspoon soda
1 teaspoon baking powder
1 teaspoon cinnamon
1 cup sugar

In a large bowl, beat eggs until light. Stir in salad oil and vanilla; add carrots, coconut, raisins, and nuts, and mix until well blended.

Combine flour, salt, soda, baking powder, cinnamon, and sugar; sift into the first mixture. Stir just until well blended. Spoon into a 9″ × 5″ loaf pan that has been well buttered and dusted with flour. Bake in a moderate oven (350° F.) for about 1 hour, or until bread tests done. Remove from pan and cool thoroughly. The flavor and texture improve if bread is wrapped and refrigerated for several days.

MAKES 1 LOAF

Desserts

CARROT COOKIES

¾ cup shortening
¾ cup sugar
1 egg
1 cup cooked, mashed carrots
2 cups flour
2 teaspoons baking powder
1 teaspoon salt
1 teaspoon vanilla
1 tablespoon orange juice

FROSTING

Juice of 1 orange
1 teaspoon butter
1 1-pound box powdered sugar

Combine shortening, ¾ cup sugar, egg, carrots, flour, baking powder, salt, vanilla, and 1 tablespoon orange juice. Place small spoonfuls of mixture on an ungreased cookie sheet. Bake at 350° F. for 15 minutes. Cool.

Blend juice of 1 orange, butter, and powdered sugar together to make frosting; frost cooled cookies.

MAKES 36 COOKIES

CARROT COOKIES WITH ORANGE JUICE FROSTING

No salt in these cookies for those watching salt intake.

¾ cup shortening
¾ cup sugar
1 egg
1 cup cooked, mashed carrots
1 cup nuts
2 cups flour
1 teaspoon baking powder
1 teaspoon vanilla
Orange juice frosting (see above recipe)

Mix all ingredients except frosting together. Drop from spoon on cookie sheet and bake at 350° F. for 10 to 12 minutes. While cookies are hot, frost with mixture of powdered sugar, butter, and orange juice, as in preceding recipe.

MAKES 36 COOKIES

CARROT-OATMEAL COOKIES

A healthy cookie made with soy flour.

1 cup finely grated carrots (packed lightly) and water

½ cup brown sugar
½ cup oil
2 cups rolled oats
1 cup macaroon coconut
¼ cup soy flour
1 teaspoon vanilla
½ teaspoon salt

Pack carrots lightly in cup; add water to fill to cup mark. Combine carrots, sugar, and oil. Beat until oil is emulsified.

Add remaining ingredients. Mix well and let stand 10 minutes or longer to absorb moisture.

Drop from teaspoon on a greased cookie sheet. Heat oven to 400°F. Put cookies in oven and reduce heat to 350°F. Bake 20 to 25 minutes until nicely browned. Loosen cookies with spatula and let cool on cookie sheet.

MAKES ABOUT 24 COOKIES

FROSTED CARROT BARS

4 eggs
2 cups sugar
1½ cups salad oil
2 cups sifted flour
2 teaspoons baking soda
2 teaspoons ground cinnamon
1 teaspoon salt
3 cups finely grated carrots (9 medium)
1½ cups flaked coconut
1½ cups chopped walnuts

CHEAM CHEESE FROSTING

1 3-ounce package cream cheese
4 tablespoons dairy half-and-half or whole milk
⅛ teaspoon salt
2½ cups sifted confectioners' sugar
1 teaspoon vanilla

Beat eggs until light; gradually beat in 2 cups sugar. Alternately add salad oil and flour sifted with soda, cinnamon, and 1 teaspoon salt. Mix well. Fold in carrots, coconut, and walnuts. Spread evenly in 2 greased 13″ × 9″ × 2″ pans. Bake in moderate oven (350°F.) for 25 to 30 minutes. Set pans on racks to cool.

Prepare Cream Cheese Frosting by beating together cream cheese, half-and-half, ⅛ teaspoon salt, confectioners' sugar, and vanilla. Spread on carrot cake, then cut into 3″ × 1″ bars. Remove from pans and place in covered container. Store in refrigerator or freezer.

MAKES 6 DOZEN

HOLIDAY CARROT CAKE

Candied fruit makes this almost a fruitcake in appearance and taste.

3 medium carrots, grated
1½ cups sugar
1 teaspoon cinnamon
1 teaspoon cloves
1 teaspoon nutmeg
1 cup raisins
2 tablespoons shortening
1½ cups water
Pinch salt
1 cup chopped walnuts
2 cups flour
2 teaspoons baking soda
Candied pineapple
Candied cherries

Combine carrots, sugar, spices, raisins, shortening, water, and salt; boil 5 minutes. When cool, add walnuts, flour, and soda. Pour into a greased bread loaf pan. Cover surface with candied fruit. Bake in a 250°F. to 325°F. oven for about 1¼ hours. Flavor is improved if cake is allowed to stand 2 days before serving.

MAKES 1 LOAF

FIVE KARRIT KAKE

This cake is an heirloom recipe from one of our favorite families.

5 eggs, separated
1 cup sugar
1 cup mashed carrots
Rind and juice of 1 lemon
Salt to taste
¾ cup ground almonds
1 lemon, sliced thin

Beat egg yolks and sugar until lemon colored. Add carrots, lemon, salt, and nuts. Beat egg whites stiff, but not dry. Fold into yolk mixture. Pour into a greased springform pan. Bake at 350°F. for 40 to 45 minutes, or until light golden brown. A thin lemon slice is very good on this but should not be too sweet.

MAKES 1 CAKE

CARROT CAKE

The best!

2 cups sugar
2 cups flour, sifted
2 teaspoons baking soda
2 teaspoons cinnamon
1 teaspoon baking powder
1 teaspoon salt
1 teaspoon cloves or allspice (optional)
4 eggs, beaten
1½ cups vegetable oil
3 cups carrots, grated
¾ cup raisins (optional)
1 cup walnuts, chopped (optional)

FROSTING

1 8-ounce package cream cheese, softened
½ cup butter, softened
1 16-ounce package powdered sugar
1 teaspoon vanilla
Chopped walnuts

Combine 2 cups sugar, flour, baking soda, cinnamon, baking powder, salt, and cloves or allspice. Stir in eggs, oil, and carrots. Mix in raisins and walnuts, if desired. Pour into a greased 9″ × 13″ pan. Bake at 325°F. for 35 to 40 minutes, or until toothpick comes out clean. Cool.

Combine all frosting ingredients except nuts. Blend well. Frost cake and sprinkle with chopped walnuts.

SERVES 12 to 16

BAKED CARROT PUDDING WITH DATES

PUDDING

2 cups grated carrots
1½ cups water
½ cup dates or raisins
1½ cups sugar
⅓ cup shortening
2 cups flour
1½ teaspoons soda
½ teaspoon salt
½ teaspoon cloves
½ teaspoon allspice
1 teaspoon cinnamon
1 teaspoon vanilla
½ cup nuts

BROWN SUGAR SAUCE

1 cup brown sugar
2 tablespoons cornstarch
1½ cups boiling water
½ stick butter (⅛ pound)
Dash salt
⅛ teaspoon nutmeg

To make pudding, grate carrots in blender with water. Add to dates, sugar, and shortening in saucepan; bring to a boil and simmer 5 minutes. Let cool, then add remaining pudding ingredients. Bake in a 9″ × 12″ pan at 350°F. for 40 to 45 minutes.

To make Brown Sugar Sauce, combine sugar and cornstarch. Pour boiling water over this mixture; cook until clear. Add butter, salt, and nutmeg. Steam pudding over hot water to reheat and serve with Brown Sugar Sauce.

SERVES 8

STEAMED HOLIDAY CARROT PUDDING

Christmas pudding at its best!

PUDDING

1 teaspoon baking soda (try 2 teaspoons at sea level)
¼ cup warm water
2 cups bread crumbs
1½ cups brown sugar, firmly packed
1 cup evaporated milk
1 cup raisins
1 cup suet, finely chopped
1 cup currants
1 cup carrots, grated
1 cup almonds, chopped
1 apple, peeled and chopped
2 eggs, beaten
1 teaspoon cinnamon
1 teaspoon nutmeg
½ teaspoon cloves
¼ teaspoon salt

TOPPING

1 cup heavy cream
¼ cup powdered sugar
Dash nutmeg

Dissolve baking soda in warm water. Set aside. Mix all remaining ingredients for pudding. Stir in baking soda and water. Fill greased 3-pound molds ½ full. Put on tightly fitting lids. Set a trivet in a large pot containing 1 inch boiling water. Place molds on trivet. Cover large pot tightly. Turn heat to high until steam escapes. Adjust to low boil and cook 3 hours, maintaining 1 inch boiling water in pot. Remove mold lids. Cool. Remove pudding from molds.

Whip cream with sugar and nutmeg to make topping. Serve with pudding.

SERVES 12

Pickles and Relishes

PICKLED CARROTS

A great relish, cold vegetable, or side dish with barbecued chicken or beef.

5 cups carrots, sliced
1 purple onion, cut into round slices
1 green pepper, cut into round slices
1 10¼-ounce can tomato soup
¾ cup vinegar
¾ cup sugar
½ cup vegetable oil
1 teaspoon prepared mustard
1 teaspoon Worcestershire sauce
1 teaspoon salt
1 teaspoon pepper

Cook carrots in boiling salted water for 10 minutes, until crispy tender. Drain and cool. Combine with onion and green pepper; set aside. Combine remaining ingredients and pour over vegetables. Cover. Refrigerate 12 hours or up to 2 weeks. Drain and serve.

SERVES 8

CARROT-CUCUMBER RELISH

12 carrots, pared (3 cups ground)
10 cucumbers, unpared (7 cups ground)
4 onions, peeled (2 cups ground)
¼ cup salt
5 cups sugar
3 cups vinegar
1 tablespoon celery seed
1 tablespoon mustard seed

Coarsely grind carrots, cucumbers, and onions. Mix in a large bowl with salt. Let stand 3 hours. Drain.

In a large kettle, combine sugar, vinegar, celery seed, and mustard seed. Bring to a boil. Stir in drained vegetables. Simmer 20 minutes. Pour into hot, sterilized jars. Wipe rims clean. Seal; screw bands on tightly with hands. Put jars in a canning pot and boil water around jars for 15 minutes (10 minutes at sea level) to seal the lids.

MAKES 5 PINTS

CARROT-RAISIN MARMALADE

Serve with baked ham and smoked meats, with peanut butter in a sandwich, as a stuffing for baked apples, or melted with butter, as a sauce over your choice of vegetables.

2 medium oranges
3½ cups coarsely shredded carrots
1½ cups water
¼ cup lemon juice
1 cup raisins
4 cups sugar

With a potato peeler, peel off the outer rind from oranges, taking care not to pick up any of the white skin; then cut peel into slivers. Squeeze oranges and strain. Combine rind and orange juice, shredded carrots (easily done in electric food processor), and water in a heavy saucepan. Bring to boil. Reduce heat; cover pan and simmer 15 minutes.

Add remaining ingredients. Return to boil. Cook for 30 minutes over medium heat, stirring frequently, until jelly stage is reached. Pour at once into hot sterilized jars, leaving a ¼-inch head space. Seal with clean, dry metal lids. Cool, label, and store.

MAKES ABOUT 2 PINTS

Cauliflower

1 pound = 1 4-inch head = 4 cups flowerets = 5 servings
1 cup cooked = 28 calories, 2.9 grams protein, 5.1 grams carbohydrates, 295 milligrams potassium, 60 units vitamin A, 78 milligrams vitamin C

Cauliflower is another member of the cabbage family, although it is more temperamental than its cabbage cousins. If the temperature goes much above 75°F. it will not head. If the weather looks grim, pull up a plant and hang it upside down in a cool dark place for a few weeks. You may save a cauliflower!

Be careful when you pick your cauliflower; they bruise easily. You can pop them in a plastic bag without washing and they will keep in the refrigerator 4 to 5 days and still taste fresh. You may still use them after that until the flowerets become woody.

To cook cauliflower, always soak 30 minutes in salted water first, to ensure crispness and drive out bugs. Adding some lemon juice to the water will keep the cauliflower white. Steam whole cauliflower 30 minutes, flowerets 10 minutes. You can also sauté flowerets in butter and garlic for 10 minutes. Cauliflower is great with lemon butter, hollandaise, or cheese sauce.

To freeze: Cut into 1-inch flowerets and soak in salted water. Scald 4 minutes. Chill in cold water. Drain. Package and freeze. Keeps frozen up to 6 months. (When using, cook frozen cauliflower 4 minutes in boiling water.)

Soups

CREAM OF CAULIFLOWER SOUP

1 cauliflower (about 2 pounds)
4 tablespoons butter
4 tablespoons flour
1½ pints chicken stock
1 onion, coarsely chopped
1 stalk celery, coarsely chopped
2 sprigs chopped parsley
2 egg yolks
¼ pint heavy or whipping cream
Salt and pepper to taste
Grated nutmeg

Poach cauliflower in boiling salted water for 5 minutes and drain. Melt butter in saucepan; add flour and cook, stirring continuously, until a smooth paste is formed. Add chicken stock, onion, celery, and parsley and simmer for 20 minutes. Strain stock. Add cauliflower and cook until it is softened. Rub soup through sieve. Bring back to a boil; stir in 2 egg yolks and cream. Simmer, stirring, for 3 minutes (take care soup does not boil or it will curdle). Season with salt and pepper and a little grated nutmeg.

SERVES 4

POTAGE CHOU-FLEUR

Quick to make—but good.

1 10½-ounce can cream of potato soup
1 whole cauliflower, broken, cooked, drained, and mashed
Paprika

Prepare potato soup according to can directions. Combine cooked cauliflower with soup and simmer 4 minutes. Top with dash of paprika when ready to serve.

SERVES 4

Salads

CHINESE CAULIFLOWER VEGETABLE SALAD

1 package frozen Chinese peas
2 cups cauliflower flowerets

1 5-ounce can water chestnuts, sliced
1 tablespoon chopped pimiento

SESAME SEED DRESSING

½ cup sesame seeds
3 tablespoons oil
1 tablespoon butter
Juice of 1 lemon

Cook peas in boiling salted water until barely tender, about 1 minute after water boils. Drain. Cook cauliflower until tender but still crisp. Drain. Combine with water chestnuts and pimiento; cover and chill.

Just before serving, prepare sesame seed dressing. Brown sesame seeds in oil. Add butter and lemon juice. Mix about 3 tablespoons sesame seed dressing into vegetable mixture and serve.

SERVES 4 to 6

CAULIFLOWER GARDEN SALAD

A marinated salad.

1 10-ounce package frozen fordhook limas
1 10-ounce package frozen cut green beans
1 10-ounce package frozen cut asparagus
1 cup thinly sliced raw cauliflower flowerets
1 8-ounce bottle Italian dressing

Cook all frozen vegetables as directed. Cool. Marinate with raw cauliflower in Italian dressing at least 24 hours. Refrigerate.

SERVES 8 to 10

WHOLE CAULIFLOWER SALAD

1 medium-sized cauliflower, about 1½ pounds

DRESSING

¼ cup lemon juice
¼ cup salad oil or olive oil
½ teaspoon thyme
½ teaspoon dry mustard
1 teaspoon salt
⅛ teaspoon white pepper

GARNISH

Radishes, sliced
Parsley sprigs

Rinse cauliflower and trim stem. Place in a steamer basket and cook over boiling water until tender, about 10 minutes. Cool in running cold water; drain.

For the dressing, combine in a deep bowl lemon juice, olive oil, thyme, dry mustard, salt, and pepper; mix well. Turn cauliflower in bowl several times until well saturated with dressing. Cover and marinate for several hours at room temperature or overnight in refrigerator. Turn cauliflower several more times.

Serve at room temperature with remaining dressing to spoon over servings. Garnish with radishes cut in decorative shapes or sliced, and parsley sprigs or chopped parsley.

SERVES 6

SALAD MAISON

A main dish gourmet salad made with chicken.

1 cup cooked cauliflower flowerets
1 cup cooked string beans
1 cup sliced cooked chicken
2 tomatoes, peeled and chopped
2 hard-cooked eggs
1 teaspoon dry mustard
Salt and pepper to taste
¾ tablespoon vinegar
6 tablespoons olive oil
½ teaspoon *fines herbes*

Mix together in a salad bowl the cauliflower, string beans, chicken, and tomatoes. Separate eggs; cut the whites in julienne and add them to the bowl.

Crush the egg yolks and combine them with dry mustard and salt and pepper; mix to a smooth paste with vinegar. Gradually mix in olive oil. Add this dressing to the salad bowl and toss the mixture well. Sprinkle the top with ½ teaspoon *fines herbes.*

SERVES 4

Side Dishes

CAULIFLOWER WITH ANCHOVY BUTTER

A simple way to serve the season's best cauliflower.

1 whole cauliflower
Water
Salt
1 tablespoon lemon juice
Dash mace
½ pound butter
½ teaspoon anchovy paste
Chives

Discard the coarse outer leaves from a large cauliflower. Cover cauliflower with tepid water and let it stand for 15 minutes. Drain; rinse it in cold water and drain again. Wrap it in a piece of cheesecloth and cook in a little boiling salted water with lemon juice and a generous dash of mace for 20 to 25 minutes, or until tender. Drain thoroughly and put in a serving dish. Combine butter with anchovy paste and spoon it over the cauliflower. Sprinkle generously with finely chopped chives.

SERVES 4

CAULIFLOWER WITH GREEN GRAPES

Looks pretty—an unusual combination.

1 large head cauliflower
1½ cups boiling water
3 teaspoons salt
2 tablespoons butter or margarine
1 cup seedless grapes
½ cup slivered toasted almonds

Break cauliflower into flowerets and then slice lengthwise into ¼-inch slices. Place in boiling water in a skillet, add salt, and simmer covered 5 minutes or until tender. Fold in butter, seedless grapes, and toasted almonds.

SERVES 6

Main Dishes

CAULIFLOWER QUICHE

2 medium-sized cauliflower (about 1 pound each)
2 medium-sized bunches broccoli (about 1½ pounds each)
Boiling salted water
2 tablespoons butter or margarine
2 medium-sized onions, chopped
3 cloves garlic, minced or pressed
1½ teaspoons *each* dry basil, oregano, and salt
½ teaspoon *each* pepper and liquid hot pepper seasoning
4 tomatoes, chopped
8 eggs
⅔ cup half-and-half (light cream) or milk
½ cup grated Parmesan cheese
2½ cups shredded Swiss cheese

Wash and trim cauliflower and broccoli into flowerets. In a 5-quart saucepan, cook vegetables in boiling salted water until tender, about 6 to 8 minutes. Drain well, coarsely chop, and set aside.

In a wide frying pan, melt butter over medium heat. Sauté onions and garlic until tender. Add cooked vegetables, basil, oregano, salt, pepper, liquid hot pepper seasoning, and tomatoes; cook, stirring occasionally, until mixture is heated through, about 4 minutes. Remove from heat.

In a large bowl, beat eggs and half-and-half just to blend. Stir in vegetable mixture, Parmesan cheese, and 2 cups of the Swiss cheese. Pour into a greased 10″ × 15″ jelly-roll pan and spread evenly. Top with remaining cheese.

Bake in a 375°F. oven for 30 to 35 minutes, or until a knife inserted in the center comes out clean. Let stand 10 minutes.

SERVES 12 to 18

EASY GARDEN VEGETABLE PIE

2 cups sliced fresh cauliflowerets
Salted water
½ cup chopped onion
½ cup chopped green pepper
1 cup shredded Cheddar cheese (about 4 ounces)
1½ cups milk
¾ cup biscuit mix
3 eggs
1 teaspoon salt
¼ teaspoon pepper

Heat oven to 400°F. Lightly grease a 10″ × 1½″ pie plate. Heat 1 inch salted water to boiling (½ teaspoon salt to 1 cup water). Add cauliflower; cover and heat again to boiling. Cook until almost tender, about 5 minutes; drain thoroughly. Mix cauliflower, onion, green pepper, and cheese in pie plate. Beat remaining ingredients until smooth, 15 seconds in blender at high speed, or 1 minute with hand beater. Pour into pie plate. Bake until golden brown and a knife inserted halfway between center and edge comes out clean, about 35 to 40 minutes. Let stand 5 minutes before cutting. Garnish as desired. Refrigerate any remaining pie.

A 10-ounce package frozen cauliflower, thawed and drained, can be substituted for the fresh cauliflower. Do not cook.

SERVES 6

CAULIFLOWER À LA BELGIQUE

A cold main dish—good for buffet entree.

1 head cauliflower
Tarragon vinegar to marinate
1 pound cooked ham
Mayonnaise

GARNISH

Watercress
Sliced cucumbers
Tomatoes

Cook cauliflower in slightly salted water until firm but not overcooked. Drain and cool. Marinate whole cauliflower in tarragon vinegar for 30 minutes. Cut ham in small wedges 2 inches long, about 1 inch wide at top. Insert ham wedges between each floweret of cauliflower. Cover with mayonnaise (much better if mayonnaise is homemade). Garnish with watercress, sliced cucumbers, and tomatoes.

This can be used as an entree for a buffet supper on a hot night, or as the first course for a formal dinner. An excellent way of using up leftover ham.

SERVES 4 to 6

Pickles and Relishes

MIXED CAULIFLOWER PICKLES

5 quarts cauliflower, cut in small pieces or chunks

2 quarts little pickling onions
1 quart cucumbers, cut into small pieces or chunks
1 cup salt in 4 quarts water
1 quart vinegar
2 quarts water
2 teaspoons turmeric

SYRUP FOR PICKLES

9 cups sugar
5 cups vinegar
4 cups water
1 handful mixed whole pickling spices
A few cloves
A few pieces cinnamon (broken)
Mustard seeds

Combine cauliflower, onions, and cucumbers. Pour salted 4 quarts of water over vegetables and let stand 4 hours; drain. Boil drained vegetables 20 minutes in 1 quart vinegar, 2 quarts water, and turmeric. Remove vegetables; drain and rinse in cold water. Pack into bottles.

Prepare syrup by heating together all syrup ingredients until sugar is dissolved. Pour hot syrup over vegetables and seal.

MAKES 10 QUARTS

PICKLED CAULIFLOWER

Hot, hot, hot!

2 large cloves garlic
10 to 12 small dried hot chili peppers
3 teaspoons pickling spice
1½ pounds carrots
3 medium onions
2 medium-sized green peppers
2 large heads cauliflower
6¼ cups water
2½ cups white wine vinegar
4 tablespoons salt

Peel and crush the garlic cloves, but leave whole; drop 1 clove into each of 2 ½-gallon jars. Break each chili pepper in half and drop 10 to 12 halves into each jar; spoon in 1½ teaspoons pickling spice into each.

Peel carrots, cut in half lengthwise, then cut into 2-inch pieces. Cut onions and green peppers into 1-inch squares. Break cauliflower into flowerets.

Distribute vegetables equally in jars, packing in as many as possible. Heat the water, vinegar, and salt to boiling, then pour over vegetables. Put lids on jars, cool, and refrigerate for at least 2 weeks before sampling.

MAKES ABOUT 4 QUARTS

VIRGINIA CAULIFLOWER RELISH

Red and green peppers give this zip!

1 pint canned sweet red pepper
1 pint canned sweet green pepper
1 pint white onions
1 large cauliflower
12 medium cucumbers
¼ cup salt
4 cups vinegar
3½ cups sugar
4 tablespoons mustard seed
2 teaspoons salt
2 teaspoons celery seed
½ teaspoon red pepper
1 teaspoon turmeric
1 teaspoon ginger
Powdered alum

Chop fine red pepper, green pepper, onions, cauliflower, and cucumber, or put through coarse blade of meat chopper. Place in a large enameled kettle or bowl and cover with ¼ cup salt. Let stand overnight. Drain and rinse well.

Bring all remaining ingredients except alum to boil. Add vegetables to boiling mixture. Bring again to boil. Pack in sterile jars and seal. Put ¼ teaspoon powdered alum into each jar.

MAKES 4 PINTS

Corn

1 6-inch ear = ½ cup kernels = 1 serving
1 6-inch ear cooked = 100 calories, 3.3 grams protein, 21 grams carbohydrates

Corn covers a lot of territory—literally! Each plant takes room to grow, 3 months of sunny weather to mature, and will only give 2 or 3 ears at the most. The sweet taste of corn straight from the garden is unmatched, so pick it only moments before you want to eat it. (As soon as it is picked, the sugar turns to starch and it loses the fresh succulent taste.) There is only a 24-hour period when corn is at its harvest peak. You can tell it is ready when the silks at the ears turn brown. If you pull back the husk, poke one kernel and if it produces a milky liquid, it's ready.

It is best to cook or freeze immediately. Refrigeration doesn't do corn any good. Corn on the cob was originally roasted (and is still great that way) but now most people boil it in water. Do not let it boil for more than 3 to 4 minutes and never salt the water—it hardens the kernels.

To freeze: Freeze only the best ears of corn. You can freeze right on the cob (clean and trim ends) or in kernels. Either way, scald for 4 minutes, plunge in ice water, drain, then freeze in plastic freezer bags.

Soups

CORN AND CHEESE CHOWDER

A good autumn soup—a meal in itself.

½ pound bacon, sliced
½ cup onion, chopped
½ cup celery, chopped
¼ cup celery leaves, chopped
½ cup green pepper, chopped
½ bay leaf, crumbled
2 tablespoons flour
3 or 4 cups whole kernel corn, fresh or canned
3 cups milk
1¼ teaspoons salt
Pepper to taste
1½ cups Monterey Jack cheese, grated

Fry bacon, drain, and crumble; set aside. Put 3 tablespoons bacon fat in frying pan; add onion, celery, celery leaves, green pepper, and bay leaf. Sauté about 8 minutes until vegetables are tender crisp. Mix in flour. Add undrained corn, milk, salt, and pepper.

Cook, stirring, until soup boils and is slightly thickened. Before serving, stir in 1 cup of the cheese. Pass remaining cheese and crumbled bacon pieces to spoon over individual servings.

SERVES 4

CORN CHOWDER

You can freeze this.

4 slices diced raw bacon
1 large onion, chopped coarsely
3 cups peeled, diced raw potatoes
3 cups water
3 tablespoons butter
¼ cup flour
2 cups milk
2 cups diced cooked ham
4 cups whole kernel corn, *or* 1 12-ounce can whole kernel corn
2 teaspoons salt
¼ teaspoon pepper
2 tablespoons dried parsley or fresh chopped

GARNISH

Fresh parsley or paprika

In a large skillet over moderate heat, cook bacon until almost crisp. Add onion; cook until soft. Add potatoes and water and cook until fork tender, about 10 minutes.

Melt butter in a heavy Dutch oven. Blend in flour and gradually add milk, stirring until mix is thick and smooth. To this white sauce add potato mix, diced ham, corn, salt, pepper, and parsley. Bring just to a boil. Garnish with fresh parsley or paprika. You may desire to add milk to make a thinner soup. Will keep frozen for several months.

MAKES 3 QUARTS

Side Dishes

GARDEN JAMBALAYA

The best of the mixed vegetable side dishes.

⅓ cup thinly sliced onion
½ cup diced celery
3 tablespoons oil
2 cups hot bouillon
1 teaspoon salt
4 cups sliced or diced fresh vegetables (zucchini, green beans, cucumber, green pepper, corn, tomatoes, etc.)
1 tablespoon lemon juice
1 tablespoon cornstarch
2 tablespoons water
1⅓ cups uncooked instant white rice

Sauté onion and celery in oil until tender. Stir in 1 cup bouillon, salt, assorted vegetables, and lemon juice. Blend cornstarch with water until smooth, then gradually stir into vegetables. Form a well in the center of the vegetables and place rice in center. Carefully pour remaining cup of bouillon over rice, moistening evenly. Cover and simmer until rice and vegetables are tender.

SERVES 6 to 8

GREEN CORN PAPRIKA

3 cups corn kernels
1 cup light cream
1 teaspoon paprika
1 teaspoon salt
Cayenne
2 tablespoons sweet butter

Cut from the cob enough corn to make 3 cups and put kernels in the top of a double boiler over boiling water. Add light cream, paprika, salt, and a few grains of cayenne. Cover the pan and cook the corn for 12 to 15 minutes, or until it is tender. Just before serving, stir in 2 tablespoons sweet butter.

SERVES 6

CORN IN SOUR CREAM

A good Sunday brunch dish served on toast points.

6 strips bacon
3 tablespoons onion
1 teaspoon sugar
2 cups corn pulp
1 tablespoon chopped pimiento
Salt and pepper to taste
1½ cups sour cream
Toast points or croutons

Sauté diced strips of bacon over low heat, stirring frequently until they are crisp and brown. Remove the bacon and sauté onion in the bacon fat. Add sugar, freshly scraped corn pulp, pimiento, salt, and pepper. Cook this mixture for 10 minutes. Add sour cream, reheat the mixture, and add diced bacon. Serve on toast points or on a bed of croutons, and garnish with curls of crisp bacon.

SERVES 4 to 6

FRESH CORN IN CREAM

Corn on the cob
Salt and pepper
Heavy cream

Cut enough fresh corn from the cobs to fill a 1½-quart buttered earthenware casserole. Sprinkle the corn with salt and freshly ground pepper and add heavy cream almost to cover. Cover the casserole and simmer the corn on top of the grill for 5 minutes.

SERVES 4

CORN SOUFFLÉ

2 tablespoons butter
2 tablespoons flour
1 cup milk
1 cup corn pulp
4 eggs, separated
Salt and pepper to taste
Corn kernels for garnish

Make cream sauce from butter, flour, and hot milk. Add freshly cooked and scraped corn pulp. Add 4 egg yolks, well beaten, and heat without boiling. Add salt and pepper and fold in 5 stiffly beaten egg whites. Pour the mixture into a 1½-quart baking dish or soufflé dish, buttered and floured, and bake it in a moderately hot oven (375° F.) for about 30 minutes, or until the soufflé is well puffed and nicely browned. The soufflé may be garnished before baking with a few whole kernels of corn cut from the cob.

SERVES 4

BARBECUED CORN

An unusual way to serve corn at a barbecue.

1 ear corn
Butter or margarine, *or* 2 tablespoons water

Open corn husks on each ear and remove corn silk and outside layer of corn husk. Cover corn kernels with butter or margarine, or sprinkle with 2 tablespoons water. Replace corn husks around corn; wrap in aluminum foil. Place on barbecue around outside for 20 to 30 minutes, turning occasionally. (Time depends on size of ear and heat of coals.)

MAKES 1 EAR

Puddings and Custards

CORN PUDDING

Good served with chicken.

12 ears corn
½ cup milk
1 teaspoon salt
1½ tablespoons sugar
3 tablespoons melted butter
5 eggs, beaten lightly
6 crackers, crushed

Remove corn from ears with coarse grater. Stir all ingredients together and pour into a greased 2-quart casserole. Bake 1 hour at 375° F., then ½ hour at 350° F. Top will be slightly brown.

SERVES 6

GREEN CORN PUDDING

Nutmeg gives this pudding flavor.

12 ears corn
1 cup light cream
Salt and pepper
Nutmeg
2 tablespoons butter
3 eggs, separated

Grate uncooked ears of corn, and with the back of a dinner knife scrape out all the milk remaining on the cobs. Add light cream seasoned with salt, pepper, and nutmeg to taste. Stir in 2 tablespoons melted butter, fold in 3 egg yolks, beaten, and 3 egg whites, stiffly beaten, and pour the mixture into a generously buttered 9″ × 13″ baking dish. Bake the pudding for 35 to 40 minutes in a slow oven (300° F.), then raise the heat to 375° F. and brown the top for 10 to 15 minutes. Serve either hot or cold.

SERVES 8 to 10

CORN CUSTARD

2 eggs, beaten
2 cups canned niblets or fresh corn
¼ cup sugar
½ teaspoon salt
¼ teaspoon pepper
1½ cups milk

Mix all ingredients together and bake in a buttered dish at 350° F. until custard is firm, about 1½ hours.

SERVES 6

Main Dishes

CRACKED WHEAT AND CORN PILAF

Vegetarian's delight.

1 cup bulgur
1 cup regular-strength chicken, beef, or vegetable broth (or water)
2 tablespoons chopped parsley
¼ cup diced green or red bell pepper or carrot
½ cup thinly sliced green onion
2 cups finely diced Cheddar, Swiss, or Monterey Jack cheese
1 cup whole kernel corn, cut off the cob or frozen (thawed)
1 egg, lightly beaten

HERBED TOMATO SAUCE

1 8-ounce can tomato sauce
1 teaspoon dry basil
½ teaspoon oregano leaves
½ teaspoon garlic salt
¼ teaspoon pepper

In a mixing bowl, combine the bulgur and broth; let stand about 1 hour, or until liquid is absorbed, stirring occasionally. Stir in the parsley, pepper or carrot, onion, cheese, corn, and egg.

Mix together all ingredients for the Herbed Tomato Sauce; stir into vegetable mixture. Spoon mixture into a shallow greased 1½-quart casserole. Cover and chill if made ahead. Bake, covered, in a 350° F. oven for 25 minutes (35 if cold), or until hot throughout.

SERVES 6

CHEESE-CORN STRADA

Vegetarian entree.

8 slices bread, crusts trimmed and cubed into ¾-inch squares
Butter
¼ to ½ pound American or Cheddar cheese, grated
1 to 1½ cups freshly cut corn, salted
3 eggs, well beaten
2 cups milk
1 teaspoon baking powder
1 teaspoon salt

Butter bread, then cube. In a buttered 8″ × 8″ or 1½-quart Pyrex dish, place a layer of half the bread cubes, then a layer of half the grated cheese. On top of cheese put a thin layer of corn which has been well salted. Repeat bread and cheese layers.

Beat eggs; add milk, baking powder, and salt. Pour this over bread mixture. Let stand overnight in refrigerator. Remove next morning, let come to room temperature, and then bake at 350°F. for 1 hour. Recipe can also be made omitting corn; it is then Cheese Strada.

SERVES 4 to 6

MAQUE CHOUX

1 large soup bone with meat
Water
3 cups fresh corn, cut from cob
1 #2 can whole tomatoes, *or* 2½ cups cooked fresh tomatoes
2 stalks celery, chopped
1 medium onion, chopped
½ bell pepper, chopped
Salt, pepper, and red pepper to taste

Cover soup bone with water and boil until very tender. Add remaining ingredients. Boil very slowly for about 2 hours.

SERVES 6

Breads

BAKED CORN

Almost like a corn bread.

6 ears corn, grated
¼ cup half-and-half
1 tablespoon sugar
1 teaspoon salt
6 crackers, crushed
3 tablespoons melted butter
3 egg whites

Mix together all ingredients except egg whites. Beat egg whites stiff, and fold into mixture. Bake about 1 hour at 375°F.

SERVES 4 to 6

CORN FRITTERS

1 cup pancake or buscuit mix
½ cup milk
1 egg
1 cup corn

Mix all ingredients; drop from spoon and brown on grill. Grease grill before each frying.

MAKES 4 4-INCH FRITTERS

FRESH CORN CAKES

These cakes make a wonderful breakfast with crisp bacon and tomato slices.

3 ears fresh sweet corn
1 egg
1 cup thick buttermilk
½ teaspoon baking soda
½ teaspoon salt
½ teaspoon sugar
½ cup flour
2 teaspoons cooking oil

To cut kernels from corn, hold the ear upright in a shallow bowl and cut downward with a sharp knife, cutting off only the tip of each kernel. Then, using the back of the knife, scrape downward until you have removed all the milk from each kernel.

To this corn mixture add the whole egg, buttermilk, and sifted dry ingredients, beating after each addition. Stir in oil. Drop by spoonfuls onto a very hot, well oiled iron skillet. Turn when brown and eat while piping hot.

SERVES 4

Relishes

CORN RELISH

Can be refrigerated for several weeks.

6 ears cooked corn, *or* 1 #2 can whole kernel corn
½ medium green pepper, chopped
2½ tablespoons finely cut pimiento
1 cup diced celery
1 large onion, chopped
⅔ cup salad oil
2½ tablespoons wine vinegar
1¼ teaspoons dry mustard
2½ tablespoons salt
1¼ teaspoons pepper

Slice kernels from cob, or drain canned corn. Add green pepper, pimiento, celery, and onion. Mix oil, vinegar, mustard, salt, and pepper; pour over corn mixture. Allow to stand several hours to mellow.

MAKES 4 to 6 PINTS

CORN CHOW CHOW

A relish good with anything.

6 to 8 ears summer corn
1 pint little green butter beans, cooked
1 quart (12) green tomatoes
5 pounds cabbage
4 large white onions
6 green peppers
2 red peppers
2 hot peppers (optional)
1 cup salt

BRINE

1½ quarts vinegar
1 cup brown or white sugar
1 tablespoon mustard seed
1 tablespoon celery seed
1 tablespoon turmeric
1 tablespoon dry mustard
½ cup cold water
1 box pickling spices in bag

Drop corn into salted boiling water; cook 5 minutes. Slice off cob, combine with butter beans, and put aside.

Put tomatoes, cabbage, onions, and peppers through a coarse grinder. Salt down this mixture overnight with 1 cup salt; next morning squeeze dry.

Mix together all brine ingredients; boil 5 minutes. Put all vegetables except corn and beans into brine. Cook and stir over high heat 10 minutes; then add corn and beans. Place in sterile jars and cover Chow Chow with brine.

MAKES 12 to 14 PINTS

Cucumbers

1 pound = 2 6-inch cucumbers = 3 cups sliced
3.5 ounces (1 5-inch) cucumber = 16 calories, .9 grams protein, 3.6 grams carbohydrates, 168 milligrams potassium, 260 units vitamin A, 12 milligrams ascorbic acid

Rich soil and warm weather are what the basic cucumber loves. They can quickly spread all over your yard so you may need to control them with wire fencing. Anyone who has ever been on a diet has made good friends with the cucumber. It's 95 percent water! It is best to harvest every 3 to 5 inches. The tasty ones are bright green, becoming darker as they age. Wash them off and they will keep up to 3 weeks in the refrigerator.

Cucumbers are most usually eaten raw. They can be scored or you can thin slice with the skin still on to add color to a salad.

To freeze: Forget it! The cucumber has too much water and you end up with a green ice cube.

Appetizers and Dips

CUCUMBERS AND SOUR CREAM

We could live on these alone!

Unpeeled cucumbers
1 cup sour cream
1 teaspoon mayonnaise
⅛ teaspoon pepper
Horseradish to taste
Parsley or dill, finely chopped

Score unpeeled cucumbers by drawing the tines of a silver fork down their length. Slice the cucumbers very thinly; chill.

Combine sour cream, mayonnaise, pepper, and horseradish to make dressing. Serve chilled cucumbers with dressing, garnished with finely chopped parsley or dill.

CUCUMBERS IN YOGURT

Low calorie but doesn't taste it.

3 cucumbers, peeled and cubed
3 cups yogurt
2 cloves garlic, crushed
½ teaspoon salt
Freshly ground pepper
1 tablespoon melted butter
1 tablespoon oil
1 tablespoon wine vinegar
2 tablespoons chopped fresh dill, *or* 1 tablespoon dried dillweed
2 tablespoons chopped fresh parsley
½ cup walnuts, chopped
2 hard-cooked egg yolks, crumbled

Mix all ingredients together in bowl. Chill in refrigerator 1 hour. Serve with coarse brown bread.

SERVES 4

CUCUMBER DIP

A good fresh vegetable dip.

2 large cucumbers, unpeeled and grated
½ cup sour cream
½ cup mayonnaise
¼ cup grated raw carrot
3 tablespoons chopped radishes
1 tablespoon chopped parsley
Salt and red papper to taste

Mix all ingredients together. Chill.

MAKES ABOUT 2 CUPS

CUCUMBER CANAPE

Good for a tea or luncheon sandwich.

2 tablespoons butter
2 tablespoons Roquefort or blue cheese

1 teaspoon lemon juice
20 toasted bread rounds
20 slices cucumber, soaked in salted ice water
Salt to taste
1 tablespoon chopped parsley

Cream together butter, cheese, and lemon juice. Spread on toasted bread rounds and cover each with a slice of cucumber. Sprinkle with salt and parsley.

SERVES 20

Soups

COLD CUCUMBER SOUP

An easy version.

½ pint dairy sour cream
½ pint plain yogurt
¼ teaspoon curry powder or to taste
½ cucumber, peeled and diced
2 tablespoons diced onion
4 tablespoons honey
Chopped chives

Combine all ingredients except chives and chill for at least 1 hour or overnight. Serve in ½-cup portions, as it is very rich. Garnish with chopped chives.

SERVES 6

COLD CUCUMBER AND BUTTERMILK SOUP

If you like buttermilk, you'll love this!

2 medium cucumbers
1 quart buttermilk
1 tablespoon green onion, minced
1 teaspoon salt
½ teaspoon monosodium glutamate
¼ cup parsley, minced
White pepper

GARNISH

2 to 4 thin slices cucumber
2 to 4 parsley sprigs

Peel cucumbers, cut into small pieces, and put in blender. Add buttermilk, onion, salt, monosodium glutamate, parsley, and white pepper. Blend until well mixed. Serve icy cold. Float a small thin slice of cucumber on each serving with a sprig of parsley.

SERVES 4 AS APPETIZER; 2 AS MAIN DISH

YOGURT CUCUMBER SOUP

Low calorie cold soup.

1 pint yogurt
1 cup milk
½ cup chicken broth
1 tablespoon salad oil
Dash garlic powder
1 medium cucumber
Salt and hot red pepper sauce to taste
1 teaspoon finely cut chives

Combine yogurt, milk, broth, oil, and garlic powder in a blender, food processor, or mixing bowl. Pare and thinly slice cucumber, then dice coarsely for machine or chop finely for bowl to make ½ cup pulp. Add to yogurt mixture; cover and whirl briefly to mix contents. Do not overmix. Season to taste with salt and pepper sauce. Add chives. Chill.

SERVES 4

Salads

EUROPEAN CUCUMBER SALAD

2 teaspoons salt
3 cucumbers, peeled and thinly sliced

3 tablespoons white vinegar
2 tablespoons minced green onions
3 tablespoons snipped fresh dill, *or* 2 teaspoons dried dill
Freshly ground pepper
½ cup sour cream
Paprika

Sprinkle salt on cucumbers; let stand for an hour. Squeeze to remove the liquid, and mix with vinegar, onions, dill, pepper, and sour cream. Sprinkle with paprika for color, and chill.

SERVES 4 to 6

MELON, CUCUMBER, AND TOMATO SALAD

A wonderful fruit/vegetable combination.

1 honeydew or casaba melon
1 cucumber
4 large, firm, ripe tomatoes (about 2 pounds)

DRESSING

½ cup salad oil
¼ cup lemon or lime juice
2 teaspoons sugar
½ teaspoon salt
Dash pepper
1 tablespoon parsley, chopped
1 tablespoon mint leaves, chopped

About 1 hour before serving, cut honeydew or casaba melon in half, scoop out seeds, and peel off rind. Cut each half into thin wedges and place in a salad bowl along with thinly sliced cucumber, peeled if desired, and tomatoes, peeled and cubed.

Prepare dressing. In a small jar, combine salad oil, lemon or lime juice, sugar, salt, pepper, parsley, and mint; cover and shake well. (If made ahead, cover and refrigerate.) Pour dressing over salad, and stir gently to mix. Cover and let stand at room temperature until serving time, stirring once or twice.

SERVES 6 to 8

GAZPACHO SALAD

Main dish summer meal.

2 medium cucumbers, peeled and sliced
Salt
⅔ cup olive oil
⅓ cup wine vinegar
1 garlic clove, minced
1 teaspoon dried basil
1 teaspoon salt
½ teaspoon pepper
10 medium mushrooms, sliced
4 scallions, sliced
½ cup minced parsley
3 large tomatoes, minced
1 medium green pepper, minced
½ pound Swiss cheese, cut into thin strips
4 hard-cooked eggs, sliced

Sprinkle cucumbers with salt; let stand ½ hour. In large bowl, combine oil, vinegar, garlic, basil, 1 teaspoon salt, and pepper. Add mushrooms, scallions, and drained cucumbers. Top mixture with parsley and mix gently. Add a layer of tomatoes and green pepper. Cover bowl and chill for 4 hours. Just before serving, add cheese strips and toss slightly. Garnish with egg slices.

SERVES 8

CREAMY CUCUMBER SALAD MOLD

2 medium-sized cucumbers
1 3-ounce package lime gelatin
1 teaspoon beef-flavored instant bouillon
1 cup boiling water
1 cup sour cream
½ teaspoon dry mustard
⅛ teaspoon dill weed
3 tablespoons tarragon vinegar
Lettuce leaves
Tomato wedges

Cut cucumbers in half lengthwise and scrape out seeds. Coarsely shred cucumbers; drain in a colander.

Meanwhile, in a bowl, combine gelatin and bouillon; add water and stir until completely dissolved. Mix sour cream, mustard, dill, and vinegar until smooth; add with cucumbers to gelatin and mix well. Pour into a lightly oiled 1-quart mold or 8 individual ½-cup molds. Chill until firm.

To serve, unmold and garnish with lettuce and tomato.

SERVES 8

CUCUMBER MOUSSE

3 3-ounce packages apple or lime gelatin
1 tablespoon salt
2 cups boiling water
1 tablespoon onion, grated
⅓ cup vinegar
1½ pints commercial sour cream
¾ cup mayonnaise
3 cups finely chopped, drained cucumber

Prepare gelatin with salted boiling water, stirring until dissolved; add onion and vinegar. Refrigerate until as thick as egg white. With egg beater, beat in sour cream and mayonnaise. Stir in cucumber. Pour into 2-quart mold and refrigerate overnight.

SERVES 12

AVOCADO-CUCUMBER SALAD MOLD

1 3-ounce package lime gelatin
1½ cups boiling water
1 large ripe avocado, sieved
1 medium cucumber, pared and diced
1 cup creamed cottage cheese
1 teaspoon grated onion
2 teaspoons lemon juice
½ teaspoon salt
Watercress or lettuce

Dissolve gelatin in boiling water. Divide ½ cup gelatin among 6 oiled individual molds or pour into a 9-inch square pan. Chill until firm.

Stir together avocado, cucumber, cottage cheese, onion, lemon juice, and salt. Add remaining gelatin mixture. Pour on top of firm gelatin and chill. Unmold or cut into squares. Serve on watercress or lettuce.

SERVES 6

Main Dishes

MOLDED CUCUMBER SALAD

This is one of the best—to be served with shrimp or lobster in the center.

1 package lime gelatin
¾ cup boiling water
2 3-ounce packages cream cheese
1 cup mayonnaise
2 teaspoons horseradish
2 teaspoons lemon juice
1 grated cucumber
½ cup chopped green onions (use the whole onion)
Shrimp or lobster

GARNISH

Tomatoes
Parsley

Dissolve gelatin in boiling water; let cool.

Soften cream cheese; mix with mayonnaise, horseradish, lemon juice, and cucumber; add to gelatin mixture. When mixture begins to thicken, fold in onions. Pour into an 8- or 9-inch ring mold.

To serve, fill center of mold with shrimp or lobster. Garnish with tomatoes and parsley.

SERVES 6

SALMON LUNCHEON MOLD

With cucumber sauce—a Newport Beach favorite. The best salmon luncheon mold!

1 10½-ounce can tomato soup
1 3-ounce package cream cheese
2 tablespoons plain gelatin
¼ cup water
1 cup diced celery
1 1-pound can salmon (or fresh cooked if possible)
1 green pepper, diced
1 cup mayonnaise
1 tablespoon Worcestershire sauce
1 medium onion, grated
2 tablespoons sweet pickle relish
½ teaspoon salt
Lettuce or other greens
Cooked broccoli tips for garnish

SOUR CREAM CUCUMBER SAUCE

1½ tablespoons vinegar
¾ teaspoon salt
1 tablespoon sugar
2 tablespoons chopped chives or green onions
1 tablespoon dill seed
1 teaspoon celery seed
¼ teaspoon dry mustard
1 cup dairy sour cream
2 cucumbers, pared, sliced thin

Heat soup until steaming; add cream cheese and dissolve; blend. Soften gelatin in water; add to soup and cheese mixture. Stir well. Combine with celery, salmon, green pepper, mayonnaise, Worcestershire, onion, pickle relish, and ½ teaspoon salt. Pour into a 6-cup oiled mold (a fish mold is very attractive) and place in refrigerator at least 3 hours. Unmold on greens and garnish with cooked broccoli tips.

Prepare Sour Cream Cucumber Sauce. Mix vinegar with salt and sugar; add chopped chives or green onions, dill seed, celery seed, and mustard. Add all this to sour cream. Slice cucumbers very thin and add to dressing. Let stand 2 hours in refrigerator. Serve salmon mold with sauce at side.

SERVES 4 to 6

HOT-WEATHER CUCUMBER AND SALMON SALAD

A meal in itself with bread or rolls.

1 tablespoon gelatin
½ cup cold water
½ cup hot water
1 large can salmon, *or* 2 cans tuna fish
½ cup chopped green peppers
½ cup chopped celery
¼ cup chopped scallions
1 cup chopped cucumbers
1 teaspoon lemon juice

SAUCE

1 pint sour cream
1 bunch radishes, sliced

Dissolve gelatin in cold water; add hot water. Add fish, peppers, celery, scallions, cucumbers, and lemon juice. Place in refrigerator to jell.

Prepare sauce by mixing sour cream with sliced radishes, and serve with cucumber-salmon mold.

SERVES 6

SALMON WITH CUCUMBER SAUCE

We have this on Christmas day with the traditional turkey.

4 to 6 pound salmon
Salt and pepper
Sprinkle lemon juice
Handful cut parsley, onion tops, and celery tops

CUCUMBER IN SOUR CREAM SAUCE

4 cucumbers
Vinegar
½ cup sugar
Salt and pepper to taste
1 tablespoon Worcestershire sauce
1 cup sour cream

Wash salmon and place on a piece of cheesecloth cut large enough that ends can be used to pick up fish. Salt and pepper insides and sprinkle with lemon juice. Place a handful of cut parsley, onion tops, and celery tops in the cavity. Place fish in large roasting pan with ½ inch of water. Cover and steam until fish flakes, or approximately 45 minutes at 350°F. Remove salmon with cheesecloth. Skin the fish while it is hot, remove stuffing, and roll fish onto serving platter. Let cool.

Prepare Cucumber in Sour Cream Sauce. Peel and dice cucumbers into small cubes. Cover with vinegar. Add sugar and let stand in refrigerator 2 or 3 hours. Pour off vinegar and add salt, pepper, Worcestershire, and sour cream. Cover salmon with sauce.

SERVES 6

Side Dishes

COOKED CUCUMBERS

Good with chicken.

4 cucumbers
Sugar
Salt
Red wine vinegar
Butter
Shallots
Heavy cream (optional)

Peel, halve, and remove seeds from cucumbers. Cut lengthwise into strips, then crosswise into thirds. Place cucumbers in bowl and cover with ¼ teaspoon sugar, 1½ teaspoons salt, and 1 teaspoon red wine vinegar for each cup of cucumbers. (Number of cups yielded by four cucumbers will depend on the size of the cucumbers.) Let sit for 30 minutes, then drain. Sauté cucumbers in butter until not quite brown. Sprinkle with chopped shallots. May be drenched in heavy cream.

SERVES 4 to 6

FRIED CUCUMBERS

This is a good and unusual way to use young cucumbers as a hot vegetable.

½ cup flour (scant)
Pinch salt
1 egg, beaten
8 tablespoons chicken stock
12 cucumbers
Cooking oil
Sour cream
Fresh dill or parsley

Mix flour with salt, egg, and chicken stock. Mix well to make a batter.

Get young, small cucumbers, allowing about 3 per person. Cut off the tips and scrub thoroughly. Dip cucumbers in the batter and drop, a few at a time, in a kettle of hot fat (360°F.). Fry until crisp and golden.

Serve hot with commercial sour cream and a sprinkle of fresh dill or parsley. These are usually eaten with boiled new potatoes, heavily buttered.

SERVES 4

STUFFED CUCUMBERS

4 cucumbers
Salt
Lemon juice
1 cup Italian-style bread crumbs or plain crumbs
2 tablespoons green onions, chopped
2 tablespoons celery, chopped
2 tablespoons parsley, chopped
1 clove garlic, finely chopped, *or* garlic powder to taste
Olive oil
Worcestershire sauce
Salt and pepper to taste
Parmesan cheese, grated

Parboil cucumbers until just tender when pierced with fork. Cut in half. Scoop out seeds, leaving meat; drain well. Sprinkle generously with salt and lemon juice.

Mix bread crumbs with onions, celery, parsley, and garlic, and moisten well with olive oil. Add a small amount of Worcestershire sauce and season with salt and pepper and grated Parmesan cheese. Lightly stuff into cucumbers. Sprinkle more Parmesan cheese on top.

Grease a shallow pan with cooking oil. Add a small amount of water to prevent sticking and place stuffed cucumbers in pan. Bake at 350°F. until top is brown and crusty, about 15 to 20 minutes.

MAKES 8 HALVES

Pickles and Relishes

MARINATED FRESH VEGETABLES

This colorful, crisp relish can double as a salad.

2 tomatoes
2 stalks celery
1 zucchini
1 onion
1 green pepper
½ cucumber, peeled
½ cup sugar
½ cup cider vinegar
½ teaspoon salt
½ teaspoon pepper

Peel tomatoes. Discard seeds. Dice into ½-inch squares. Dice remaining vegetables. Toss together. Combine sugar, vinegar, salt, and pepper. Thoroughly blend into vegetables. Refrigerate 4 or more hours. Drain and serve in chilled bowl.

SERVES 8

CUCUMBER COOLER

May be kept for several weeks in the refrigerator.

¼ cup vinegar
1 tablespoon lemon juice
1 teaspoon celery seed
2 tablespoons sugar
1 teaspoon salt
⅛ teaspoon black pepper
¼ cup onion, chopped
2 tablespoons parsley
3 medium cucumbers, sliced thin

Mix together all ingredients except cucumbers in a jar or large container with a lid. Add cucumber slices. Toss to coat with dressing mixture. Chill. Turn or shake container several times. Keep refrigerated.

MAKES 1 QUART

MARINATED CUCUMBERS

This is a very tasty accompaniment to a roast.

1 or 2 cucumbers
5 tablespoons sugar
½ cup vinegar
½ teaspoon salt

Slice the cucumbers paper thin. Combine sugar, vinegar, and salt. Marinate cucumbers in this mixture for only a few hours; if marinated longer, cucumbers will get limp.

SERVES 4

SPICY 7-DAY REFRIGERATOR PICKLES

7 or 8 medium-sized cucumbers (about 3½ pounds)

Boiling water
4 cups sugar
2 cups white distilled vinegar
1 tablespoon mixed pickling spice
2 teaspoons salt

Scrub cucumbers; leave whole. Place in a deep bowl and cover with boiling water. Let stand overnight. The next day, drain cucumbers, again cover with boiling water, and let stand overnight. Repeat this process on the third and fourth days. On the fifth day, cut cucumbers into ¼-inch slices and return them to the clean deep bowl.

In a 3-quart saucepan, combine sugar, vinegar, pickling spice, and salt. Bring to a boil to dissolve sugar; pour over cucumbers. Cool, then cover bowl and refrigerate two days.

On the seventh day bring cucumbers and syrup just to a boil, then pack into hot clean jars; place on lids. Allow to cool, then store in the refrigerator.

MAKES ABOUT 5 PINTS

SWEET FREEZER CHIPS

If you love pickles and hate canning, freeze these.

5 medium cucumbers (about 2½ pounds)
1 medium-sized white onion
Salt
2 quarts ice cubes
4 cups sugar
2 cups cider vinegar

Cut cucumbers into ⅛-inch slices; you should have 2 quarts. Also thinly slice onion. Mix the cucumber and onion slices with salt in a large bowl; cover mixture with about 2 quarts ice cubes and refrigerate 2 to 3 hours. Drain off water and discard unmelted ice cubes; do not rinse. Pack cucumber and onion slices in freezer containers or canning jars to within 1½ inches from top.

In a 2-quart pan, combine sugar and vinegar and quickly bring to a boil, stirring, until sugar dissolves. Pour just enough hot syrup over cucumbers to cover. Place on lids and freeze at least one week.

To serve, place container to thaw in the refrigerator at least 8 hours.

MAKES ABOUT 3 PINTS

GRANDMA TANNER'S FAVORITE MUSTARD PICKLES

This recipe is 100 years old—and a winner at several Utah state fairs!

3 large cucumbers, peeled and seeds removed
6 cups onions
3 green peppers
2 red peppers
1 head celery
1 head cauliflower
3 quarts green tomatoes
3 cups vinegar
6 cups water
6 cups sugar
1 cup flour
½ cup mustard seed
2 teaspoons turmeric
1 teaspoon mustard

Cut cucumbers, onions, peppers, celery, cauliflower, and tomatoes into small pieces. Soak in salt water overnight, rinse with cold water, and drain. Heat ingredients with 3 cups vinegar and 6 cups water.

Mix together sugar, flour, mustard seed, turmeric, and mustard with a little water and vinegar. Pour over vegetables, cook 15 minutes, and seal in hot jars.

MAKES 6 to 8 QUARTS

BREAD AND BUTTER PICKLES

12 medium cucumbers
6 medium onions
Salted water
2 cups sugar
3 cups vinegar
1 cup water
1 teaspoon mustard
1 teaspoon salt
1 teaspoon celery seed
2 green peppers, chopped

Slice cucumbers and onions, and let stand overnight in salt water. Drain.

Mix together sugar, vinegar, 1 cup water, mustard, salt, celery seed, and green peppers. Pour over cucumbers and onions. Bring to boil. Seal in jars.

MAKES 4 to 6 QUARTS

CHOPPED MUSTARD PICKLES

1 quart cauliflower
1 quart onions
1 quart green tomatoes
1 quart celery
1 quart cucumbers
3 red peppers
3 cups vinegar
1 pound brown sugar
3 cups sugar
3 cups water
6 tablespoons flour
6 tablespoons dry mustard
3 tablespoons salt
1 tablespoon turmeric

Cut all vegetables to the size of thumb and measure. Steam cauliflower until tender and drain. Add remaining vegetables, combine with vinegar, sugar, and water, and bring to boil.

Sift flour, mustard, salt, and turmeric, make into a paste with water, and add to vegetables. Cook 20 minutes and bottle.

Note: We have sometimes substituted cucumbers for tomatoes.

MAKES 6 to 8 QUARTS

DILL PICKLES

Blue ribbon winner in the Lincoln County Fair—the secret is the coarse salt and fresh stalk of dill in each jar.

3 cups water
1 cup white vinegar
¼ cup coarse salt (like the salt you use to make ice cream)
2 quarts pickling cucumbers
2 stalks fresh dill
2 cloves garlic
2 teaspoons alum

Be sure measurements are accurate. Bring water, vinegar, and salt to a good rolling boil. Put cleaned cucumbers, a stalk of dill, and a clove of garlic into each of 2 1-quart bottles. Add 1 teaspoon alum to each quart, then add hot liquid and seal. The liquid is enough for 2 quarts.

Never double the ingredients or your pickles may not turn out right. If for some reason either of the bottles does not seal after cooling, just drain juice off, reheat, and, using a new lid, reseal. Do not use for 6 weeks; the longer the pickles age, the better they are.

MAKES 2 QUARTS

HOT DILL PICKLES

Cucumbers to fill a 1-quart jar
3 dill heads
4 large garlic buttons
4 pods hot pepper
2 tablespoons bulk or meat salt
1 cup red vinegar
Boiling water

Pack cucumbers in jar. (Use medium-sized cucumbers if you want to pack them vertically.) Add dill heads, garlic, hot pepper, and bulk salt. Heat red vinegar and bring to a boil. Pour over cucumbers and finish filling with boiling water. Seal and set aside for 2 weeks.

MAKES 1 QUART

Eggplant

1 pound = 1 large eggplant = 3–3½ cups cooked
1 cup cooked = 38 calories, 2 grams protein, 8.2 grams carbohydrates, 300 milligrams potassium, 20 units vitamin A, 6 milligrams vitamin C

This beautiful purple plant is easy to grow. Don't be put off by the unusual name; try it—to grow and eat! In Europe it is loved and used in every dish under the sun. Eggplants can get huge, but it is by far the best at the small 4- to 6-inch stage. A good eggplant is shiny. If it is dull and there are brown seeds inside, it is overripe and not good to eat.

Eggplant will keep a week in the refrigerator and a young, superfresh eggplant doesn't need to be peeled when you cook it. It can be boiled, baked, or fried. It generally is served with something else, or breaded and served with lemon.

To freeze: This is tricky because of the eggplant's high water content. You can freeze in series or by cubes by dropping in cold salt water first to preserve color, then scalding for 4 minutes. We've had the best luck freezing eggplant puree which we use in many casseroles. Prepare eggplant pieces and scald 10 minutes, drain, puree in blender, and freeze.

Appetizers and Salads

EGGPLANT SPREAD

1 large or 2 medium eggplants
2 cloves garlic, minced
Salt and pepper to taste
Nutmeg, freshly grated
¼ cup oil
Parsley, chopped
Juice of ½ lemon

Grill eggplants in their skins in 450° F. oven for 35 to 40 minutes. Peel soft eggplant and mash in a food processor or pound in a mortar with garlic, salt, pepper, and freshly grated nutmeg. Drop by drop, beat in oil for a thick puree. Add parsley and lemon juice. Serve chilled with crackers.

SERVES 8

EGGPLANT CHIPS

1 very small eggplant
Hot deep fat
Salt to taste

Peel and cut eggplant into paper-thin slices and drop the slices at once into hot deep fat (375° F.). Fry the chips until they are golden. Drain them on absorbent paper and sprinkle with salt.

SERVES 2

EGGPLANT SLICES IN VINEGAR

1 medium-sized eggplant
Salt
3 teaspoons white wine vinegar

Trim, slice, and oven bake eggplant until tender. Arrange half the slices in a 7″ × 11″ baking dish (cut large slices in half). Sprinkle lightly with salt and drizzle with half the vinegar. Top with remaining slices; sprinkle with salt and remaining vinegar. Cover and chill up to 3 days.

MAKES ABOUT 8 SLICES

EGGPLANT SALAD

Dressing II may also be used as a party dip; it is especially good with fish or seafood.

3 medium eggplants
1 cup chopped green onions or dehydrated green onions
4 cloves garlic, crushed
1 cup chopped bell pepper
1 cup finely chopped fresh parsley
Salt to taste
Red pepper to taste

DRESSING I

½ cup olive oil
¼ cup lemon juice
Garlic, crushed

DRESSING II

½ cup sesame seed dressing (tahini)
Garlic, crushed
¼ cup lemon juice
Water

Place unpeeled eggplants in 450°F. oven and bake until they are soft and the skin crinkles. Remove from the oven and allow to cool. Peel and beat thoroughly with a mixer until it has a very smooth consistency. Add onions, garlic, bell pepper, parsley, and seasonings to taste.

There are two dressings which can be used for this very tasty salad.

For Dressing I, combine olive oil, lemon juice, and garlic, mixing thoroughly, and add to eggplant mixture. Blend again. Chill and serve.

For Dressing II, mix sesame seed dressing, which can be obtained from almost any imported food store, with crushed garlic and lemon juice (water may be added if it is too thick). Add to eggplant mixture, blend again, and chill. Dressing II may also be used as a party dip.

SERVES 8 to 10

VEGETABLE EGGPLANT SALAD

1 medium eggplant
3 tablespoons olive oil or salad oil
1 large green pepper
1 large tomato
½ cucumber
5 green onions
4 tablespoons lemon juice
1 clove garlic
Salt to taste

Trim ends from eggplant, then cut into 1-inch slices. Arrange slices in a single layer in a rimmed 10″ × 15″ baking pan. Brush cut sides with oil. Bake in a 425°F. oven for 25 to 30 minutes or until well browned; let cool.

Cut eggplant slices into ¾-inch cubes; you should have 2 cups. Combine in a bowl with green pepper, seeded and cut into strips; tomato, peeled, seeded, and diced; cucumber, peeled and diced; green onions, thinly sliced; lemon juice; and garlic, minced or pressed. Stir gently to mix; season with salt. Cover and chill up to 3 days.

MAKES ABOUT 5 CUPS

Side Dishes

LAYERED EGGPLANT CASSEROLE

Make this ahead—slip into the oven an hour before serving.

3 pounds eggplant (2 medium-sized or 3 small)
6 tablespoons olive oil or salad oil
1 medium-sized onion, finely chopped
1 clove garlic, minced or pressed
1 16-ounce can tomatoes
3 tablespoons tomato paste
4 to 5 mushrooms (about ⅛ pound), sliced

2 teaspoons sugar
1 beef bouillon cube
Salt and pepper
1 tablespoon flour
1 cup plain yogurt
Nutmeg
Grated Parmesan cheese

Cut eggplant (peeled if desired) into ½-inch slices; brush both sides lightly with about 4 tablespoons of the oil and arrange in single layers on 2 rimmed baking sheets. Bake in a 450°F. oven until slices are browned and very soft, about 30 minutes; set aside to cool.

Meanwhile, place 2 tablespoons of the oil in a saucepan and set over medium heat; when hot, add onion and garlic; cook, stirring, until onion is limp, about 10 minutes. Stir in tomatoes and their liquid (break up tomatoes with a spoon), tomato paste, mushrooms, sugar, and the bouillon cube; reduce heat and simmer, uncovered, until thick, 40 to 45 minutes; add salt and pepper to taste. Set aside 1 cup of this tomato sauce to use later.

Stir flour into the yogurt and add to remaining tomato sauce; cook, stirring, until thickened, about 10 minutes.

Arrange a third of the eggplant slices in the bottom of a shallow, 1½-quart baking dish; sprinkle lightly with nutmeg and spoon half the yogurt-tomato sauce over top. Repeat with another third of the eggplant and the remaining yogurt-tomato sauce to form a second layer; top with remaining eggplant. (If made ahead, cover and refrigerate.)

Before serving, cover with foil and bake in a 350°F. oven until mixture is thoroughly hot, about 30 minutes (if refrigerated, about 55 minutes). Heat the reserved cup of tomato sauce and spoon over top; sprinkle with Parmesan cheese.

SERVES 4 to 6

EGGPLANT DELIGHT

1 eggplant
1½ cups water
⅓ cup chopped onion
½ cup chopped celery
1 10½-ounce can cream of mushroom soup
⅓ to ½ cup milk
⅓ cup bell pepper, chopped
½ cup grated sharp cheese
½ cup toasted plain or Progresso bread crumbs
1 teaspoon salt
3 slices bacon, partially cooked

Peel and cube eggplant. Place in cold water for 10 minutes. Drain and cook with fresh water, onions, and celery until tender. Drain and mash. Beat soup and milk into eggplant. Add bell pepper, cheese, bread crumbs, and salt. Pour into greased casserole. Top with partially cooked bacon and bake uncovered at 350°F. for 35 minutes.

SERVES 4 to 6

SCALLOPED EGGPLANT

A Southern favorite made with corn bread crumbs.

1 large eggplant (or 2 small)
½ teaspoon salt
Dash black pepper
2 cups canned whole tomatoes, drained
½ cup onion, finely chopped
2 eggs, well beaten
2 cups corn bread crumbs
2 tablespoons butter
½ cup milk
½ cup grated Cheddar cheese

Peel eggplant and cut into cubes. Cook in a little water until tender. Drain thoroughly. Add salt and pepper, and mash with potato masher. Mash drained tomatoes and chopped onion, and combine with the mashed eggplant. Add the beaten eggs and corn bread crumbs. Grease casserole with butter. Pour in the mixture, adding enough milk to cover well. Top with grated cheese and bake at 375°F. until bubbly, about 20 minutes.

SERVES 6

BROILED EGGPLANT

Great as a side dish for breakfast or brunch.

1 large eggplant
Salted water
¼ cup melted butter
6 slices large ripe tomato
Salt and pepper to taste
1 cup grated American cheese
6 slices bacon, broiled and chopped

Peel eggplant and slice crosswise ½ inch thick. Soak slices in salted water for ½ hour. Brush slices with melted butter on both sides. Broil lightly, turn, and broil until almost tender. Top each slice with a thick slice of tomato. Salt and pepper to season; cover with generous amount of grated cheese and bacon pieces. Broil under flame until cheese melts and bacon browns. Serve at once, allowing one slice per serving.

SERVES 6

BAKED EGGPLANT PARMESAN

2 eggplants
½ teaspoon salt
Flour
2 eggs, slightly beaten
1 cup olive oil
1 15-ounce can tomato sauce
¼ cup grated Parmesan cheese
¾ pound mozzarella cheese, thinly sliced

Peel eggplant. Cut into ¼-inch slices. Sprinkle each slice with salt. Draw out juices by stacking slices between 2 plates topped with a weight. Let stand 1 hour. Coat with flour. Dip in egg. Fry in hot olive oil until golden brown. Drain on paper towel.

In a 9″ × 13″ baking dish, spread a thick layer of tomato sauce, then eggplant; sauce again, then Parmesan cheese, and finally mozzarella slices. Repeat twice or until all eggplant is used, ending with mozzarella. Bake at 400°F. for 15 to 20 minutes, or until cheese is melted.

SERVES 8

EGGPLANT ITALIANO

Easy to freeze.

2 medium-sized eggplants
Salted water
Flour
Oil
2 15-ounce cans pizza sauce or spaghetti sauce
1 16-ounce can grated Parmesan cheese

Wash and peel eggplant and slice ¼ inch thick. Place slices in salted water and leave until removed to skillet. Roll each slice of eggplant in flour and place in skillet with enough oil to cover; cook until golden brown on both sides.

Place cooked eggplant in a casserole in layers. Coat each layer with 4 tablespoons pizza sauce or spaghetti sauce and a thick layer of Parmesan cheese. Repeat until all the eggplant is used. Coat top layer with sauce and Parmesan cheese. Cook in medium oven (350° F.) until bubbling hot and cheese on top is golden brown, approximately 15 minutes.

SERVES 6

EGGPLANT WITH SWISS CHEESE

2 medium eggplants
Salted water (1½ teaspoons per 2 quarts water)
½ cup butter
Swiss cheese
Pepper

Slice eggplant ¼ inch thick and soak the slices in salted water for 20 minutes. Drain, cover with boiling water, and drain again. Dry the slices thoroughly.

Melt butter in a skillet and sauté the eggplant in it for about 2 minutes on each side, or until browned. Arrange the slices in a 9″ × 13″ baking dish, alternating the layers with layers of thinly sliced Swiss cheese and a sprinkling of freshly ground pepper. Bake the casserole in a moderate oven (350° F.) for 30 minutes, or until the cheese is melted and bubbly.

SERVES 8

EGGPLANT SANDWICH

2 medium eggplants
Flour
1 cup olive oil
2 egg yolks
½ pound mozzarella cheese
2 tablespoons Parmesan cheese
1 egg, beaten
Bread crumbs

Peel eggplant and cut into ½-inch slices. Dip in flour and sauté in hot olive oil for about 2 minutes on each side, or until almost tender. Drain.

Combine egg yolks, mozzarella cheese, and Parmesan cheese. Spread about 1 tablespoon of this mixture on an eggplant slice and cover filling with another slice in sandwich fashion. Dip whole sandwich in beaten egg, roll in bread crumbs, and brown on both sides in oil remaining in skillet.

SERVES 4

EGGPLANT FRITTERS

2 eggplants
1 large onion, chopped fine
½ bell pepper, chopped fine
2 cloves garlic, chopped fine
2 or 3 green onion tops
1 tablespoon chopped parsley
2 eggs, well beaten
4 teaspoons butter
Salt and pepper to taste
Flour
Cooking oil

Boil eggplant until tender. Peel and mash well. Add onion, bell pepper, garlic, onion tops, and parsley. Add eggs, butter, salt, and pepper. Add enough flour to make a good batter. Drop from spoon into hot oil. Brown and drain on brown paper. Serve hot.

SERVES 6 to 8

GRILLED EGGPLANT

A good choice for outdoor cooking.

1 large eggplant
Butter
Seasoned flour
Parmesan cheese

Peel eggplant and cut into ½-inch slices. Dip the slices in melted butter and seasoned flour. Broil the slices over hot coals until the underside is brown, turn, dot with butter, and brown the other side. If desired, the half-cooked eggplant may be generously sprinkled with grated Parmesan cheese; the cheese will melt as the underside of the eggplant browns.

SERVES 4

Main Dishes

EGGPLANT ROAST

A vegetarian main dish.

1 large eggplant
Salted water
3 eggs, well beaten
1 large onion, diced
2 cloves garlic, sliced
1½ cups white cracker crumbs
1 teaspoon salt
1 teaspoon poultry seasoning
Cheese slices, American or Monterey Jack
Half-and-half or light cream

Peel and cube eggplant. Cook in salted water until tender, about 20 minutes. Drain and combine with eggs, onion, garlic, cracker crumbs, salt, and poultry seasoning. Place half of mixture in a casserole. Cover with 1 layer of sliced cheese. Add remainder of mixture and top with another layer of cheese. Form a moat around the edge by pushing mixture to center. Pour half-and-half around edge. Bake in a 325°F. oven for 45 to 60 minutes until brown on edges.

SERVES 6 to 8

EGGPLANT CASSEROLE

Quick to fix—and good!

1 small onion, chopped
Butter
2 to 3 pounds hamburger
2 large eggplants
3 28-ounce cans tomatoes, drained
1 8-ounce package herb stuffing mix
Bread crumbs

Sauté onion in butter. Brown meat and drain. Peel and dice eggplant, then boil until translucent. Mix in the drained tomatoes, meat, onion, and stuffing. Put in a casserole and top with crumbs. Bake 1 hour at 325°F.

SERVES 10 to 12

ONE-DISH SUPPER

1 pound ground beef or lamb
4 tablespoons oil
2 tablespoons butter or margarine
1 small eggplant, cut into small cubes
3 onions, chopped
1 clove garlic, chopped
2 cups cooked macaroni or rice
3 large ripe tomatoes (2 cups canned)
1 teaspoon salt
Pepper, thyme, oregano to taste
Greens for garnish

In a large skillet, cook ground meat, stirring, until browned. Drain fat; set meat aside.

Heat oil and butter in same skillet; add cubed eggplant, onions, and garlic. Stir to brown. Return meat to pan; add macaroni, tomatoes, salt, pepper, thyme, and oregano. Cook, stirring, about 10 minutes. Garnish with greens.

SERVES 4

POLO CLUB EGGPLANT

Nutmeg gives this Southern dish a distinctive flavor—from a famous Southern polo club.

2 eggplants
Salted water
½ pound chicken livers (or to taste)
½ stick butter
Salt and pepper
2 eggs
⅓ cup cream
¼ teaspoon nutmeg
Salt and pepper to taste
1 7½-ounce can mushrooms
½ cup bread crumbs
½ cup grated cheese

Peel and cut the eggplant into cubes. Cook until tender in salted water. Drain well and mash. Broil livers in small amount of butter, reserving enough butter to dot top of casserole. Season with salt and pepper while broiling. Chop fine.

Beat eggs, cream, nutmeg, salt, and pepper together. Add drained mushrooms, eggplant, and liver with the butter it was cooked in; mix well. Put into a 1-quart casserole. Cover with bread crumbs and cheese, dot with butter, and cook in a 350°F. oven for 20 to 30 minutes. You will find this casserole slightly liquid before cooking, but don't worry, it will thicken.

SERVES 6 to 8

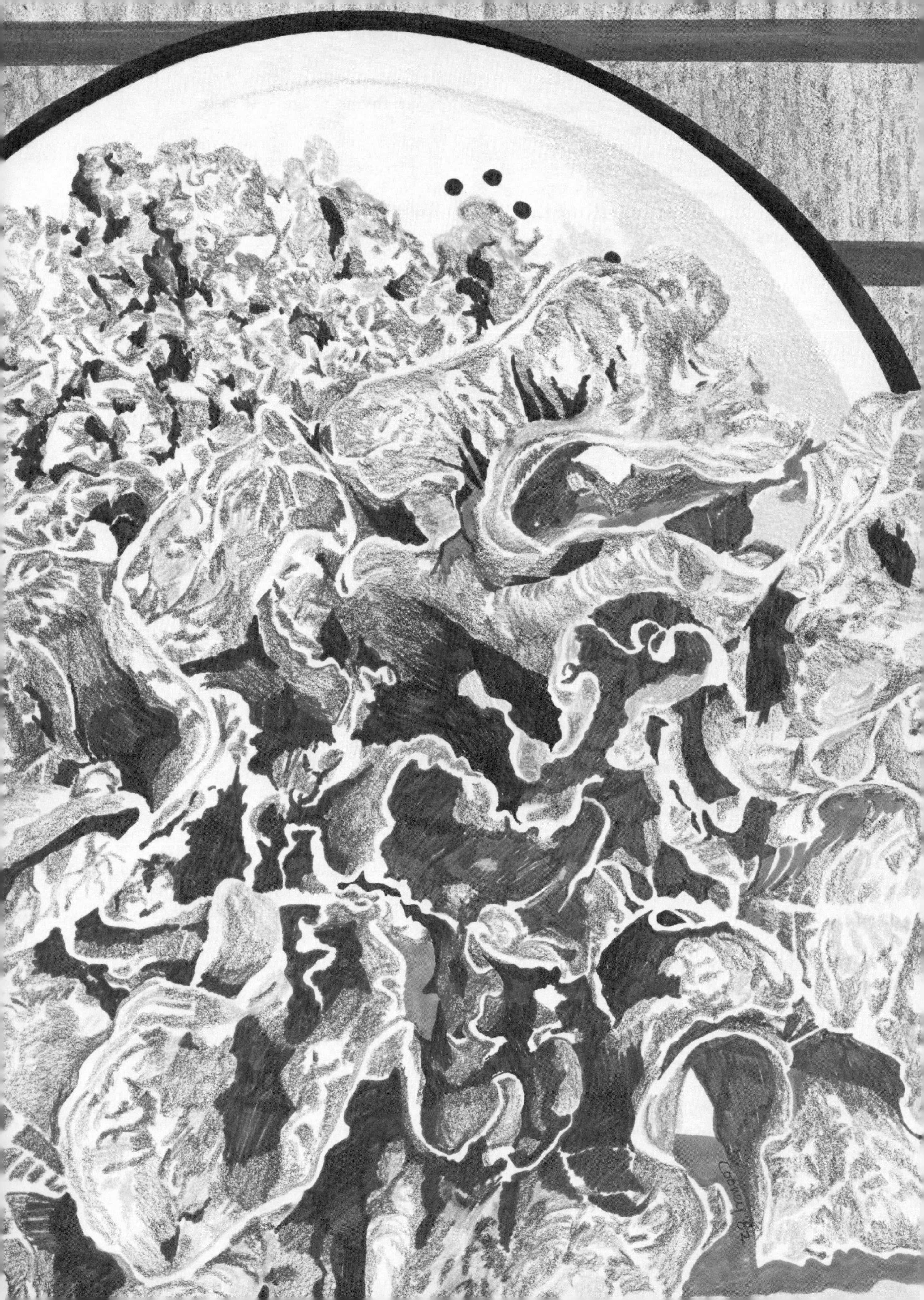
Cooney '82

Lettuce

1 pound = 1 medium head = 3½ cups torn
1 cup torn lettuce = 18 calories, 1.5 grams protein, 3 grams carbohydrates, 145 milligrams potassium, 1,050 units vitamin A, 10 milligrams vitamin C

The lettuce you buy at the market can't hold a candle to the lovely, leafy stuff you can grow. Boston lettuce and buttercrunch lettuce have been our favorites to grow, although there are many varied kinds. Lettuce grows fast and you can tuck it throughout your garden.

You can harvest outer leaves as the head grows. The outer leaves have the most vitamins and minerals. To harvest the whole head, pull up from the ground and cut off the root. To store, core, wash, and drain. Lettuce will store well in a plastic bag in your refrigerator for a week. A couple of paper towels in the bag help absorb moisture. Lettuce is usually eaten raw, although it can be braised.

To freeze: The closest you can get to freezing lettuce is a crisp salad on a chilled plate!

Soups

LETTUCE SOUP

You will never guess there is lettuce in this soup.

1 tablespoon onion, minced
1 tablespoon butter
1 tablespoon flour
½ teaspoon salt
¼ teaspoon pepper
3½ cups chicken broth, canned or fresh
1 head iceberg lettuce, shredded
½ cup heavy cream
1 egg yolk

Sauté onion in butter until tender. Blend in flour, salt, and pepper. Gradually stir in chicken broth. Cook and stir until thick and bubbling. Add lettuce. Cover pot and simmer 3 minutes. Combine cream and egg yolk. Stir small amount of hot mixture into the yolk mixture. Stir warmed yolk mixture back into hot mixture. Cook and stir just to boil. Taste for seasoning.

SERVES 6

CREAM OF LETTUCE SOUP

1 head romaine lettuce
1 bunch watercress
¼ cup butter
1 clove garlic (or garlic powder)
1 teaspoon tarragon
½ teaspoon dried parsley
3 tablespoons chopped onion (or onion flakes)
2 tablespoons chopped green peppers
4 cups beef bouillon or stock
Salt and pepper
1 cup milk, scalded
2 egg yolks
1 cup heavy cream

Shred a fairly large head of romaine as finely as possible. Chop watercress.

Cream butter; gradually add garlic clove, finely chopped; tarragon; and dried parsley and blend well. Heat the herb butter in a soup kettle and add onion and green pepper, both finely chopped. Cook the mixture for 3 to 4 minutes, stirring constantly, and add the chopped watercress and the shredded lettuce. Again cook the mixture for 3 to 4 minutes, stirring constantly. Add bouillon and cook for 25 minutes longer. Season to taste with salt and pepper and cook the soup for 15 more minutes. Remove the kettle from the heat and stir in scalded milk. Just before serving, stir in egg yolks, slightly beaten, mixed with cream.

SERVES 4

LETTUCE AND SOUR CREAM SOUP

3 tablespoons butter
2 tablespoons flour
1 cup chicken stock or bouillon
Salt and pepper
2 heads lettuce, shredded
1 cup sour cream
2 tablespoons capers
1 tablespoon cider vinegar

In a large skillet mix butter with flour and cook, stirring constantly, over very low heat until it bubbles. Add chicken stock, stirring mixture constantly until it is smooth. Season to taste with salt and pepper.

Shred lettuce. Wash the leaves in cold water; drain and pat dry. To sauce in skillet add lettuce and sour cream mixed with capers and cider vinegar. Cover skillet tightly and simmer lettuce gently for 10 minutes. Serve very hot.

SERVES 6 to 8

STUFFED LETTUCE

Looks beautiful on a table, fun for a dinner party.

1 small head iceberg lettuce
½ pound blue cheese
1 3-ounce package cream cheese
2 tablespoons milk
1 tablespoon chopped chives (or green onion tops)
1 whole pimiento, chopped
French dressing (make your own or use your favorite commercial brand)

Hollow out center of heart of lettuce, leaving a 1-inch shell of green. Beat cheeses and milk together until smooth. Add chives and pimiento and mix thoroughly. Fill lettuce hollow and chill in refrigerator until cheese mixture is solid. When ready to serve, cut in crosswise slices about ¾ inch thick and serve with French dressing.

SERVES 4 OR MORE, DEPENDING ON SIZE OF HEAD OF LETTUCE

Salads

GREENS FOR SALAD BOWL

A new way of looking at just what really can go into a salad bowl!

Use any combination of these salad greens: romaine (cos), Simpson, Bibb, Boston, or iceberg lettuce; escarole, chicory, endive, sorrel, garden cress, watercress, field salad, dandelions, young spinach, chard, beet tops, new nasturtium leaves.

Add: chives, shallots, parsley, tarragon, chervil.

For texture contrast, make use of other vegetables: cabbage, Chinese cabbage, radishes, cucumbers, celery, hearts of palm.

24-HOUR GREEN SALAD

This is a crisp, fresh green salad and can be done ahead.

6 cups chopped lettuce
Salt, pepper, sugar
6 hard-cooked eggs, sliced
1 10-ounce package frozen baby peas, thawed, not cooked
1 pound bacon, crisp-cooked, crumbled
½ cup sliced green onions
8 ounces Swiss cheese, shredded
1 cup mayonnaise
Paprika

In a large bowl (that you will serve in) place 3 cups lettuce; sprinkle with salt, pepper, and sugar. Add all the sliced eggs, all the thawed peas, all the bacon. Place remaining 3 cups lettuce over this; add green onions and top with shredded cheese. Frost with mayonnaise, being sure salad is completely covered. Top with paprika. Refrigerate 24 hours.

SERVES 12

7-LAYER SALAD

1 medium head lettuce, shredded (about 6 cups)
1 cup coarsely chopped celery
1 cup coarsely chopped green pepper
1½ cups coarsely chopped onion
1 cup cooked peas
1½ cups mayonnaise
2 teaspoons sugar
2½ cups shredded Cheddar cheese
8 strips bacon, cooked, drained, and crumbled, *or* bacon bits

Arrange lettuce in bottom of a deep bowl. In layers add celery, green pepper, onion, and peas; do not toss. Spread mayonnaise evenly over layer of peas. Sprinkle with sugar and cheese. Cover and refrigerate for at least 4 hours. Sprinkle bacon over salad before serving.

SERVES 10 to 12

WILTED LETTUCE

8 slices bacon cut into quarters, fried
½ cup vinegar
¼ cup sugar
¼ cup water
Bacon fat from fried bacon
1½ pounds leaf lettuce (early spring type)
3 tender green onions with green tops, chopped
Salt and pepper

Fry the bacon in a heavy frying pan until crisp. Remove from pan and drain on paper towels.

Add the vinegar, sugar, and water to the bacon fat, and boil for about 5 minutes to make a sauce. Set aside.

Tear greens into bite-sized pieces and place in a large salad bowl; add green onions, bacon, salt, and pepper. Boil the sauce once more. Pour over greens, toss quickly, and serve.

SERVES 6

LETTUCE–MANDARIN ORANGE SALAD

Colorful and different.

1 large head lettuce, *or* same amount of leaf lettuce
2 7½-ounce cans mandarin oranges
⅛ cup slivered almonds
Onion rings to taste

POPPY SEED DRESSING

½ cup sugar
½ teaspoon salt
1 tablespoon dry mustard
1 tablespoon paprika
1 teaspoon poppy seeds
4 tablespoons vinegar
2 teaspoons grated onion
1 cup salad oil

Tear lettuce into bite-sized pieces. Drain oranges and chill. Toast almonds to light brown in 300°F. oven.

Prepare Poppy Seed Dressing. With mixer, blend in all dressing ingredients except oil. Add salad oil in thirds, blending well after each addition. Toss dressing lightly with lettuce, oranges, almonds, and onion rings just before serving.

SERVES 6

ROMAINE AND APPLE SALAD

1 large head romaine, about 1½ pounds
⅔ cup sliced celery
¼ cup thinly sliced green onion
¼ cup raisins
6 slices bacon
3-red-skinned apples
¼ cup cider vinegar
¼ cup water
1 package Italian salad dressing mix (0.60 ounce)
2 teaspoons sugar
½ teaspoon dry mustard
½ teaspoon basil
Salt and pepper

Rinse and pat dry romaine leaves; break into bite-sized pieces. Combine the romaine, celery, green onion, and raisins. Cover and chill 2 to 4 hours.

In a wide frying pan over medium heat, cook the bacon until crisp; lift out, drain, and crumble. Set bacon aside and reserve drippings.

Just before serving, core but do not peel the apples; cut into thin slices. Heat the bacon drippings and stir in vinegar, water, salad dressing mix, sugar, dry mustard, and basil until well blended. Add apple slices, bacon, and hot dressing to the romaine mixture and mix well. Season to taste with salt and pepper. Serve at once.

SERVES 6 to 8

Main Dishes

MEXICAN CHEF SALAD

1 or 1½ pounds ground chuck, cooked and seasoned
1 head lettuce, chopped
1 large onion, chopped
1 15-ounce can red kidney beans
2 large tomatoes, chopped
1 large avocado, diced
1 3¼-ounce bag Dorito chips or other corn chips
1 10-ounce package mild Cheddar cheese, grated
1 bottle Thousand Island dressing
Salt and pepper to taste

Combine chuck, lettuce, onion, beans, tomatoes, avocado, Dorita chips, and cheese. Toss lightly. Add Thousand Island dressing and toss again. Season to taste with salt and pepper.

This is good with French bread for a late snack.

SERVES 12

CALIFORNIA SALAD BOWL

From a well-known California department store luncheon menu—has a Mexican flavor.

½ head lettuce, torn in pieces
2 tomatoes, in pieces
½ cup sliced black olives
½ cup green onions, chopped
1 7-ounce can tuna
½ cup mashed avocado
1 tablespoon lemon juice
⅛ cup salad oil
½ cup sour cream
½ teaspoon salt
¼ teaspoon pepper
½ cup corn chips
½ cup shredded Cheddar cheese

Combine lettuce, tomatoes, olives, onions, and tuna. Make a dressing by mixing together the avocado, lemon juice, salad oil, sour cream, salt, and pepper. Mix ½ cup regular-sized corn chips and ½ cup shredded cheese for top of salad. Serve with other chips to the side of salad.

SERVES 2

OVERNIGHT LAYERED CHICKEN SALAD

6 cups shredded iceberg lettuce
¼ pound bean sprouts
1 8-ounce can water chestnuts, drained and sliced
1½ cups thinly sliced green onions
1 medium-sized cucumber, thinly sliced
4 cups cooked chicken, cut into 2- to 3-inch strips
2 6-ounce packages frozen edible pea pods, thawed
2 cups mayonnaise
2 teaspoons curry powder
1 tablespoon sugar
½ teaspoon ground ginger
½ cup Spanish-style peanuts
1 to 1½ dozen cherry tomatoes, halved

In a shallow 4-quart serving dish, distribute shredded lettuce in an even layer. Top with the bean sprouts, water chestnuts, green onion, cucumber, and then chicken. Pat pea pods dry and arrange them on top.

In a small bowl, stir together the mayonnaise, curry powder, sugar, and ginger. Spread mayonnaise mixture evenly over pea pods, cover dish, and refrigerate as long as 24 hours.

To serve, garnish salad with peanuts and cherry tomato halves. Let each guest help himself to the salad, scooping down to the bottom of the dish and lifting out a portion of all the layers.

SERVES 10 to 12

BELLEVUE TUNA SALAD

You can use chicken instead.

½ cup mayonnaise
⅓ cup chopped chutney
1 teaspoon curry powder
1 tablespoon white wine vinegar
¼ teaspoon ground ginger
Salt and pepper to taste
2 quarts torn salad greens (spinach, red leaf lettuce, romaine, or butter lettuce, or a combination)
2 cups thinly sliced celery
½ cup thinly sliced green onion
1 8-ounce can pineapple chunks
2 6½-ounce cans chunk-style tuna
⅔ cup Spanish-style peanuts

In a small bowl, stir together mayonnaise, chutney, curry powder, wine vinegar, ginger, salt, and pepper. Cover and refrigerate as long as overnight.

In a large salad bowl, combine salad greens, celery, and green onion. Drain pineapple and tuna thoroughly, then add to salad mixture. Cover and chill 1 to 2 hours.

To serve, stir dressing well and pour over salad. Toss well to thoroughly coat the greens. Sprinkle peanuts over top and serve immediately.

SERVES 4 to 6

LAYERED VEGETABLE SALAD

Use this to generously fill taco shells or pocket bread.

1 head (1 pound) romaine or iceberg lettuce, *or* use 1 pound spinach, *or* ½ medium-sized head cabbage
2 large tomatoes, seeded and chopped
1½ cups chopped or diced cooked chicken, turkey, ham, or roast beef, *or* 1½ cups diced cheese (Swiss, Cheddar, or Monterey Jack)
⅓ cup chopped parsley or alfalfa sprouts
1 small green or red bell pepper, chopped, *or* 1 cup shredded carrot, *or* 1 cup thinly sliced celery
1 2¼-ounce can sliced ripe olives, drained
3 green onions, chopped, *or* ½ cup chopped red onion
¼ cup toasted slivered almonds or chopped walnuts
Dressing of your choice

LEMON-TAHINI DRESSING

¼ cup tahini (ground sesame seed)
2 tablespoons soy sauce
2 tablespoons lemon juice
½ cup salad oil
1 tablespoon water
Liquid hot pepper seasoning

CHILI-CUMIN DRESSING

⅓ cup salad oil
2 tablespoons red wine vinegar
1 clove garlic, minced or pressed
1 teaspoon chili powder
½ teaspoon ground cumin
½ teaspoon salt
¼ teaspoon pepper

Wash lettuce well, drain, and pat dry (or remove tough spinach stems or core the cabbage). Cut greens into thin strips, then coarsely chop (about 6 cups). Place greens in the bottom of a salad bowl and top with layers of tomatoes, meat or cheese, parsley, peppers, olives, and onions. Cover and chill if assembled ahead.

Prepare dressing of your choice. For Lemon-Tahini Dressing, whirl 1 15-ounce can tahini in a blender until smooth. Measure out ¼ cup; return remainder to can. In the blender, combine whirled tahini with soy sauce and lemon juice; blend until smooth. With motor running, slowly add salad oil in a slow, steady stream. Add water to thin slightly. Season to taste with hot pepper seasoning.

To prepare Chili-Cumin Dressing, thoroughly mix all ingredients together.

Just before serving, sprinkle salad with nuts. At the table, pour your choice of dressing over salad and toss.

SERVES 5

Onions

1 pound = 4 2-inch globe onions = 2 cups chopped
1 cup chopped onion = 38 calories, 1.5 grams protein, 8.7 grams carbohydrates, some vitamin C

Keep this basic ingredient for so many recipes unwashed in a dark, cool, dry place. They will last for months. The onions with the strongest flavor will last the longest. Onions are a member of the lili family (don't let that ruin their appeal for you) and have been around since "the dawn of time."

When the leaves start to turn yellow, bend all the stems level with the ground. That stops the stems from growing and sends all the energy to the onion. It helps to dig away a little dirt at the top of the onion to encourage it to ripen. Lift the onion out of the ground when the leaves turn brown and let it sit out in the sun for a week to dry.

To freeze: You can freeze small packages of chopped onion. They don't have much texture when thawed, but they are fine in casseroles, etc.

Soups

ONION SOUP

You may add thick slices of French bread to this soup if desired.

4 large onions, chopped
3 tablespoons bacon fat
2 tablespoons flour
1 clove garlic, mashed
½ teaspoon salt
⅛ teaspoon pepper
4 cups beef or chicken stock
1 cup dry white wine (substitute ¾ cup water and ¼ cup wine vinegar if desired)
Sprig parsley
Pinch thyme
Grated Parmesan cheese

Sauté onions in bacon fat just until soft. Stir in flour, garlic, salt, and pepper. Simmer just until mixture is golden brown. Stir in stock, wine, parsley, and thyme. Simmer 30 minutes. Serve immediately or make ahead and reheat. You can garnish with grated cheese. Put under broiler until cheese melts.

SERVES 6

HOT ONION BOUILLON

3 12-ounce cans mixed vegetable juice (V-8 juice may be used)
2 small onions, sliced
Celery leaves
Sprig parsley
4 whole cloves
4 peppercorns
¼ teaspoon salt

BLUE CHEESE GARNISH

¼ cup blue or Roquefort cheese, sieved
½ cup sour cream

Heat vegetable juice in a saucepan. Add onions, a few celery leaves, sprig of parsley, cloves, peppercorns, and salt. Simmer 10 to 15 minutes. Strain and serve very hot.

Mix Blue Cheese Garnish ingredients together. Add a spoonful of garnish to each bowl of soup.

SERVES 6

SOUTH OF THE BORDER ONION SOUP

2 large onions, chopped
1 clove garlic, minced

4 tablespoons butter
1 #2½ can tomatoes (about 29 ounces or 3½ cups)
2 peeled and chopped green chilies, *or* 1 small can diced chilies
2 cups water
½ pound grated Cheddar cheese
2 eggs, beaten

Brown onions and garlic in the butter. Add tomatoes with their liquid, chilies, and water. Bring to a simmer, breaking up tomatoes with a spoon. You may set it aside at this point.

To complete soup, reheat, add the cheese, and stir until the cheese melts. Take off heat and stir in the beaten eggs; return to heat and cook gently for a few minutes. Do not allow it to boil or the eggs will scramble.

SERVES 4 to 6

FRENCH ONION SOUP

Different and good.

1 large beef soup bone
3½ quarts water
2 stalks celery, chopped with leaves
2 carrots, thinly sliced
1 large onion, chopped
¼ cup parsley, chopped
1 bay leaf
Salt and pepper to taste
6 medium onions, sliced
¼ cup butter
1 1⅛-ounce package dry onion soup mix
⅛ cup soy sauce
French bread, toasted and buttered
Parmesan cheese

Brown soup bone on all sides. Add water, celery, carrots, 1 chopped onion, parsley, bay leaf, salt, and pepper. Simmer several hours. Strain. Cool and remove fat from top. Set aside.

Sauté 6 sliced onions in butter until transparent. Add dry onion soup mix and soy sauce. Simmer 2 hours; combine with beef stock.

Place buttered toasted French bread slice in bottom of each bowl. Fill with soup. Garnish with Parmesan cheese.

SERVES 12

FRENCH ONION SOUP WITH SWISS CHEESE

6 large white or yellow onions, sliced
½ cup cooking oil
6 cups chicken stock, *or* 6 chicken bouillon cubes in 6 cups water
Salt and pepper
6 slices French bread or toast
½ cup grated Swiss cheese
¼ cup Parmesan cheese

Melt onions in oil by cooking in deep skillet, covered, very slowly 2 to 3 hours. Heat should be low enough to simmer but not fry. Add chicken stock and heat thoroughly. Add salt and pepper to taste. In each serving bowl place a piece of toasted bread and sprinkle with Swiss cheese. Pour on soup and top with Parmesan cheese.

SERVES 6

Salads

WEEPING ONION SALAD

The sugar makes the onions weep and the juice mixes with the mayonnaise to make the dressing for this super salad.

1 head lettuce
Mayonnaise
1 red onion, sliced
Sugar
1 16-ounce can English peas
Swiss cheese
3 slices bacon, fried and crumbled

Tear some of the lettuce into small pieces and place in a large salad bowl. Spread enough mayonnaise on lettuce to cover. Slice a red onion and put a few slices on the lettuce. Sprinkle a little sugar over the onion. Put some drained English peas over this and top with small slices of Swiss cheese. Repeat layers until everything is used. Put foil or a light cover over the bowl and refrigerate for 1½ to 2 hours to properly combine flavors. Do not use any additional dressing on this salad.

Before serving, sprinkle with crumbled bacon.

SERVES 6 to 8

TANGERINE, WALNUT, AND ONION TOSS

WALNUT CROUTONS

3 tablespoons butter
¼ teaspoon salt
½ cup walnuts

7 cups romaine lettuce, torn into bite-sized pieces
2 cups tangarine sections, white membrane removed
1 red onion, sliced and separated into rings
⅓ cup Italian dressing

Prepare Walnut Croutons by melting butter in saucepan. Add salt and walnuts. Stir until walnuts are crisp and butter-browned.

Combine romaine, tangerines, and red onion; toss with dressing, and top with croutons.

SERVES 4 to 6

SLIVERED CHICKEN LIVER AND ONION SALAD

Certainly this could serve as an entree.

¼ cup olive oil or salad oil
3 tablespoons lemon juice
½ teaspoon salt
½ teaspoon sugar
¼ teaspoon dry chervil
¼ teaspoon thyme leaves
¼ teaspoon dry mustard
⅛ teaspoon white pepper
2 quarts lightly packed curly endive or Australian lettuce, or a combination
1 small mild red or white onion, thinly sliced
1 cup thinly sliced celery
¼ cup chopped parsley
1 tablespoon olive oil or salad oil
1 tablespoon butter or margarine
1 pound chicken livers

In a measuring cup, stir together ¼ cup olive oil, lemon juice, salt, sugar, chervil, thyme, mustard, and pepper; cover and set dressing aside.

In a large salad bowl, combine the endive, onion, celery, and parsley. Cover and chill 2 to 4 hours.

Just before serving, heat 1 tablespoon olive oil and butter in a wide frying pan over medium-high heat. Add the chicken livers and cook until browned on all sides but still pink in the center. Lift livers out and quickly cut into thin slivers. Return to pan and stir to coat with drippings, then pour into the salad mixture. Stir dressing and pour over all; toss to mix well.

SERVES 8

Side Dishes

ONION AND ORANGE

Thin orange slices
Sugar
Raw onion slices
Salt and pepper
French dressing

In a salad bowl arrange a layer of thin orange slices; sprinkle them lightly with sugar, and add a layer of raw onion slices seasoned with salt and pepper. Repeat the layers and pour over them French dressing to taste. Let the salad stand 1 hour in the refrigerator to marinate and chill.

ONIONS GLACÉ

18 to 20 young tender white onions
1 stick butter
1½ teaspoons powdered sugar
1 quart canned consommé

Clean onions, leaving whole. Fry in butter until brown; add sugar. Continue to fry until quite brown; then put in baking dish with consommé. Cook in 325° F. oven for about 1 hour. Onions must be so well cooked they will glaze in their own juice.

SERVES 4

GOURMET ONIONS

Great with beef.

4 cups sliced onions (about 3 large)
5 tablespoons butter
2 eggs
1 cup sour cream
Salt and pepper to taste
⅔ cup Parmesan cheese, grated

Sauté onions in butter until transparent. Place in a 1½- or 2-quart casserole. Beat eggs until light; add sour cream, salt, and pepper. Pour over onions and sprinkle with Parmesan cheese. Bake at 425° F. for 20 to 25 minutes. Serve with roasts, steaks, or ham. The top of the onions turns a lovely brown.

SERVES 4

ONIONS CELESTE

A great way to show off sweet, juicy onions.

2 large Bermuda onions, sliced and separated into rings
2 tablespoons butter
½ pound Swiss cheese, grated
1 10-ounce can cream of chicken soup
½ cup milk
8 slices French bread, buttered and cubed

Cook onions in butter. Do not brown; onions should remain clear.

Spoon onions into a baking dish and cover with grated Swiss cheese. Mix cream of chicken soup with milk and add to baking dish. Top with French bread. Bake 30 minutes at 350° F.

SERVES 6

STUFFED ONIONS WITH SPINACH

8 large mild onions
1 10-ounce package frozen chopped spinach
½ pound sausage
2 teaspoons lemon juice (optional)
Salt and pepper

Wash and peel onions. Cover with water and cook 20 to 25 minutes; do not overcook or onions will fall apart. Drain, cut root end off, remove centers from root end, and chop centers fine. Set aside outer shells of onions. Cook spinach; drain.

In a skillet, break sausage into small pieces, cook, and crumble; add spinach, lemon juice, chopped onion, and salt and pepper to taste.

Fill onion shells with stuffing. Arrange in a greased baking dish and bake at 250° F. for 25 minutes. This is better if the onions are stuffed hours before serving.

SERVES 8

ONION-APPLE SURPRISE

A wonderful accompaniment to Christmas dinner.

3 large onions
1 tablespoon salt
4 tart medium apples
3 tablespoons sugar
1 teaspoon cinnamon
⅓ cup butter, melted

Peel onions and slice ¼ inch thick. Cook covered in ½ inch boiling water with ½ teaspoon salt for 20 minutes. Peel and core apples; cut into ⅛-inch slices. Drain onions, reserving liquid. Fill a 1-quart casserole with alternate layers of onions and apples, sprinkling each layer with mixture of sugar, cinnamon, and remainder of salt. Add ⅓ cup reserved onion liquid and melted butter. Cover and bake 45 minutes in a 350°F. oven.

SERVES 6

ONION FRITO DISH

1 large onion
1 or 2 cloves garlic
Butter for browning
1 green pepper, chopped
1 #2 can tomatoes
1 teaspoon Worcestershire sauce
Cayenne and Tabasco to taste
1 4¼-ounce package corn chips
1½ cups sharp cheese

Chop onion; brown with garlic in butter in a skillet. Add green pepper, tomatoes, Worcestershire, and cayenne and Tabasco to taste. Cook over medium heat. Add corn chips and 1 cup of cheese; let corn chips absorb liquid. Pour into casserole. Sprinkle remaining ½ cup cheese on top. Bake in 375°F. oven until cheese melts.

SERVES 4 to 6

ONION RINGS

2 eggs, beaten
1 cup milk
1 cup flour
1 teaspoon salt
1 teaspoon baking powder
4 to 6 onions, sliced into rings

Mix batter ingredients together. Dip onions that have been sliced and separated into rings into batter. Fry in hot oil until brown. Make ½ this recipe for small family as batter goes a long way.

SERVES 6

BROILED ONION SLICES

3 large onions
¾ cup cooking oil
⅓ cup red wine vinegar
½ teaspoon thyme, crushed
½ teaspoon oregano, crushed
Dash salt and pepper

Cut onions into ½-inch-thick rings and place in a shallow baking dish. Combine oil, vinegar, thyme, oregano, salt, and pepper, and mix well. Pour over onions and marinate at least 1 hour at room temperature. Drain onions and broil about 4 inches below heat for 20 minutes.

SERVES 4 to 6

COAL-ROASTED ONIONS

Wash large sweet onions, but do not peel them. Wrap each onion in aluminum foil and bury the packages in hot coals to roast for 45 to 60 minutes.

Main Dishes

SOY CREAM–ONION PIE

Vegetarian entree.

2 cups small boiling onions, or wedges of large onions
1 tablespoon oil
½ cup water
1 teaspoon salt
2 cups raw soy cream or sour cream or low-calorie imitation sour cream
½ cup cashew nuts
1 9-inch pastry shell

Simmer onions briefly in oil at low temperature. Add water and salt. Bring to boiling point and boil gently until tender. Add soy cream to onions; then add cashew nuts. Heat until thickened. Fill pastry shell and garnish with one whole cashew.

Variation: Cooked garbanzos, chicken, or other protein food with texture may be used.

SERVES 6

HAMBURGER-ONION PIE

Quick! Made with Bisquick mix.

2 cups Bisquick mix
3 tablespoons butter or margarine
1 cup onion
1¼ pound ground beef
1 teaspoon salt
½ teaspoon pepper
2 tablespoons flour
1 cup sour cream
¼ teaspoon salt
2 beaten eggs
¼ teaspoon paprika

Make dough; roll to fit a 9-inch pie pan.

Melt butter and cook onion until yellow. Add beef; cook until it loses its redness. Pour off fat. Add 1 teaspoon salt, pepper, and flour. Spread onto dough.

Blend sour cream, ¼ teaspoon salt, and eggs. Pour over meat mixture and top with paprika. Bake in a 375°F. oven for 30 minutes or until done.

SERVES 6

SWISS ONION PIE

Serve while warm as an hors d'oeuvre or as the first course.

2 or 3 small onions, chopped fine
Butter
3 eggs
2 cups milk
½ teaspoon salt
1 teaspoon paprika
2 tablespoons Swiss cheese, grated
1 9-inch baked pie shell

Cook onions in butter until soft. Beat eggs slightly; add milk, onions, salt, paprika, and cheese. Pour into pie crust and bake until brown in 350°F. oven.

SERVES 6

BEEF-FILLED ONIONS

Serve with mushroom sauce for lunch or a special supper.

4 large, mild white or red onions (3 to 3½ inches in diameter)
½ pound lean ground beef
⅓ cup grated Parmesan cheese
4 tablespoons chopped parsley
¼ teaspoon oregano
¼ teaspoon thyme leaves
Salt and pepper to taste

MUSHROOM SAUCE

2 tablespoons butter or margarine
¼ pound mushrooms, sliced
1 tablespoon all-purpose flour

1 cup milk
2 tablespoons dry sherry or additional milk
2 tablespoons parsley
Salt and pepper to taste

Place unpeeled onions in a 5-quart kettle, add water to cover, and boil for 20 minutes. Drain, cool, and peel. Cut off top and bottom, then push out the center from each onion and set aside, leaving about a ½-inch shell. Arrange shells in a 9-inch square baking pan; set aside.

Finely chop enough of the onion centers to make 1 cup (save remaining onion for other uses). Mix chopped onion, beef, cheese, 4 tablespoons parsley, oregano, thyme, salt, and pepper. Stuff meat mixture into onion shells, cover, and bake in a 375°F. oven for 1 hour or until onion is fork tender.

To make the sauce, melt butter in a wide frying pan over medium heat; add mushrooms and cook until golden. Stir in flour and cook, stirring, 1 minute, then gradually add milk and cook until thickened. Stir in sherry, 2 tablespoons parsley, salt, and pepper. Spoon some sauce over each onion and pass remaining sauce at the table.

SERVES 4

Breads

GREEN ONION CHEESE BREAD

1 loaf French bread
⅓ cup grated Cheddar cheese
⅓ cup chopped green onions
⅓ cup homemade or commercial blue cheese or Roquefort salad dressing

Slice loaf of French bread lengthwise. Cut in diagonal slices and hold together in foil wrapping. Combine cheese, green onions, and salad dressing; cover bread with this mixture and let warm in oven until bubbly.

SERVES 6 to 8

ONION TWIST

An onion lover's delight—a beautiful loaf of bread

1 package dry yeast
¼ cup warm water
4 cups flour
½ cup butter or margarine, melted
½ cup milk
½ cup hot water
¼ cup sugar
1½ teaspoons salt
1 egg, beaten

FILLING

1 cup onion, finely chopped (or ¼ cup dried onion—but fresh is best)
¼ cup butter, melted
1 tablespoon Parmesan cheese
1 tablespoon sesame seeds
1 tablespoon poppy seeds
1 teaspoon garlic salt
1 teaspoon paprika

In a large mixing bowl, mix yeast and ¼ cup warm water. Let stand 10 minutes. Stir in 2 cups flour, melted butter, milk, ½ cup hot water, sugar, salt, and egg. Blend at low speed until moistened. Beat 2 minutes at medium speed. Stir in remaining flour. Cover and let rise in warm place until double in bulk (about 1 hour).

While dough is rising, mix all filling ingredients. Set aside. Stir down dough. Toss on a floured surface until dough is no longer sticky. Roll into a 12″ × 18″ rectangle. Cut lengthwise into 3 4″ × 18″ strips. Spread on filling. Starting with 18-inch side, roll each strip around filling. Seal edges and ends. Place strips on greased cookie sheet. Press strips together at one end. Braid, keeping seams inside the braid whenever possible. Cover and let rise in warm place until double in size. Bake at 350°F. for 30 minutes until golden brown.

MAKES 1 LARGE LOAF or 2 SMALL

ONION SQUARES

2 packages refrigerated biscuits
2 tablespoons butter
2 cups sliced onions
Salt and pepper
Cayenne
1 egg
¾ cup sour cream

Pat the dough for biscuits into an 8- or 9-inch square baking pan. Heat 2 tablespoons butter in a skillet, add onions and cook, stirring constantly, until the onions are browned. Add salt, pepper, and a dash of cayenne to taste; drain off the butter, and spread onions over biscuit dough.

Beat egg with sour cream, season with salt and pepper, and pour mixture over onions. Bake dough in a hot oven (400°F.) for 20 minutes, or until the topping is well browned. Cut into squares and serve very hot.

MAKES 6 to 8

Pickles and Sauces

FRESH VEGETABLE SAUCE (SALSA)

Very good.

1 medium-sized green pepper, seeded and chopped
4 green onions, thinly sliced
1 4-ounce can diced green chilies
1 cup thinly sliced celery
2 medium-sized tomatoes, seeded and chopped
1 tablespoon cider vinegar
1 tablespoon Worcestershire sauce
1 tablespoon sugar
Salt

Combine green pepper, onions, chilies, celery, and tomatoes. Add vinegar, Worcestershire, and sugar, mixing well. Then season to taste with salt. Cover and chill at least 4 hours; stir several times. You can store any leftover salsa in the refrigerator as long as 1 week.

MAKES ABOUT 3 CUPS

SPICED ONIONS

1 pound small white onions
1 cup white wine vinegar
1 cup sugar
1 cup seedless white raisins
Nutmeg
Cinnamon
Peppercorns
½ teaspoon paprika

Clean onions and put them in a saucepan with white wine vinegar, sugar, and seedless white raisins, a little grated nutmeg and cinnamon, a few peppercorns, and paprika. Bring the mixture to a boil and simmer until it reaches a jamlike consistency. Serve cold.

MAKES 4 PINTS

PICKLED ONIONS

7 quarts onions
2 cups salt
7 cups vinegar
4 teaspoons celery seed
4 teaspoons mustard seed
3 teaspoons turmeric
5 cups sugar
7 cups water
1 4-ounce jar sliced pimiento, or if whole, slice in strips (optional)

Peel onions and slice. Add salt and let stand overnight either in the refrigerator or covered for several hours to wilt. Drain; rinse off salt thoroughly. Heat vinegar, celery seed, mustard seed, turmeric, sugar, water, and pimiento. Add onions and boil about 45 minutes or 1 hour, until tender to your taste. Pack in jars and seal while hot. May be eaten anytime, but best when cold.

MAKES 8 QUARTS

Cooney '82

Peas

1 pound peas = 1 to 2 cups shelled
1 cup shelled peas = 114 calories, 8.6 grams protein, 19.4 grams carbohydrates, 314 milligrams potassium, 860 units vitamin A, 32 milligrams vitamin C

Peas, like corn, turn from sugar to starch the minute they are picked, so there is nothing to match the taste of peas fresh from the garden. They are ready to harvest when the pod is bulging with peas, but still bright green. Don't let them go beyond that point or you will have tough, mature peas. Try snow peas along with regular peas in your garden—they have pods that are delightful eating.

Peas lose sugar, vitamins, and texture when stored. But if you must, store them unshelled in a plastic bag. A couple of cooking tricks: When boiling peas add a pinch of sugar and some of the pea pods. Cook about 4 minutes and remove pods. It does wonderful things for the flavor!

To freeze: Shell peas and scald 1 minute. Chill in cold water, drain, freeze in plastic freezer bags.

Soups

FRESH PEA SOUP

4 small onions, finely chopped
½ cup butter
2 large potatoes, peeled, cubed
2 teaspoons salt
2 cups water
6 cups peas
2 cups milk
¼ teaspoon pepper
½ cup sour cream

Sauté onions in butter until limp but not brown, stirring frequently. Add potatoes, 1 teaspoon salt, and 1 cup water; cover and cook until very tender.

In another pan, pour the other cup water, heated to boiling, over peas; combine with ingredients in first pan, including all liquid. Put in blender and blend until smooth. Pour back into pan; add milk, pepper, and sour cream. Adjust seasonings to taste. Heat slowly until hot. If soup gets too thick while standing, add a little more milk.

SERVES 12

SPRING PEA SOUP

4 pounds peas
1 whole onion
Salt and pepper
1 white onion, finely chopped
1 tablespoon butter
1 tablespoon flour
1 egg yolk
⅓ cup heavy cream
Finely chopped parsley

Shell freshly picked peas and cook; reserve 1½ cups. Put the pods and remaining peas in a large kettle and cover with water. Add 1 whole onion and salt and pepper to taste. Cover the kettle and simmer the soup gently for about 1 hour, or until pods are tender. Strain the broth.

In a saucepan, sauté chopped white onion in butter until onion is tender but not brown. Blend in flour. Measure 6 cups of pod stock and add it to the saucepan, stirring constantly. Simmer the soup for a few minutes. Just before serving, mix a little of it into the egg yolk lightly beaten with cream. Stir egg mixture into soup and add reserved peas. Sprinkle each serving with finely chopped parsley.

SERVES 8 to 10

CREAM OF PEA POD SOUP

1 quart fresh pea pods
3 cups cold water
½ cup soy cream or evaporated milk with 1 tablespoon flour
½ to 1 teaspoon salt
1 tablespoon margarine, *or* 1 tablespoon oil with 2 drops butter flavoring
4 tablespoons sour cream
4 tablespoons cooked peas
4 tablespoons grated carrots

Blend half of pea pods with 1½ cups water until pulp separates from fiber. Pour into strainer over saucepan. Press out all liquid possible. Rinse with half the water and press out all liquid. Repeat with second half of pods. Discard fibers. Heat liquid and add cream or milk, salt, and margarine. Let simmer, being careful not to boil. Dish into bowls and serve with 1 tablespoon sour cream, 1 tablespoon cooked peas, and 1 tablespoon grated carrots in each bowl.

SERVES 4

Salads

FRESH PEA SALAD

So good.

DRESSING

1 cup mayonnaise
¼ cup parsley, chopped
¼ cup vinegar
¼ cup (2 ounces) blue cheese, crumbled
½ cup sour cream
2 tablespoons green onions, chopped
1 tablespoon lemon juice
1 clove garlic, minced
Salt to taste
Pepper, freshly ground to taste

SALAD

1 head romaine lettuce
1 head iceberg lettuce
3 tomatoes, in sections
4 eggs, hard-cooked, in wedges
3 cups fresh peas

Combine all dressing ingredients. Refrigerate.

Shred romaine and iceberg lettuce. Toss with tomatoes and eggs. Add peas and dressing. Toss again.

SERVES 10

COOKED PEA SALAD

A way to use leftover peas in a high protein salad—a nice main course on a hot summer day.

2 or 3 cups fresh peas, cooked, or leftover cooked peas
5 strips bacon, crisply cooked
2 hard-cooked eggs, sliced
½ cup salted peanuts
Cheddar cheese
Mayonnaise

Chill peas. Add bacon, eggs, peanuts, and some small chunks of Cheddar cheese. Toss with mayonnaise.

SERVES 8

FRESH PEA AND GREEN BEAN SALAD

Like a marinated bean salad—keeps well in the refrigerator.

¾ cup sugar
2 or 3 tablespoons wine vinegar
1 teaspoon salt

½ cup vinegar
½ cup vegetable oil
Pepper to taste
1 cup fresh peas, rinsed and drained
1 15-ounce can whole green beans, drained
1 green pepper, sliced thin
1 2-ounce jar chopped pimiento
1 onion, sliced thin
4 ribs celery, chopped

In a saucepan, add sugar, wine vinegar, salt, vinegar, vegetable oil, and pepper. Bring to a boil. Pour over peas, beans, green pepper, pimiento, onion, and celery. Chill overnight.

SERVES 8

CRUNCHY GREEN PEA SALAD

Water chestnuts add the crunch—a good choice for a buffet scooped into lettuce leaves.

1 1-pound package frozen green peas
Water
2 hard-cooked eggs, chopped
1 8-ounce can water chestnuts, drained and sliced
2 tablespoons chopped pimiento, drained
⅓ cup thinly sliced green onion
½ cup sliced celery
⅓ cup mayonnaise
1 tablespoon Dijon mustard
½ teaspoon garlic salt
¼ teaspoon pepper
Lettuce leaves
Sliced hard-cooked egg (optional)

Cook peas in boiling water as package directs until just barely tender; drain. Rinse briefly with cold water to cool quickly; drain again. In a bowl, combine the cooled peas, eggs, water chestnuts, pimiento, onion, and celery. Stir together the mayonnaise, mustard, garlic salt, and pepper. Stir gently into salad; cover and chill 24 hours.

To serve, spoon onto a lettuce-lined serving plate and garnish with sliced hard-cooked egg (optional).

SERVES 4 to 6

ROMAINE LETTUCE WITH PEAS

A hot salad.

2 heads romaine lettuce
1 10-ounce package frozen peas, *or* 1 pound fresh peas
1½ cups salted water
2 tablespoons parsley, chopped
1 tablespoon onion, chopped
2 tablespoons flour
2 tablespoons butter
½ cup beef broth
Salt and pepper to taste
1 teaspoon sugar (optional)

Quarter lettuce; wash and drain. Simmer uncovered in enough salted water to cover for 10 minutes, or until just tender. Cook peas uncovered in 1½ cups salted water 10 minutes, or until just tender. Drain and discard lettuce liquid. Dice lettuce. Drain peas, saving pea stock. Set aside.

Sauté parsley and onion with flour in butter just until onion is limp. Blend in reserved pea stock and beef broth until smooth. Add peas, diced lettuce, salt, and pepper. Stir and simmer 4 minutes. Add sugar if needed.

SERVES 6

REDLANDS WATERCRESS, ARTICHOKE, AND SWEET PEA SALAD

This is a beautiful green salad and great for a luncheon. You make it early in the morning.

1 bunch watercress
1 14-ounce can artichoke hearts
1 cup frozen peas (1 10-ounce package)
Well-seasoned French dressing

Wash, drain, and dry watercress thoroughly. Use only the tender leaves. Chill thoroughly. Drain artichokes and chill. Cook peas 1 or 2 minutes, until thawed. Chill.

To assemble and garnish, combine artichoke hearts and peas in a bowl and marinate in French dressing 1 hour before serving. Toss with watercress and more dressing if needed and serve very cold.

If salad is assembled in the morning, cover with a damp towel and refrigerate. Add more dressing if needed before serving.

SERVES 6

CURRIED VEGETABLE RICE AND PEA MOLD

1 6-ounce package curried rice
2 cups water
1 10-ounce package frozen peas, *or* 1 pound fresh peas
½ cup mayonnaise
1 envelope sour cream sauce mix
⅓ cup milk
1 cup diced celery

Prepare rice according to package directions, using 2 cups water. Cool. Cook peas. Combine mayonnaise, sour cream mix, and milk. Add more milk if it seems too thick. Toss rice, peas, dressing, and celery together, and chill for 1 to 2 hours.

SERVES 6

Side Dishes

MINTED NEW PEAS

A fresh taste.

1½ pounds fresh new peas, *or* 1 10-ounce package frozen peas
1 bunch fresh mint leaves
2 tablespoons butter

Cook new peas in slightly salted boiling water with a bunch of fresh mint leaves. When peas are tender, drain. Remove mint leaves and add butter.

SERVES 4

FRESH PEAS OREGANO

Oregano does great things for fresh peas.

¼ cup butter
2 pounds fresh peas, shelled, *or* 1 10-ounce package frozen peas
½ teaspoon salt
1 teaspoon lemon juice
1 tablespoon dried onion flakes
½ teaspoon dried oregano leaves

Slowly melt butter in a medium-sized skillet. Add remaining ingredients. Cook, covered, over medium heat for 10 to 15 minutes or just until peas are tender.

SERVES 4 to 6

GREEN PEAS WITH CARROTS

2 pounds peas
6 tablespoons butter
2 or 3 small heads lettuce
4 medium-sized carrots
2 bunches green onions
¼ cup water
½ teaspoon sugar
Salt to taste
¾ cup heavy cream

Shell peas. Melt butter in a saucepan and add the hearts of young lettuce, young carrots scraped and cut into 1-inch strips, onions with 1 or 2 inches of their green stems, the peas, ¼ cup water, sugar, and salt to taste. Cover pan and cook vegetables over low heat until tender. There should be enough liquid so that vegetables can steam and not be in danger of burning, but it should be almost absorbed when they are done.

Heat ¾ cup cream in another pan until it is slightly reduced and pour it over the vegetables before serving.

SERVES 4

SPRING PEAS AND HERBS

Mint, basil, oregano, and other herbs may be used to flavor green peas as desired.

PEAS À LA BONNE FEMME

A good way to use pea pods.

¼ head lettuce in small chunks
2 green onions, chopped
1 teaspoon sugar
2 tablespoons butter
1 teaspoon monosodium glutamate
⅛ teaspoon Java cracked pepper (regular ground pepper can be used)
1 bay leaf (optional)
¼ pound fresh peas and pods
2 10-ounce packages frozen peas
2 tablespoons chopped chives
3 tablespoons chopped parsley
4 tablespoons butter

Put lettuce, chopped onion, sugar, 2 tablespoons butter, monosodium glutamate, pepper, bay leaf, and fresh peas and pods into a frying pan. Break frozen peas in as small bits as possible. (This is easily done if peas are unwrapped 15 minutes before you are ready to cook.) Add to above mixture in frying pan. Put lid on, bring to a quick boil (about 5 minutes), lower heat and cook 20 to 25 minutes longer, or until peas are tender. Turn off heat and allow to steam 1 minute. Add chives, parsley, and 4 tablespoons butter. Stir well. Remove pods and serve at once.

SERVES 6 to 8

PEA PODS

Wonderful Oriental pea pods are picked and used sweet and tender before the peas form. Ordinary pea pods can be used if they are gathered young and tender.

4 pounds pea pods
1 small head lettuce, finely shredded
3 tablespoons raw bacon, chopped
3 tablespoons butter
Salt and pepper to taste
Nutmeg
1 teaspoon sugar (optional)

Wash and trim the stems from pods and put pods in a large saucepan with ½ a small head of lettuce, raw bacon, butter, salt and pepper to taste, a dash of nutmeg, and enough water to barely cover. Cook the mixture gently until the pods are tender. There should be almost no water left when they are done. If the pods are not sweet enough, stir in 1 scant teaspoon sugar.

SERVES 6 to 8

SNOW PEAS

1 pound Chinese pea pods, *or* 1 10-ounce package frozen pea pods
1 tablespoon soy sauce
3 tablespoons chopped green onion
2 tablespoons margarine or oil

Wash pods, break off ends, and remove string that runs along spine. Cut pods in half if too large. Sprinkle with soy sauce and sauté quickly with a few chopped onions in margarine or oil.

SERVES 4

MOLD OF PEAS WITH ARTICHOKE HEARTS

2 pounds fresh green peas
2 tablespoons butter
2 tablespoons flour
½ cup light cream
1 teaspoon grated onion
1 teaspoon salt

4 eggs, separated
½ cup fine soda cracker crumbs
Buttered cooked artichoke hearts
Chopped parsley

Shell peas and cook in salted water to cover for 20 minutes, or until peas are tender. Transfer peas to container of an electric blender. Add ½ cup of the pea liquid, cover, and blend on high speed for 20 minutes, stopping to stir down if necessary. Strain through a coarse sieve. This should make 2 cups of fresh pea puree.

Butter a 6-cup ring mold. Cover bottom of mold with a band of waxed paper and butter the paper.

Melt butter in a saucepan. Stir in flour and cook, stirring, for 2 minutes. Stir in cream and cook, stirring, until sauce is smooth and thick. Stir in onion and salt, and let mixture cool slightly.

Stir in egg yolks and cracker crumbs. Fold in the pea puree. Preheat oven to moderate (350° F.).

Beat egg whites until stiff but not dry and fold into the pea mixture. Fold lightly but thoroughly. Pour the mixture into prepared ring mold and bake in preheated oven for 40 minutes, or until set.

Remove ring from oven and let stand for a few minutes. Unmold on platter and remove waxed paper from bottom. Fill center with buttered cooked artichoke hearts and sprinkle with chopped parsley.

SERVES 8

FETTUCCINI AMERICANA

Can be a vegetarian entree.

1 10-ounce package frozen baby peas, *or* 1 pound fresh peas
½ cup dairy sour cream
¼ cup grated Parmesan cheese
½ teaspoon salt
1 8-ounce package broad noodles

Cook frozen peas as directed on package, or boil fresh peas in lightly salted water until just tender. Drain well. Toss lightly with sour cream, grated Parmesan cheese, and salt. Cook noodles according to package directions. Add peas to noodle mixture and sprinkle more Parmesan cheese lightly on top. Serve immediately.

SERVES 6

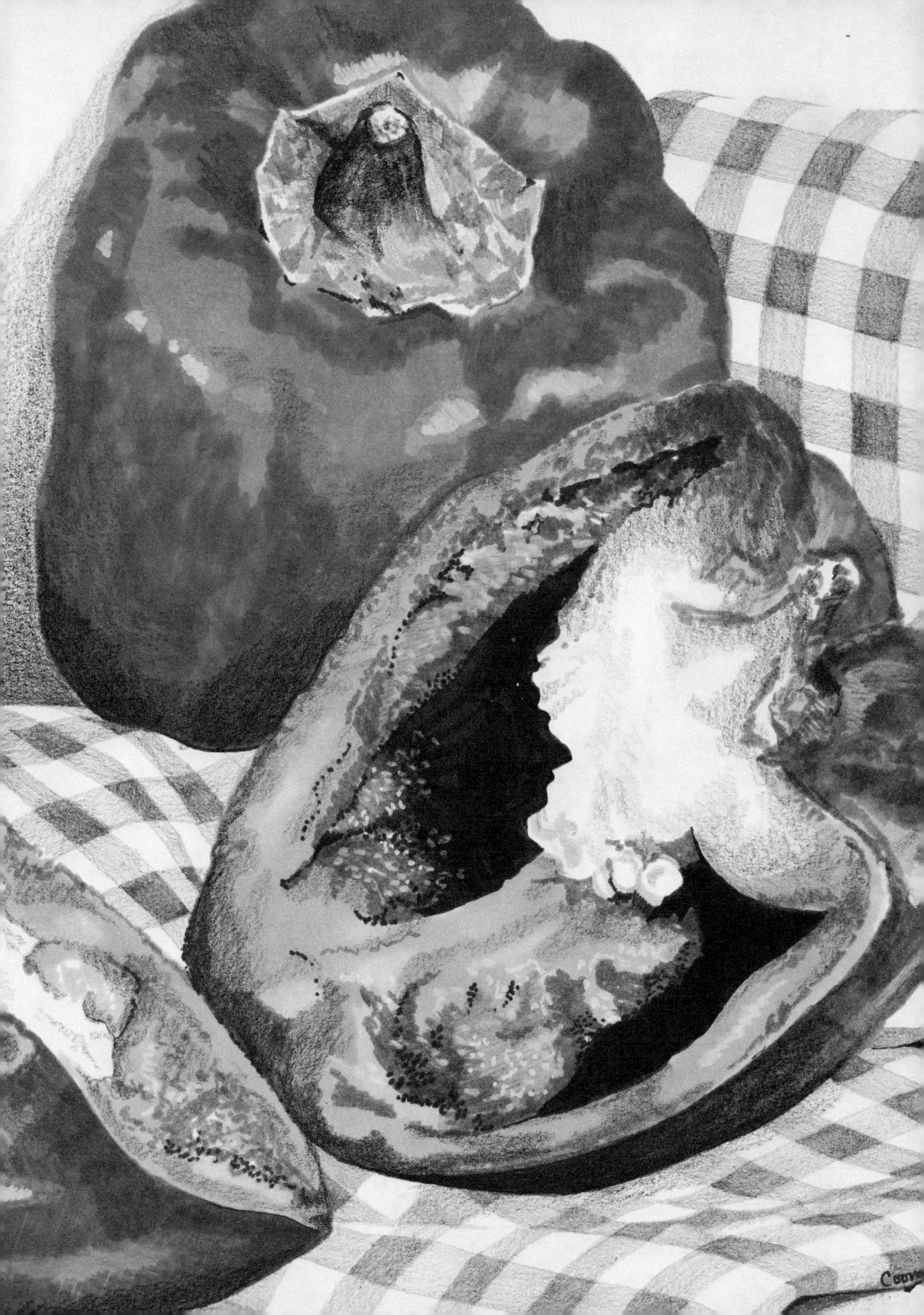

Peppers

1 pound = 2 medium sweet green peppers = 1 cup chopped
1 cup chopped pepper = 22 calories, 1.2 grams protein, 4.8 grams carbohydrates, 213 milligrams potassium, 420 units vitamin A, 120 milligrams vitamin C

Peppers come in all colors, sizes, and varieties. Life would be dull without them. They like a hot place to grow and some of the "hot" variety are guaranteed to make your eyes water!

Sweet green peppers are picked while they are still crisp and not more than 3 or 4 inches around. If you leave them they will turn red, but are still good to eat. Store them unwashed in a plastic bag in the refrigerator for up to 10 days. The hot ones are fun to string and hang out in the sun to dry, like they love to do in New Mexico. When thoroughly dry, bring them in and hang them on a kitchen wall. Along with being a colorful addition to your decor, you can snip off small amounts to use in cooking.

To freeze: Peppers are the easiest of all the vegetables to freeze. Simply chop, package, and freeze in small convenient sizes. They lose some crispness but are really handy for cooking.

Soups

SPANISH GAZPACHO

The soup served icy cold is refreshing—be sure to use very, very ripe tomatoes.

6 thin slices bread, diced
3 very ripe tomatoes, chopped
1 cucumber, chopped
3 tablespoons olive oil
1 quart water
2 cloves garlic, minced
2 tablespoons wine vinegar
2 teaspoons salt
1 teaspoon ground cumin
4 ice cubes

GARNISHES

1 red or green pepper, diced
1 large ripe tomato, diced
1 small cucumber, diced
2 slices bread, diced
Butter

Into a mixing bowl, put the bread, tomatoes, cucumber, olive oil, and water. Let soak for 1 hour, then puree in a food mill or blend, half at a time, on high speed in an electric blender for 8 seconds. Strain through a coarse sieve into a large soup bowl.

Add garlic, wine vinegar, salt, cumin, and ice cubes. Chill in refrigerator for at least half an hour.

In separate small dishes prepare garnishes. Dice 1 red or green pepper, 1 tomato, 1 cucumber, and 2 slices bread. If desired, the bread cubes may be browned in butter.

Serve the gazpacho in well-chilled bowls. Serve garnishes in the small dishes, sprinkling some of each into individual soup bowls.

SERVES 4 to 6

GAZPACHO

One of the best gazpachos.

1 16-ounce can tomatoes, diced
1 46-ounce can tomato juice
1 cup red wine vinegar
½ cup salad oil
3 tablespoons Worcestershire sauce
1½ teaspoons fresh ground pepper
½ teaspoon cumin
1 or 2 cloves garlic, minced
2 green peppers, minced
1 medium cucumber, peeled and minced
3 or 4 stalks celery, minced
1 medium onion, minced
Salt to taste
12 unpeeled cucumber slices for garnish

Combine all ingredients except cucumber slices for garnish; mix well. Season to taste. Chill for several hours; garnish each serving with one cucumber slice.

SERVES 12

Side Dishes

GOURMET GREEN VEGETABLES

1 medium bell pepper
1 10-ounce package frozen baby lima beans
1 15-ounce can French-style green beans
1 15-ounce can Petit Pois English peas
Salt and pepper to taste
½ pint whipping cream
1 cup mayonnaise
1 3-ounce can Parmesan cheese
Paprika

Slice bell pepper into thin strips and cook with lima beans. Drain. Drain liquid from canned beans and peas. Toss with salt and pepper to taste. Place in a 7″ × 10″ casserole. Whip cream and fold in mayonnaise and cheese. Spread over top of vegetables and sprinkle with paprika. Bake at 350° F. for 20 minutes.

SERVES 6

FRIED GREEN PEPPERS

Delicious with meat loaf.

4 green peppers
Butter
Salt and pepper

Wash and remove seeds from green peppers. Cut in long strips about ½ inch wide. Sauté in butter in a skillet until tender and edges are slightly brown. Drain on absorbent paper; salt and pepper to taste. Serve piping hot.

SERVES 4 to 6

BAKED GREEN PEPPERS

Especially good with barbecued meat.

6 bell peppers
Monterey Jack cheese (or cottage cheese)
1 cup tomato sauce
3 eggs
Salt and pepper to taste

Cut peppers in half and remove seeds. Drop in a large saucepan of boiling water and blanch for about ½ minute. Remove from heat and let stand 6 minutes, covered. Place peppers in a greased baking dish. Fill with Monterey Jack cheese. Add tomato sauce and bake at 350° F. for 20 minutes. Beat eggs, season with salt and pepper, and pour over peppers. Bake 20 minutes longer at same heat.

SERVES 6

Main Dishes

CHILIES RELLENOS (STUFFED PEPPERS)

From a favorite Palm Springs restaurant.

6 long green peppers (Anaheim chilies)
3 eggs, separated
Salt to taste
1 small package cream cheese, *or* 12 slices Monterey Jack cheese ⅛ inch thick
Oil for frying
½ cup flour

SAUCE

2 tablespoons chopped onion
1 tablespoon peanut oil
1½ cups tomato sauce
Salt
Pepper
¼ teaspoon oregano

Slit peppers at lower end. Remove seeds and pulp but leave stems. Parboil until tender.

Separate eggs. Beat whites to soft peaks, then add yolks and beat until fluffy. Add salt to taste. Stuff each pepper with 2 pieces of cheese ⅛ inch thick. Heat oil in frying pan. Roll chilies in flour, then dip in egg batter and fry until golden.

To make sauce, sauté onion in oil, add tomato sauce, salt, pepper, and oregano and simmer about 5 minutes. Pour sauce over each *relleno* and serve.

SERVES 4

GREEN PEPPER TOSTADAS

2 sweet green peppers, diced
1 medium onion, diced
3 whole canned or fresh tomatoes, diced
1 tablespoon oil
¼ cup whipped cottage cheese
4 tortillas
½ cup grated mozzarella cheese
½ cup shredded lettuce

Sauté green peppers, onion, and tomatoes in oil; add whipped cheese and cook for 5 minutes.

Broil tortillas until slightly crisp; tortillas will curl up and form pocket. Place 3 tablespoons pepper-tomato mixture in center of each tortilla. Sprinkle with grated cheese and broil until cheese is melted. Serve topped with shredded lettuce.

SERVES 4

PEPPER STEAK

Soy sauce makes this so tasty.

1 1- to 2-pound piece round steak
Meat tenderizer
2 tablespoons fat
2 tablespoons flour
1 cup hot water
1 bouillon cube
3 tablespoons soy sauce
3 tablespoons catsup
⅛ teaspoon pepper
1 onion, cut into rings
1 7-ounce can mushrooms and liquid
2 green peppers, cut into rings

Sprinkle steak with tenderizer; cut into 1½-inch cubes and brown in fat. When brown, remove meat from pan. Stir flour into pan, then add hot water in which bouillon cube has been dissolved, soy sauce, catsup, and pepper. Stir and cook until you have a smooth gravy. Add browned meat to gravy; add onion rings. Cover and simmer 2 to 3 hours, adding a little water if needed. Last 10 minutes before ready to serve, add mushrooms and their liquid; place green pepper rings on top of meat. Peppers should be slightly crisp after cooking. Serve with rice or noodles.

SERVES 4 to 6

WOODCHUCK

Vegetarian main course.

1 pint milk
¼ pound butter
6 tablespoons flour
½ cup grated Cheddar cheese
1 4-ounce can mushrooms
1 small green pepper, finely chopped
Butter for sautéing
6 hard-cooked eggs, chopped
2 tablespoons chopped pimiento
Salt to taste
1 large can Chinese noodles

Make cheese sauce by heating together milk, butter, flour, and cheese; do not boil. Blend well.

Sauté mushrooms and green pepper in a small amount of butter. Toss with eggs, pimiento, and cheese sauce; add salt to taste. Serve immediately over warmed Chinese noodles.

SERVES 4 to 6

STUFFED PEPPER CUPS

You can freeze these.

6 medium green peppers
Salt
1 pound ground beef
⅓ cup chopped onion
2 cups stewed tomatoes (about a 1-pound can)
1 cup precooked rice
2 tablespoons Worcestershire sauce
Salt and pepper to taste
1 cup shredded American cheese

Cut tops off peppers; remove seeds. Precook in boiling water, salted, about 5 minutes, or steam; drain. Sprinkle inside with salt.

Brown meat and onion; add tomatoes, rice, Worcestershire sauce, salt, and pepper. Cover and simmer until rice is almost tender. Add cheese. Stuff peppers. Stand upright in baking dish. Bake, uncovered, at 350° F. for 25 minutes.

SERVES 6

STUFFED BELL PEPPER CREOLE

Southern main dish—yummy.

4 onions, chopped
2 cloves garlic
16 medium-sized peppers
1 stick butter
1 #2 can tomatoes
1 cup tomato juice
1 cup chopped ham
Salt and pepper to taste
Dash Tabasco
1 cup water
4 cups cracker crumbs
2 eggs
1 teaspoon sugar
Dash paprika

Wash and chop onions, garlic, and 4 peppers, leaving in the seeds. Cook with butter in a skillet until tender. Add tomatoes, tomato juice, ham, salt, pepper, Tabasco, and water, and cook until all ingredients go to the bottom. Take off heat; add cracker crumbs. Beat eggs well and add to mixture.

Scald the remaining 12 peppers with a pinch of salt and a little sugar. Stuff the peppers with the filling, sprinkle cracker crumbs over, and add a little melted butter and a dash of paprika. Bake 20 minutes at 350° F.

SERVES 12

Pickles and Jellies

PICKLED GREEN PEPPERS

Enough green peppers to fill 3 1-quart jars
3 cloves garlic
3 tablespoons oil
3 teaspoons salt
1 quart vinegar
1 quart water
3 cups sugar

Wash and take seeds from peppers. Cut peppers in lengthwise strips and stand in hot jars. To each quart jar add 1 clove garlic, 1 tablespoon oil, and 1 teaspoon salt.

Bring to a boil the vinegar, water, and sugar. Pour over peppers in hot jars and seal. Stand bottles in a kettle of hot water until cool.

MAKES 3 QUARTS

PEPPER JELLY

An unusual, beautiful jelly that complements poultry, corn bread, or toast.

2½ pounds (7 large) red bell peppers or green peppers (mild)

2 cups cider vinegar
2 teaspoons salt
2 teaspoons chili powder
10 cups sugar
⅔ cup lemon juice
1 6-ounce bottle liquid pectin

Cut peppers into chunks, discarding stems and seeds. Finely chop small amounts at a time in electric blender to get 4 cups. Mix chopped pepper, vinegar, salt, and chili powder in a large saucepan. Bring to a boil. Boil for 10 minutes, stirring occasionally. Stir in sugar and lemon juice and return to boil. Add pectin; stir constantly for exactly 1 minute. Lower heat and skim off foam. Quickly ladle into hot, sterilized jars to within ⅛ inch of rim. Wipe rims clean. Seal with parafin wax.

MAKES 7 PINTS

HOT VEGETABLE PICKLES

Very hot—will make your eyes water.

24 pickling cucumbers, cut into chunks
24 green tomatoes, quartered (optional)
12 cloves garlic
6 green peppers, cut into strips
6 hot peppers, cut into halves
2 cauliflowers, in flowerets
2 bunches celery, thickly sliced
2 pounds carrots, cut into ¼-inch slices
2 pounds pearl onions, peeled
9 cups vinegar
9 cups water
1 cup salt

Mix all vegetables. Put into sterilized quart jars. Bring the vinegar, water, and salt to a boil. Pour into jars. Wipe rims clean. Seal. Screw bands on tightly with hands. Put jars in a canning pot and boil water around jars for 15 minutes (10 minutes at sea level) to seal the lids.

MAKES 12 QUARTS

ROASTED RED AND GREEN PEPPERS

4 large red bell peppers
4 large green bell peppers

MARINADE

4 tablespoons olive oil
2 tablespoons white wine vinegar
1 clove garlic, minced or pressed
Salt and pepper to taste

Set the peppers, 4 at a time, on a broiler pan so they are about 1 inch below the broiler element. Broil, turning often with tongs, until peppers are well blistered and charred on all sides, about 30 minutes.

Place peppers in a paper bag, close tightly, and let sweat for 15 to 20 minutes to loosen skins. Cool and strip off skins. Cut peppers lengthwise in quarters; remove and discard stems and seeds. Cut pepper quarters into strips about ½ inch wide. Place in a bowl.

Combine all marinade ingredients. Pour over peppers; chill up to 3 days. Serve at room temperature.

MAKES 4 CUPS

NASHVILLE CHILI SAUCE

24 ripe tomatoes
6 chopped green peppers
8 sliced onions
4 cups vinegar
8 tablespoons sugar
6 tablespoons salt
1 tablespoon cinnamon
1 tablespoon cloves
1 tablespoon allspice
1 tablespoon nutmeg

Boil all ingredients together until thick. Mash with a potato masher to distribute flavor. Seal in sterile jars while hot.

MAKES 6 PINTS

Potatoes

1 pound = 3 4-inch white potatoes = 2 cups sliced
1 cup potatoes = 118 calories, 3.3 grams protein, 26.5 grams carbohydrates, 630 milligrams potassium, 25 milligrams vitamin C

Potatoes have taken the blame for that extra ten pounds we're all trying to lose for far too long. It's not the potato; it's all the stuff we load on top of it!

There are 3 basic kinds of potatoes: the baking potato (Idaho spud) which is dry and mealy; the white potato, long and thin-skinned; and the small new or red potato, firm and the best for potato salad. There is also the sweet potato (it is called a yam, but isn't!), without which no Thanksgiving is complete. You can harvest anytime after the plant flowers. Young potatoes (1 to 2 inches) can be eaten raw because they are so sweet. Store your potatoes in a cool, dark place. Just a note: the tomatolike fruit on the plant top and the sprouts are mildly poisonous so take care to remove and dispose of these, especially around small children.

To freeze: Raw potatoes don't freeze well, but cooked potatoes do fine. Our favorite way to freeze potatoes is to make casseroles, stuffed potatoes, etc. and take them right from freezer to oven. Don't let them thaw first; they go mealy.

Soups

DUTCH POTATO SOUP

1 small onion, thinly sliced
2 tablespoons oil
2 or 3 medium potatoes, thinly sliced
1 cup evaporated milk
½ pound fine curd cottage cheese
Chopped parsley

Sauté onion in oil in a soup kettle. Add potatoes and enough water to cover; simmer until tender. Add evaporated milk, bring just to a boil, and gently stir in cottage cheese. Top with chopped parsley to serve.

SERVES 4

BACON AND POTATO SOUP

A quick and perfect dish for a cold, wintry Sunday night.

½ pound bacon
4 to 6 medium potatoes, diced
1 medium onion, chopped
Water to cover
4 hard-cooked eggs, cubed
2 cups scalded milk
Salt and pepper to taste

Fry bacon until crisp. Remove from pan and crumble. Pour off all but 2 tablespoons bacon fat. Add diced potatoes and onions to fat. Cover with water and cook until done. Add crumbled bacon, cubed eggs, scalded milk, salt, and pepper.

SERVES 4

Salads

HERBED POTATO SALAD

An excellent red potato salad.

8 medium potatoes
3 tablespoons white wine vinegar
1 teaspoon salt
¼ teaspoon pepper
¼ teaspoon dry mustard
½ cup oil
1 teaspoon tarragon leaves, dried
6 green onions, sliced
2 teaspoons minced parsley

Cook potatoes in their skins until tender but still firm. Peel potatoes while warm and cut into ⅛-inch slices. Layer into a large bowl, sprinkling each layer with some of the vinegar. Combine remaining vinegar, salt, pepper, and mustard, and mix well. Slowly beat oil into vinegar mixture until dressing is creamy. Add tarragon. Add green onions, parsley, and dressing to potatoes and toss gently. Serve at room temperature (best), or chill thoroughly.

SERVES 8

HOT SOUR CREAM POTATO SALAD

A superb summer dinner.

6 medium potatoes
1 cup sour cream
1 cup mayonnaise
2 tablespoons flour
2 tablespoons chopped onion
3 tablespoons fine bread crumbs
Salt and pepper to taste
4 to 6 hard-cooked eggs, sliced
2 tablespoons melted butter

Boil and slice potatoes. Mix sour cream, mayonnaise, flour, and onion.

Put half the bread crumbs on bottom of a 2-quart casserole; layer half the potatoes seasoned with salt and pepper, half the eggs, and half the cream mixture. Repeat layers, starting with potatoes; then top with remaining bread crumbs and butter. Bake at 350° F. for 25 minutes. May be made ahead of time and stored in refrigerator.

SERVES 8

Baked and Stuffed Potatoes

OVEN POTATOES

6 unpeeled baking potatoes
8 tablespoons butter
½ portion dried onion soup mix
Foil

Slice potatoes vertically into ¼-inch slices, *not cutting quite through.* Mix butter and soup mix and spread between slices. Wrap in foil and bake for 1 hour at 350° F.

SERVES 6

STUFFED POTATOES

You can freeze these and have them on hand to pop in the microwave for emergencies.

12 medium potatoes, baked
½ cup butter
1 cup sour cream
¼ to ½ cup cream
2 teaspoons salt
1 cup Cheddar cheese, grated
1 tablespoon dehydrated chives

Remove top sides of potatoes; scoop out centers into a large bowl. Reserve boat-shaped skins. With an electric mixer, combine potatoes, butter, sour cream, and ¼ cup cream. Beat until smooth, adding more cream if necessary. Add salt, cheese, and chives, and beat just to blend. Spoon into skins. Store in refrigerator until mealtime. Bake at 400° F. for 30 minutes or until heated and browned.

To freeze: Place on flat tray in freezer; package and label. To serve, place frozen potatoes in oven and bake at 400° F. for 45 minutes or until heated and browned.

SERVES 12

BARBECUED STUFFED POTATOES

Potatoes, baked
Salt and pepper to taste
Butter
Grated onion
Milk
Foil

Bake potatoes in the usual way, split them, and scoop out the pulp. Mash and season pulp with salt, pepper, butter, and a little grated onion, and add enough milk to make a smooth mixture. Pack the shells with the seasoned potatoes and put the halves together. Wrap each potato separately in aluminum foil. Heat the stuffed potatoes on the back of the grate while the meat is cooking, for 20 to 30 minutes.

Side Dishes

MAXINE'S SOUR CREAM SCALLOPED POTATOES

1 2-pound bag frozen hash browns
2 10-ounce cans cream of chicken soup
2 cups sour cream
1 cup shredded Cheddar cheese
Crushed corn flakes, or buttered crumbs

Mix together hash browns, cooked according to package directions; soup; sour cream; and cheese. Place in baking dish; cover with crushed corn flakes or buttered crumbs. Heat through in 350° F. oven (about 10 minutes).

SERVES 8

HOT SWISS SCALLOPED POTATOES

1½ cups shredded Swiss cheese
½ cup sliced green onions
1 tablespoon dill weed
2 tablespoons butter
2 tablespoons flour
1 teaspoon salt
1 cup milk
1 cup sour cream
4 large potatoes, cooked, peeled, and sliced
3 cups cooked ham, diced
¼ cup dry bread crumbs
4 tablespoons butter

Combine 1 cup cheese, onions, and dill weed, and mix well. Set aside. Melt 2 tablespoons butter, stir in flour and salt, and gradually stir in milk. Cook until thick (about 2 minutes). Remove from heat and add sour cream. Add above cheese mixture.

Grease a 3-quart casserole. Place ⅓ potatoes in casserole, then some ham, then some cream sauce. Alternate layers. Combine remaining ½ cup cheese, bread crumbs, and 4 tablespoons butter, melted. Sprinkle over top. Bake at 350° F. for 30 to 35 minutes.

SERVES 6

EASY POTATOES AU GRATIN

3 medium potatoes, peeled, cooked, and sliced
½ cup coarsely chopped celery
1 can Cheddar cheese soup
1 tablespoon prepared mustard

In a nonstick 9″ × 9″ baking pan, combine potatoes and celery. Blend soup, undiluted, with mustard; pour over vegetables. Bake at 375° F. for 30 minutes or until hot and bubbly.

SERVES 8

POTATOES DAUPHINOIS

Good—watch for the garlic.

2 cups milk
½ cup butter
½ teaspoon salt
¼ teaspoon white pepper
3 pounds (about 4) baking potatoes
6 cloves garlic, peeled
1 cup heavy cream
1 cup grated Swiss cheese

Combine milk, butter, salt, and pepper in a large saucepan. Slowly bring to a boil. Peel potatoes. Rinse without soaking. Dry thoroughly. Slice fairly thin, letting slices drop into hot milk. Put toothpicks in garlic for easy removal later, then blend garlic and cream into milk. Slowly return to boil. Simmer 15 minutes, until potatoes are half done. Remove garlic. Pour potatoes with liquid into a buttered 1½- or 2-quart baking dish. Sprinkle with cheese. Bake at 325° F. for 10 to 15 minutes.

SERVES 6

COUNTRY COMPANY POTATOES

The potatoes we use with our Easter ham dinner.

7 large potatoes
1 cup cream of chicken soup
½ cup butter
1½ cups grated Cheddar cheese
1 pint sour cream
⅓ cup onions, minced
1 teaspoon salt
½ teaspoon pepper

TOPPING

1 cup corn flake crumbs
2 tablespoons butter

Boil potatoes with jackets until tender. Cool, peel, and grate.

Combine undiluted soup with butter and heat just until butter is melted. Add cheese, sour cream, and minced onions; combine with potatoes and add salt and pepper. Mix well. Place in a buttered 8″ × 8″ casserole or sheet cake pan; top with mixture of corn flakes and melted butter. Refrigerate overnight and bake at 350° F. for 45 to 60 minutes, uncovered; bake at 325° F. for 45 to 60 minutes if using a glass utensil.

SERVES 12

APPLE ZODIAC CASSEROLE

Sweet potatoes, apples, sausage—perfect for brunch.

4 cups thinly sliced sweet potatoes
4 cups thinly sliced tart apples
2 tablespoons instant minced onions
2 teaspoons salt
¾ cup maple blended syrup
¾ cup apple cider
½ cup melted butter
12 brown-and-serve sausages (optional)

Arrange alternate layers of sweet potatoes and apple slices in a greased 2-quart casserole. Sprinkle each layer with instant minced onion and salt. Combine syrup, cider, and melted butter; pour over all. Cover and bake in a 350° F. oven for 1 hour. Arrange sausages on top and bake uncovered for 20 minutes longer, or until sausages are brown and tender.

SERVES 6

Sweet Potatoes and Yams

MEXICAN SWEET POTATOES

2 cups cooked sweet potatoes, cubed
½ cup chopped green pepper
½ cup chopped onion
½ cup butter
Salt to taste

Toss all vegetables together and fry in butter until potatoes are brown and crisp. Salt to taste. A delicious way to use leftover sweet potatoes!

SERVES 4

SWEET POTATO CROQUETTES

Wrap this mixture around a marshmallow to make a hit with the children. A Thanksgiving day treat.

4 large sweet potatoes
1 cup broken pecan meats
1 cup crushed corn flakes
1 heaping tablespoon flour
½ cup sugar, or to taste
2 tablespoons milk
1 teaspoon cinnamon
1 teaspoon vanilla
1 egg
¼ teaspoon baking powder
Coarse corn flake crumbs for coating

Boil potatoes until thoroughly done. Drain and peel; mash until they are smooth. Add all remaining ingredients except corn flake crumbs for coating; mix well. Shape into croquettes and roll in coarse corn flake crumbs. Place in refrigerator to set. Fry in hot fat. Drain.

SERVES 8

ALMOND SWEET POTATO PUFF

2 cups mashed, cooked sweet potatoes
⅔ cup orange juice
½ teaspoon grated orange rind
¼ cup brown sugar, packed
3 tablespoons melted butter
2 eggs, separated
¼ cup chopped, blanched almonds
Salt

Combine sweet potatoes, orange juice and rind, brown sugar, and butter. Whip until light. Beat egg whites until stiff, but not dry; then beat yolks. Blend yolks into potato mixture along with ½ the almonds. Fold in whites and salt to taste. Turn into a greased 2-quart casserole and sprinkle remaining nuts over the top. Bake at 375° F. for 30 to 35 minutes.

SERVES 6

YAMS AND APPLES

6 to 8 medium yams
6 to 8 apples
½ cup butter
2 cups water
3 tablespoons cornstarch
1 cup sugar
Marshmallows

Parboil yams until tender; peel and slice ½ inch thick. Peel and slice apples. Alternate layers of yams and apples in a casserole. Combine butter, water, cornstarch, and sugar; cook until clear. Pour over the yams and apples. Bake 1 hour, covered, in a 250° F. oven. Uncover and arrange marshmallows on top and brown.

SERVES 12

Main Dish

SUPREME POTATO AND CORNED BEEF CASSEROLE

A main dish—great for potlucks.

1 10½-ounce can cream of mushroom soup
¼ cup milk
1 10½-ounce can corned beef
6 to 8 raw potatoes
1 cup shredded Cheddar cheese

Blend cream of mushroom soup and milk until smooth. Add corned beef and separate into small chunks in sauce. Blend again. Peel potatoes and slice thick; alternate layers of potatoes and sauce in a 2-quart casserole. Sprinkle cheese on top. Bake at 350° F. for 60 minutes.

SERVES 8 to 10

Pancakes, Dumplings, and Balls

POTATO PANCAKES

This is a favorite with German friends.

6 raw potatoes
3 eggs
1 small onion, grated
2 tablespoons fine bread crumbs
Salt and pepper to taste
3 tablespoons vegetable oil

Peel and grate potatoes. Drain off liquid. Mix in eggs, onion, bread crumbs, salt, and pepper. Fry like a pancake in hot vegetable oil (380° F.). Keep warm in oven.

MAKES 15 PANCAKES

POTATO BALLS

5 or 6 medium potatoes
1 medium onion, finely minced
2 7½-ounce cans chopped black olives
2 eggs
Dash onion salt
Dash garlic salt
Cracker meal
Oil
Tartar sauce

Cook and mash potatoes. Add onion, olives, 1 egg, onion salt, and garlic salt. Let mixture cool.

Form balls into about a half-dollar size. Dip balls into remaining egg that has been beaten, and roll in cracker meal. Refrigerate overnight. When ready to serve, fry in ¾ inch of very hot oil. Serve hot with tartar sauce.

SERVES 6

GNOCCHI (POTATO AND CHEESE DUMPLINGS)

A good accompaniment to a roast.

4 potatoes (about 1 pound)
1 cup water
6 tablespoons butter
Salt and pepper to taste
2 pinches nutmeg
1 cup flour
3 eggs
1 cup Parmesan cheese, grated

TOPPING

2 tablespoons melted butter
½ cup Parmesan cheese, grated

Peel and quarter potatoes. Boil until tender, drain, and dry well. Put the cooked potatoes through a ricer and set aside. (There will be about 2 cups.)

In a saucepan put 1 cup water, 6 tablespoons butter, salt, pepper, and nutmeg. Bring to a boil, remove from heat, then quickly stir in the flour. Stir rapidly with a wooden spoon until mixture leaves sides of pan and forms a ball.

Put flour mixture into electric mixer or mixing bowl and beat in eggs, one at a time. Add 1 cup Parmesan cheese, then beat in mashed potatoes. Mix all ingredients to a smooth paste. On a lightly floured board, roll a tablespoonful at a time with the palm of your hand to form small dumplings. Drop dumplings gently into a pan of simmering salted water and let them cook, uncovered, for about 15 minutes, or until they swell and are firm. Don't boil water or dumplings will disintegrate. Remove dumplings with slotted spoon. Drain on paper towels.

Place in a shallow buttered baking dish. Brush with 2 tablespoons melted butter. Sprinkle with ½ cup Parmesan cheese. Just before serving, put baking dish under broiler (about 5 inches from heat) until slightly browned.

SERVES 4

YORKSHIRE POTATO PUDDING

If you like Yorkshire pudding, this is a fun variation to try.

6 medium-sized potatoes
1 beef bouillon cube
⅓ to ½ cup hot milk
3 tablespoons melted butter
1 teaspoon salt
¼ teaspoon pepper
1 to 2 eggs, slightly beaten
½ teaspoon paprika

Boil and mash potatoes. Dissolve bouillon cube in hot milk, add butter, salt, and pepper, and beat into potatoes. Reserve 1½ tablespoons of the beaten egg; add remainder to potatoes and beat again. Pile into well greased 8- or 9-inch cake tin. Brush with remaining egg combined with the paprika. Brown in hot oven. Cut into wedges.

SERVES 6 to 8

Puddings and Pies

SWEET POTATO CUSTARD

1 cup sugar (brown is best), firmly packed
⅔ cup butter
2 eggs, beaten
2 cups grated raw sweet potato
Grated rind of 1 orange
Grated rind of ½ lemon
½ teaspoon ginger
½ teaspoon mace
Dash cinnamon

Cream together sugar and butter. Add eggs and grated raw sweet potato and beat well. Add grated rinds of orange and lemon, ginger, mace, and cinnamon. Beat the custard again well and bake it in a 1½-quart buttered baking dish in a moderate oven (350° F.) for 1 hour.

SERVES 4

SWEET POTATO PIE

Served with whipped cream, orange peel, and nutmeg—good!

4 eggs
1½ cups boiled, mashed sweet potato
⅓ cup sugar
2 tablespoons honey
½ cup crushed walnuts or pecans
⅔ cup milk
⅓ cup orange juice
1 teaspoon vanilla extract
Pinch salt
Unbaked pie shell

TOPPING

1 cup whipped cream
1 tablespoon grated orange peel
½ teaspoon nutmeg

Beat eggs until they are very light, add sweet potatoes and sugar, and beat all together. Stir in honey, walnuts or pecans, milk, orange juice, vanilla, and salt. Pour the mixture into an unbaked pie shell and bake pie in a very hot oven (450° F.) for 10 minutes. Reduce temperature to moderate (350° F.) and bake 30 minutes longer, or until a silver knife inserted near the center comes out clean.

Cool pie and spread it with whipped cream flavored with grated orange peel and nutmeg.

SERVES 6 to 8

Pumpkin

1 pound = ½ small pumpkin cleaned = 2 cups peeled and diced
½ cup cooked = 40 calories, 1.2 grams protein, 13.4 grams carbohydrates, lots of vitamin A
1 pound of pumpkin = about 1 cup of mashed, cooked pumpkin

If you think pumpkins are just for Halloween take another look. Connecticut Field, Sugar Bush, Sugar Pie, and Winter Keeper are the best for pies. Others like Cinderella and Big Max are best left as jack-o'-lanterns.

To harvest pumpkins for cooking it is best to stick to small varieties. Choose a hard, thick rind and a bright yellow-orange color. Pumpkins will store in a dark, cool place for several months. To prepare for cooking, cut and scrape away seeds and stringy portions. Put an inch of salted water in baking dish and bake at 375° F. for 40 minutes or until tender. You can also boil pieces for 5 minutes in boiling salted water. Drain and mash smooth.

To freeze: Bake or boil and mash smooth (blender or food processor works well). Pack in freezer containers leaving ½ inch at top. Seal and freeze. The pumpkin will be ready for baking when you are. It has a higher water content than canned pumpkin though, so keep that in mind when cooking.

Soups

PUMPKIN BEEF STEW

2 pounds beef stew meat
2 medium onions, sliced
¼ cup butter
2 teaspoons salt
½ teaspoon pepper
2 potatoes
3 carrots
3 cups cubed pumpkin
1 16-ounce can tomatoes
¼ cup flour
½ cup cold water

Brown the beef and onions in a kettle; add butter, salt, and pepper and cook slowly for 1½ hours or until the meat is tender. Add the vegetables and cook for 30 minutes or until the vegetables are tender. Remove meat and vegetables from the kettle and place into a bowl.

Add flour and ½ cup cold water to kettle; boil until thick. Pour over the meat and vegetables and serve in a hollowed-out pumpkin.

SERVES 8 to 10

PUMPKIN SOUP

Great autumn supper or a farewell dinner to Mr. Jack-O'-Lantern.

4 tablespoons butter
4 scallions, chopped
1 small onion, sliced
1½ pounds pumpkin, peeled and diced
4 cups chicken stock
½ teaspoon salt
2 tablespoons flour
1 cup hot light cream
Tiny toasted croutons
Whipped cream, lightly salted

Melt 2 tablespoons butter in a large saucepan. Add scallions and onion slices and cook gently until they are almost soft but not brown. Add pumpkin, chicken stock, and salt. Simmer until pumpkin is soft. Stir in flour kneaded with 1 tablespoon butter and bring soup to a boil. Press soup through a fine sieve or puree it in a blender. Correct the seasoning and add the light cream and 1 tablespoon butter. Heat soup just to the boiling point and serve it garnished with tiny toasted croutons and whipped cream.

SERVES 12 to 14

Side Dishes

PUMPKIN PUREE

You can freeze for use later in pumpkin pies.

1 ripe pumpkin
Hot water
Butter
Salt
Pepper
Sugar
Ginger (optional)

Wash pumpkin and cut into quarters, discarding seeds and fibers. Arrange the quarters on a baking pan in ½ inch hot water and bake them in a moderate oven (350° F.) for 1½ to 2 hours, or until they are tender. Scrape the pulp from the rind and rub it through a sieve, or put it through a food mill or blender.

Stir the puree over moderate heat until most of the moisture evaporates. Season it with butter, salt, pepper, and a little sugar. A pinch of ginger may also be added to taste.

MAKES 4 to 12 CUPS, DEPENDING ON SIZE OF PUMPKIN

BAKED PUMPKIN

Comes out just like squash.

2 pounds pumpkin
½ cup butter
¼ cup brown sugar
½ teaspoon cinnamon
½ teaspoon ginger
½ teaspoon allspice (optional)
Salt

Cut pumpkin into serving pieces. Peel the wedges and discard seeds and fibers. In a small saucepan melt butter and brown sugar; add cinnamon, ginger, and allspice. Score pumpkin wedges with a sharp knife, spread them with the butter-sugar mixture, and sprinkle lightly with salt. Bake pumpkin in a moderate oven (350° F.) in ½ inch water on a shallow baking pan for 1½ to 2 hours or until tender, basting the wedges frequently with melted butter.

SERVES 4 to 6

NEW ENGLAND APPLE-STUFFED PUMPKIN

1 small to medium pumpkin
2 teaspoons butter, melted
Salt
½ cup brown sugar
4 cups sliced apples
2 cups raisins
1 teaspoon cinnamon
¼ teaspoon cloves

Clean out pumpkin. Brush insides with butter; sprinkle with salt and 2 tablespoons brown sugar. Combine remaining ingredients, place in pumpkin, replace pumpkin lid, and bake at 375° F. for 2 to 2½ hours or until pumpkin is tender. Scrape pumpkin from sides to go with apple mixture when serving.

SERVES 4 to 6

PAT'S PUMPKIN WHIP

A custard that's not too sweet.

3 egg whites
3 tablespoons sugar
¼ cup chopped nuts
¾ cup canned or fresh pumpkin
⅛ teaspoon salt
⅛ teaspoon cinnamon
⅛ teaspoon ginger
1 teaspoon lemon juice

Beat egg whites until stiff. Add sugar gradually and beat until dissolved. Mix nuts, pumpkin, salt, cinnamon, ginger, and lemon juice; fold in egg whites. Pour into buttered custard cups. Set in pan of water. Bake at 350° F. for 35 minutes.

SERVES 4

Breads and Pancakes

PUMPKIN BREAD

Healthy for breakfast, lunch, and dinner.

3½ cups flour
1 tablespoon baking soda
1¼ teaspoons salt
1 teaspoon cinnamon
1 cup nuts, chopped
4 eggs
3 cups sugar
2 cups pumpkin
1 cup vegetable oil
⅔ cup water

Sift flour, baking soda, salt, and cinnamon. Mix with chopped nuts. Set aside.

Thoroughly beat eggs, sugar, pumpkin, vegetable oil, and water. Fold in flour mixture. Pour into 2 greased 4½″ × 8½″ loaf pans. Bake at 350° F. for 60 to 70 minutes or until a toothpick comes out clean.

MAKES 2 LOAVES

PUMPKIN MINCEMEAT BREAD

Rich and moist, nice bread to serve with cream cheese.

3½ cups flour
1½ cups sugar
2 tablespoons pumpkin pie spice
2 teaspoons baking soda
1½ teaspoons salt
1½ cups brown sugar, firmly packed
4 eggs, beaten
⅔ cup water
2 cups canned pumpkin, *or* 2½ cups fresh cooked and drained pumpkin
1 cup vegetable oil
1½ cups prepared mincemeat
1 cup nuts, chopped

Sift flour, sugar, pumpkin pie spice, baking soda, and salt into a large bowl. Mix in brown sugar. Make a well in the center. Pour in eggs, water, pumpkin, and oil. Stir well. Blend in mincemeat and nuts. Pour into three greased 5″ × 9″ loaf pans. Bake at 350° F. for 1 hour.

MAKES 3 LOAVES

ICED PUMPKIN BREAD

3½ cups sifted flour
3 cups sugar
2 teaspoons soda
1½ teaspoons nutmeg
1½ teaspoons salt
1½ teaspoons cinnamon
1 cup oil
4 eggs
⅔ cup water
2 cups pumpkin
1 cup nuts
1 cup raisins

ICING

¼ cup butter
½ cup brown sugar
⅛ cup canned milk
1 cup powdered sugar

Sift flour, sugar, soda, nutmeg, salt, and cinnamon together. Mix oil, eggs, water, and pumpkin; add to flour mixture. Add nuts and raisins. Put in floured and greased 9″ × 5″ × 3″ loaf pans. Fill only ¾ full—if too full, bread will take too long to cook and will get brown and crusty. Bake at 350° F. about 1 hour.

While bread is baking, prepare icing. Bring to a boil butter, brown sugar, and milk; boil for 2 minutes. Gradually add powdered sugar. Beat until thick. When bread is done, cover with icing.

MAKES 2 LOAVES

FRUITED PUMPKIN BREAD

Like fruitcake.

½ cup butter or margarine
1 cup brown sugar
2 eggs
1 cup canned pumpkin or fresh, cooked pumpkin
2 cups flour
½ cup candied fruit, chopped
½ cup raisins
½ cup walnuts, chopped
2 teaspoons baking powder
½ teaspoon soda
½ teaspoon salt
1 teaspoon cinnamon
1 teaspoon pumpkin pie spice
½ cup milk

Cream butter; gradually add brown sugar and beat until light and fluffy. Add eggs and beat well. Stir in pumpkin. Mix ½ cup flour with fruit, raisins, and walnuts. Set aside.

Sift together remaining flour, baking powder, soda, salt, cinnamon, and pumpkin pie spice. Add to creamed mixture alternately with milk. Stir in fruit mixture. Pour into a greased and wax paper–lined 9″ × 5″ × 3″ loaf pan. Bake at 350° F. for about 1 hour or until a toothpick inserted in the center comes out clean. Cool in pan on wire rack 5 minutes, then remove to cool completely.

MAKES 1 LOAF

PUMPKIN MUFFINS

¼ cup butter
½ cup sugar
½ cup milk
1 egg
½ cup pumpkin
1½ cups flour
2 teaspoons baking powder
¾ teaspoon salt
½ teaspoon cinnamon
½ teaspoon nutmeg
½ cup seedless raisins

Cream butter and sugar together until fluffy. Add milk, egg, and pumpkin. Combine flour, baking powder, salt, cinnamon, and nutmeg, and add to butter mixture. Stir just until flour is moistened. Add raisins. Fill muffin tins ⅔ full and bake at 400° F. for about 25 minutes.

MAKES 12 MUFFINS

PUMPKIN PANCAKES

1 cup pancake mix
2 tablespoons sugar
¼ teaspoon ground cinnamon
⅛ teaspoon ginger
⅛ teaspoon nutmeg
1 egg, well beaten
2 tablespoons melted shortening
1 cup pumpkin
1¼ cups milk
Butter
Syrup or powdered sugar

Combine pancake mix, sugar, cinnamon, ginger, and nutmeg. Combine egg, shortening, pumpkin, and milk. Blend mixtures together, beating until smooth. Bake on lightly greased hot griddle, turning only once. Serve hot with butter and syrup or powdered sugar.

MAKES 24 4-INCH PANCAKES

Custards, Cakes, and Cookies

PUMPKIN COOKIES

1 teaspoon vanilla
¼ cup butter
¾ cup shortening
1 cup sugar
1 cup pumpkin, cooked and strained
1 egg
2 cups flour
½ teaspoon salt
1 teaspoon baking powder
1 teaspoon soda
1 teaspoon cinnamon
½ cup chopped pecans
½ cup chopped dates

ICING

3 tablespoons butter
¼ cup milk
½ cup light brown sugar
1 cup + 2 tablespoons confectioners' sugar
½ teaspoon vanilla

Cream together vanilla, butter, shortening, sugar, pumpkin, and egg. Mix flour, salt, baking powder, soda, and cinnamon. Add to creamed mixture. Mix well. Add pecans and dates. Make into balls and place on lightly greased and floured cookie sheet. Flatten with a fork. Bake at 350° F. for 10 to 12 minutes.

Prepare icing by boiling together butter, milk, and brown sugar for 2 minutes. Cool. Stir in confectioners' sugar and vanilla; beat. Frost cookies.

MAKES 1 to 2 DOZEN

PUMPKIN BARS

4 eggs, slightly beaten
¾ cup salad oil
2 cups sugar
1 small can (about 15 ounces) pumpkin
2 teaspoons ground cinnamon
¾ teaspoons *each* ground ginger, ground cloves, ground nutmeg, and salt
2 teaspoons baking powder
1 teaspoon soda
2 cups all-purpose flour, unsifted
Whole almonds (optional)

ORANGE–CREAM CHEESE FROSTING

1 3-ounce package cream cheese
2 tablespoons butter or margarine
1½ teaspoons milk
½ teaspoon vanilla
¾ teaspoon grated orange peel
Up to ½ pound powdered sugar

With an electric mixer blend eggs, oil, sugar, and pumpkin; set aside. Stir together cinnamon, ginger, cloves, nutmeg, salt, baking powder, soda, and flour until blended; add to pumpkin mixture and beat until well blended.

Pour mixture into a greased and flour-dusted 10″ × 15″ jelly roll pan, or evenly divide into 2 9-inch square baking pans. Bake in a 350° F. oven until edges begin to pull away from sides and center springs back when lightly touched, about 35 minutes; remove and let cool in pan.

Prepare Orange–Cream Cheese Frosting. Bring cream cheese and butter or margarine to room temperature; beat until light and fluffy. Add milk, vanilla, and grated orange peel. Sift in powdered sugar a little at a time, beating until frosting is desired consistency.

To serve, spread pumpkin mixture with Orange–Cream Cheese Frosting; cut into 1″ × 2″ bars. If desired, top each bar with an almond.

MAKES ABOUT 60 BARS

PUMPKIN CUSTARD

1 cup cooked, pureed pumpkin
2 lightly beaten eggs
½ cup brown sugar
½ teaspoon salt
½ teaspoon cinnamon
¼ teaspoon ginger
1 cup heavy cream
Grated rind of ½ orange

Mix together cooked, pureed pumpkin, eggs, and brown sugar mixed with salt, cinnamon, and ginger. Stir in cream and orange rind. Pour mixture into buttered custard cups and set the cups in a pan of hot water. Bake custard in a 325° F. oven for 40 minutes, or until a knife inserted near the center comes out clean.

SERVES 4 to 6

PUMPKIN CAKE

4 eggs
2 cups sugar
1 cup cooking oil
2 cups all-purpose flour, sifted
2 teaspoons soda
2 teaspoons cinnamon
½ teaspoon salt
2 cups fresh or canned pumpkin, cooked and drained

CREAM CHEESE ICING

1 stick butter or margarine
1 3-ounce package cream cheese
1 teaspoon vanilla
1 pound confectioners' sugar
1 cup broken pecans
Milk (optional)

Beat eggs and sugar until well blended and light. Add oil and continue beating. Sift flour, soda, cinnamon, and salt together to mix. Add flour mixture to egg mixture. Add pumpkin. Bake in well greased and floured 9-inch tube pan for 55 minutes at 350° F. Remove from pan after cooling for 10 minutes on rack.

When cake is cooled, frost with Cream Cheese Icing prepared by creaming together butter, cheese, and vanilla. Add sugar and beat until creamy. Stir in pecans. If icing is a little thick, add small amount of milk until of spreading consistency.

SERVES 8 to 12

FRESH PUMPKIN BUTTERMILK CAKE

2¼ cups white flour
2 teaspoons baking powder
1 teaspoon soda
½ teaspoon cinnamon
½ teaspoon allspice
¼ teaspoon cloves
½ cup butter
1½ cups sugar
2 eggs
½ teaspoon vanilla extract
½ cup strained pumpkin
½ cup buttermilk

Sift flour with baking powder, soda, cinnamon, allspice, and cloves. Cream butter well with sugar. Beat in eggs; beat until the mixture is light and fluffy. Stir in vanilla and pumpkin.

Add buttermilk to pumpkin mixture alternately with the sifted dry ingredients to make a smooth batter. Pour the batter into 2 buttered and floured layer cake pans or into a fluted mold and bake cake in a moderate oven (350° F.) until it tests done.

SERVES 10 to 12

Pies

PUMPKIN PIE

2 eggs, slightly beaten
1¾ cups canned pumpkin, *or* 1½ cups cooked, strained fresh pumpkin
¾ cup sugar
½ teaspoon salt
1 teaspoon cinnamon
½ teaspoon ginger
¼ teaspoon cloves
1⅔ cups (1 can) evaporated milk
1 9-inch pastry shell, unbaked

Combine all filling ingredients and blend well with electric mixer. Pour into pastry shell. Bake in a 425° F. oven for 15 minutes. Reduce oven and bake at 350° F. for 45 minutes. Knife inserted in center should come out clean.

SERVES 6 to 8

PUMPKIN CHIFFON PIE

Made with walnut pie crust.

1 envelope (2 tablespoons) Knox gelatin
¼ cup cold water
¾ cup sugar
1¼ cups canned pumpkin, *or* 1 cup cooked, strained fresh pumpkin
½ cup milk
½ teaspoon *each* of salt, ginger, nutmeg, and cinnamon
3 eggs, separated
Whipped cream
Walnuts for garnish

WALNUT PIE CRUST

1½ cups ground walnut meat
½ cup chopped walnuts
3 tablespoons sugar

Soften gelatin in cold water. Combine ½ cup sugar with pumpkin, milk, and seasonings in top of double boiler. Heat, add beaten egg yolks, and cook until thick. Add gelatin to hot pumpkin mixture. Mix thoroughly. Cool and set in refrigerator. Beat egg whites until stiff. Beat in remaining sugar, and when pumpkin mixture begins to thicken, fold in egg whites.

To make pie crust, mix walnut meat and nuts with sugar. Press mixture firmly against sides and bottom of pie pan. Fill with Pumpkin Chiffon mixture. Spread with whipped cream and garnish with walnuts if desired.

SERVES 6 to 8

PUMPKIN SOUR CREAM PIE

1½ cups sour cream
1½ cups Pumpkin Puree (see Index for recipe)
3 eggs, separated
1 cup brown sugar
¾ teaspoon cinnamon
¼ teaspoon nutmeg
¼ teaspoon ground ginger
¼ teaspoon salt
1 9-inch pie shell, lightly baked and brushed with egg white
Whipped cream

Heat 1 cup sour cream in the top of a double boiler. In a mixing bowl mix together ½ cup sour cream, Pumpkin Puree, beaten egg yolks, brown sugar, cinnamon, nutmeg, ginger, and salt. Add the seasoned puree slowly to the hot sour cream and cook the mixture over hot water, stirring constantly, until it is thick. Cool the custard and fold into it stiffly beaten egg whites. Pour custard into lightly baked pie shell. Bake at 350°F. for 20 minutes or until the top is nicely browned. Serve with whipped cream.

SERVES 6 to 8

PUMPKIN–APPLE BUTTER PIE

Top this moist pie with fresh whipped cream.

SPICY PASTRY

1 cup all-purpose flour
2 tablespoons sugar
¼ teaspoon *each* ground cinnamon, nutmeg, and cloves
⅓ cup solid shortening
1½ tablespoons orange juice
1½ tablespoons vinegar

FILLING

1 1-pound can pumpkin
1 cup apple butter
½ cup packed brown sugar
1 teaspoon ground cinnamon
½ teaspoon *each* ground ginger, nutmeg, and salt
3 eggs, slightly beaten
3 5⅓ ounce cans evaporated milk

Prepare pastry. Stir together flour, sugar,

cinnamon, nutmeg, and cloves. Cut in shortening until lumps are the size of peas. Mix together orange juice and vinegar, then stir into flour mixture with a fork. Shape into ball. Roll out and fit into a 9-inch pie pan; trim edges and flute. Chill while preparing filling.

In a bowl, stir together pumpkin, apple butter, sugar, cinnamon, ginger, nutmeg, salt, eggs, and milk. Pour into pie shell. Bake on the lowest rack of a 425° F. oven for 15 minutes; reduce heat to 350° F. and bake 40 to 45 minutes longer or until a knife inserted comes out clean. Cool on a wire rack.

SERVES 6 to 8

FROZEN PUMPKIN PRALINE PIE

Melts in your mouth.

1 quart vanilla ice cream
1½ cups pumpkin, cooked and strained or canned
½ cup granulated sugar
½ teaspoon salt
1 teaspoon pumpkin pie spice
1 9-inch baked pie shell

TOPPING

4 tablespoons brown sugar
4 tablespoons butter
4 tablespoons cream
½ cup chopped nuts

Soften ice cream. Combine pumpkin, sugar, salt, and pumpkin pie spice. Fold ice cream and the pumpkin mixture together and pour into a baked pie shell. Freeze.

Combine brown sugar, butter, and cream in a saucepan; heat to boiling and cook 1 minute. Remove from heat and stir in nuts. Cool mixture to warm and spoon over top of pie. Place pie back in freezer until serving time.

SERVES 6 to 8

Seeds

SALTED PUMPKIN SEEDS

Separate the seeds of a pumpkin from the yellow fibers to which they cling, but do not wash them. Spread seeds in a shallow baking pan and sprinkle with salt. Coat the seeds with melted butter and brown lightly in a very slow oven (250° F.).

Spinach

1 pound = 2 3-inch bunches = 8 cups raw = 1½ cups cooked
1 cup raw chopped spinach = 41 calories, 5.4 grams protein, 6.5 grams carbohydrates, 583 milligrams potassium, 14,580 units vitamin A, 50 milligrams vitamin C

Popeye was right! Spinach is loaded with vitamin A and other good things. You can pick the outer leaves of spinach for salads when the plant is growing. When it is mature, uproot it and cut off leaves. You need to rinse quickly, drain, and dry off leaves with paper towels. Spinach will wilt after 1 to 2 days storage in a plastic bag. We've had better storage success by cutting the leaves for a salad, washing, drying, then storing in Tupperware with paper towels at the bottom of the container to absorb moisture.

To freeze: Prepare; scald 1 minute. Chill in ice water; drain but don't dry. It is best to freeze spinach damp. When you go to cook it, do not defrost first.

Soup

SPINACH SOUP

BASIC SOUP BASE

2 large baking potatoes, peeled
1 bunch celery
1 onion, minced
1 10½-ounce can chicken broth

FOR SPINACH SOUP

2 bunches spinach
1 clove garlic, crushed
1 10½-ounce can chicken broth
2 heaping tablespoons butter
2 heaping tablespoons sour cream
3 cups Basic Soup Base
Tarragon
Nutmeg
Lemon juice
Pepper

To prepare Basic Soup Base, wash and chop vegetables. Put into a large pot with chicken broth. Cover and cook until soft. Put through blender. Add more broth if necessary to make blend possible. Store in refrigerator or freeze for future use.

For Spinach Soup, cook spinach and garlic in chicken broth. Blend. In a saucepan, heat butter, Imo or sour cream, Basic Soup Base, and 3 cups spinach–chicken broth mixture. Add tarragon, nutmeg, lemon juice, and pepper to taste. Add more chicken broth until soup is desired consistency. Soup may be stored in refrigerator.

SERVES 4 to 6

Salads and Dips

SOUR CREAM SPINACH DIP

2 cups sour cream
1 cup mayonnaise
¾ package dry leek soup mix
1 10-ounce package frozen chopped spinach, well drained and rechopped
½ cup fresh parsley, finely chopped
½ cup green onions and tops, finely chopped
1 teaspoon dill weed
Pinch garlic powder
1 teaspoon salad seasoning mix

Combine sour cream and mayonnaise. Add soup mix and combine thoroughly. Add remaining ingredients and mix well.

MAKES 3½ to 4 CUPS

SPINACH SALAD

The dressing is fantastic.

1 pound spinach
8 slices bacon
3 hard-cooked eggs

FRENCH DRESSING

2 tablespoons lemon juice
2 tablespoons vinegar
½ cup oil
1 teaspoon sugar
½ teaspoon dry mustard
½ teaspoon paprika
½ teaspoon salt
Dash pepper
Dash cayenne pepper

Wash and dry spinach well. Cook bacon crisp and crumble. Chop hard-cooked eggs.

Combine ingredients for French Dressing and mix well in a blender. Toss spinach with French Dressing and garnish with bacon and eggs.

SERVES 8

SPINACH AND BEAN SALAD

¾ pound kidney beans (or broad beans)
6 to 8 tablespoons olive oil
3 tablespoons wine vinegar or lemon juice
1 teaspoon chopped fresh marjoram
1 teaspoon chopped fresh basil
2 teaspoons chopped fresh parsley
1 clove garlic, finely chopped
Salt and freshly ground pepper
1 pound raw spinach leaves
1 small onion, thinly sliced into rings

Cook kidney beans until tender, then cool and drain. Mix with dressing made of olive oil, wine vinegar or lemon juice, chopped herbs, garlic, salt, and pepper. Serve on spinach leaves and garnish with onion rings.

SERVES 4 to 6

CASHEW SPINACH SALAD

1 head lettuce
1 bunch spinach
⅛ cup sugar
1 teaspoon salt
1 teaspoon dry mustard
1 teaspoon grated onion
¼ cup vinegar
1 cup oil
1 teaspoon celery salt
1 6-ounce can salted cashews

Wash lettuce and spinach, dry, and break into pieces. Mix sugar, salt, and mustard; add onion and vinegar. Blend in oil, pouring slowly into mix; beat. Add celery salt. Toss greens with dressing. Add nuts.

SERVES 8 to 12

MOLDED SPINACH SALAD

A different way to serve spinach.

1 3-ounce package lime gelatin
1 cup hot water
½ cup mayonnaise
Finely chopped onion to taste
Salt and pepper
2 cups cottage cheese
1½ cups chopped raw spinach

Melt gelatin in 1 cup hot water. Mix together remaining ingredients and add to gelatin; let thicken a little, then stir to keep ingredients from settling. Refrigerate.

SERVES 4 to 6

SPINACH-APPLE TOSS

2 10-ounce bags spinach
2 tart red apples, unpeeled and sliced

8 slices bacon, crispy and crumbled
⅔ cup salad dressing or mayonnaise
⅓ cup frozen orange juice concentrate, thawed

Wash and dry spinach leaves; tear into bite sized pieces. Combine spinach, apples, and bacon. Mix salad dressing and orange juice concentrate; pour over spinach-apple mixture and toss lightly.

SERVES 12

WILTED SPINACH SALAD

Early in the day check the spinach and wash. Drain and refrigerate it.

½ pound bacon
¾ cup vinegar
¼ cup water
⅔ cup sugar
1 large bunch spinach
4 green onions, chopped
2 hard-cooked eggs, chopped fine
Salt and pepper to taste

Fry bacon in a heavy pan and drain. Pour off the fat, measure ⅓ cup, and return it to the pan. Add vinegar, water, and sugar. Bring to a boil over high heat; reduce heat and cook down about 10 minutes. Set dressing aside.

Crumble bacon. At serving time put uncooked spinach in a very large salad bowl; sprinkle top with onions; add eggs, crumbled bacon, and salt and pepper to taste (be generous with this).

Bring dressing to a boil again, pour over salad, and serve it quickly.

SERVES 4 to 6

Side Dishes

FRESH SPINACH IN A SKILLET

A similar taste to spinach salad.

8 slices bacon
8 bunches fresh spinach (2 bunches per person)
Sea salt
Juice of 1 lemon

Cook bacon in large skillet. Remove and crumble. Use 3 teaspoons bacon drippings and add washed spinach. Cover and cook 5 minutes. Salt with sea salt, toss, and finish off with lemon juice.

SERVES 4

SPINACH SUPREME

7 to 8 cups fresh spinach chopped, *or* 4 10-ounce packages chopped frozen spinach, cooked and drained
1 pint sour cream
1 package onion soup mix
1 package slivered almonds
Garlic croutons
Parmesan cheese, grated

Mix together all ingredients except Parmesan cheese and bake in a 1½- to 2-quart casserole for ½ hour. Sprinkle Parmesan cheese on top. Bake at 350°F.

SERVES 8 to 10

SPINACH-STUFFED MUSHROOMS

2 tablespoons butter
3 tablespoons flour
1 cup milk
Salt and pepper to taste
¾ pound fresh spinach
½ cup green onions, finely chopped
½ clove garlic, minced
3 tablespoons butter
¼ cup boiled ham, finely chopped
Salt and pepper to taste
30 2-inch mushroom caps, stems removed
2 tablespoons butter, in tiny pieces

Make sauce by melting 2 tablespoons butter. Using a whisk, gradually stir in flour until smooth and bubbly. Stirring constantly, add milk, salt, and pepper. Stir and simmer 5 minutes. Set sauce aside.

Cook spinach. Chop finely. Squeeze out all excess liquid. Pack to make ¼ cup. Set aside.

Sauté onions and garlic in 3 tablespoons butter for 2 minutes. Add spinach and stir fry for 3 minutes. Remove to a bowl. Stir in chopped ham, sauce, and additional salt and pepper.

Arrange mushroom caps in a shallow pan, bottoms up. Stuff each with filling. Dot with butter. Bake at 350° F. for 10 to 15 minutes in the upper third of oven.

MAKES 30 APPETIZERS OR A VEGETABLE SIDE DISH WITH BEEF

Main Dishes

LAYERED SPINACH SUPREME

Meatless main dish—good with a fruit salad for a simple meal.

1 cup Bisquick baking mix
¼ cup milk
2 eggs
¼ cup finely chopped onion
1 10-ounce package frozen chopped spinach, thawed and drained, *or* 1 bunch fresh spinach
½ cup grated Parmesan cheese
4 ounces Monterey Jack cheese, cut into ½-inch cubes
1 12-ounce carton creamed cottage cheese
½ teaspoon salt
2 cloves garlic, crushed
2 eggs

Heat oven to 375° F. Grease rectangular baking dish, 12″ × 7½″ × 2″. Mix baking mix, milk, 2 eggs, and the onion; beat vigorously 20 strokes. Spread batter in dish.

Mix remaining ingredients; spoon evenly over batter in dish. Bake until set, about 30 minutes. Let stand 5 minutes before cutting.

SERVES 6 to 8

MOCK RAVIOLI

Vegetarian main dish—but as good as the real thing.

1 pound butterfly macaroni, cooked
2 cups finely chopped spinach
1 clove garlic, crushed
½ cup finely chopped parsley
½ cup olive oil
½ cup dry bread crumbs
½ cup grated Parmesan cheese
1 teaspoon salt
½ teaspoon sage
4 eggs, well beaten
2 8-ounce cans tomato-mushroom sauce

Cook macaroni in boiling salted water; drain Combine all remaining ingredients except tomato-mushroom sauce. Using a 9″ × 12″ × 2″ baking dish, alternate layers of macaroni and mixture. Pour tomato-mushroom sauce over casserole and bake in a 325° F. oven for 45 minutes.

SERVES 8 to 10

COTTAGE CHEESE–SPINACH CASSEROLE

Another vegetarian main dish.

1 pint farmer-style cottage cheese
3 eggs, beaten
3 tablespoons flour
¼ pound American cheese, cubed
½ package (5 ounces) frozen chopped spinach
2 to 3 tablespoons butter
Salt

Mix together cottage cheese, eggs, and flour. Add American cheese. Allow spinach to thaw until it can be broken apart in chunks. Add frozen chunks to mixture. Cut butter in pieces and combine with mixture. Add salt to taste. Bake uncovered for 1 hour in a 350° F. oven. If doubling recipe, allow 2 hours for baking in a deep casserole.

SERVES 4

SPINACH AND CHEESE CUSTARD

A vegetarian main dish or lovely side dish for chicken or beef.

¼ cup butter or margarine
1 large onion, chopped
½ pound mushrooms, sliced
1 10-ounce package frozen chopped spinach, thawed
1 cup small curd cottage cheese
1 cup sour cream
8 eggs
½ teaspoon seasoned salt
½ teaspoon pepper
¼ teaspoon ground nutmeg
1 cup shredded Monterey Jack cheese
1 cup shredded Cheddar cheese

In a wide frying pan, melt butter over medium-high heat. Add onion and mushrooms and cook, stirring occasionally, until limp and most liquid has evaporated. Spread in an even layer over the bottom of a buttered 7″ × 11″ baking pan.

Squeeze out liquid from spinach. Stir together spinach, cottage cheese, and sour cream. Beat eggs with salt, pepper, and nutmeg. Add to spinach mixture. Spread over onion-mushroom layer.

Bake uncovered in a 325° F. oven 30 minutes; then sprinkle with Monterey Jack and Cheddar cheeses. Continue baking until custard is set in center, about 10 to 15 minutes more. Let stand 10 minutes before cutting.

SERVES 6 to 8

SPINACH QUICHE

Stands alone for a luncheon or as a side dish with beef.

1 10-inch pastry shell
1 beaten egg yolk
1 10-ounce package frozen chopped spinach
6 eggs
1 3-ounce package cream cheese, softened
¼ cup grated sharp Cheddar cheese
½ cup almonds, slivered
3 green onions, finely chopped (include some tops)
2 tablespoons parsley, finely chopped
½ teaspoon salt
Dash pepper
3 tablespoons grated Parmesan cheese
1 large tomato, cut into narrow wedges
1 tablespoon grated Parmesan cheese

Partially bake pastry shell in a 425° F. oven for 15 minutes. Lightly brush beaten egg yolk over shell. Return to oven for 2 minutes. Cool slightly before adding filling.

Cook spinach according to package directions. Drain and squeeze out all liquid. Combine eggs, cream cheese, and Cheddar cheese. Stir in spinach, almonds, green onions, parsley, salt, and pepper. Pour into pastry shell. Sprinkle with 2 tablespoons Parmesan cheese. Bake at 425° F. for 15 minutes or until edges are set. Top with tomato wedges and 1 tablespoon Parmesan cheese. Return to oven for 4 minutes. Let stand 10 minutes before serving.

SERVES 8

GREEN AND GOLD CASSEROLE

Perfect for a buffet party.

4½ cups chopped spinach, cooked and drained
1 5-ounce can water chestnuts, drained and thinly sliced (⅔ cup)
1 10-ounce package frozen Welsh rarebit, thawed
8 slices bacon, crisp cooked, drained, and crumbled
½ 3½-ounce can french-fried onion rings

Combine spinach, water chestnuts, and ⅓ of Welsh rarebit in a 10″ × 6″ × 1½″ baking dish. Top with crumbled bacon. Spread remaining rarebit evenly over all, and top with onion rings. Bake, uncovered, in a moderate oven (350° F.) for 15 minutes or until heated through.

SERVES 6 to 8

Squash

1 pound = 4 medium summer squash = 2 cups sliced
½ cup cooked = 16 calories, 9 grams protein, 3.1 grams carbohydrates, some vitamins A and C

Plant a few seeds and stand back! This plant approaches life with vigor, and before you know it you'll be up to your neck in squash. There are summer and winter squashes, but they both grow after the weather has warmed. Squash can be harvested when they are young and small. If you allow one squash to grow to maturity it will stop the rest of the vine from producing. Giant squash are no surprise if you've let the garden go for a week. Hubbard squash will store for up to 4 months in a cool, dark place, and all hard-shelled squash stores well.

To freeze: Cooked puree is the best way to freeze squash, although precooked squash casseroles can be frozen with some success.

Soup

SQUASH SOUP

Creamy—like pumpkin soup.

3 tablespoons chopped onion
2 tablespoons butter
1 cup cooked squash
2 cups chicken broth
2 cups half-and-half cream
Salt and pepper to taste
1 tablespoon sugar

Sauté onion in butter until soft but not browned. Blend with squash and a little chicken broth in blender. Place in a saucepan with remaining broth, half-and-half, and seasonings. Bring to boiling point over medium heat, stirring constantly.

SERVES 6

Side Dishes

NANA'S BAKED SQUASH CASSEROLE

2 pounds yellow summer squash
3 tablespoons chopped onion
3 eggs, beaten
½ teaspoon Tabasco sauce
2 tablespoons parsley flakes
Salt and pepper to taste
½ cup melted butter or margarine
2 cups cracker crumbs

Slice squash and boil for 3 minutes. Drain; add onion, Tabasco, parsley, salt, and pepper. Mix well. Pour into a 1-quart casserole. Mix butter and cracker crumbs and sprinkle over squash. Bake at 350°F. for 35 to 45 minutes or until browned.

SERVES 4 to 6

SQUASH CREOLE

A Southern favorite.

2 pounds yellow butter and zucchini squash (in combination)
1 tablespoon butter
½ cup chopped green onion
1 1-pound can stewed tomatoes
1 teaspoon salt
Dash pepper

Wash squashes and cut diagonally into slices ¼ inch thick. In hot butter sauté green onion until tender, about 3 minutes. Add the sliced squash, tomatoes, salt, and pepper; toss lightly. Cook covered 1 minute longer, or until mixture is heated through.

SERVES 8

YELLOW SQUASH WITH SOUR CREAM

Freezes well.

5 pounds tender yellow squash
1 large white onion, chopped
2 sticks butter or margarine
4 tablespoons sugar
Salt and pepper to taste
1 1½-ounce can seasoned bread crumbs
2 8-ounce cartons sour cream

Chop squash and cook slowly with onion, butter, sugar, salt, and pepper until squash is very tender. Shortly before serving add bread crumbs; only slightly stir in sour cream. Place in a baking dish or pan and sprinkle more crumbs over top. Bake at 350° F. for about 20 minutes. Serve hot.

SERVES 10

CROOKNECK SQUASH AND PEA PODS

2 10-ounce packages frozen sliced yellow summer squash, crookneck style (or use equivalent amount of fresh)
1 7-ounce package frozen Chinese pea pods or pea pods and water chestnuts
Butter
Salt to taste

Cook each vegetable separately according to package directions. Do not overcook. Combine vegetables with butter and salt. Serve immediately.

SERVES 4 to 6

NANA'S BAKED CROOKNECK SQUASH

2 pounds crookneck squash
Salt, pepper, butter to taste
1 tablespoon Worcestershire sauce
1 egg
½ cup grated cheese
1 cup cracker crumbs

Slice and cook squash. Mash and add salt, pepper, butter, Worcestershire, egg, and cheese. Put into an 8-inch square baking dish and sprinkle with cracker crumbs. Bake 20 minutes at 350° F.

SERVES 6 to 8

PECAN-CRUSTED WINTER SQUASH

Sweet—could almost be a dessert.

1 1-pound package frozen winter squash, *or* 1½ pounds fresh squash puree
4 tablespoons melted margarine
2 tablespoons cream
4 tablespoons brown sugar
¼ teaspoon salt
⅛ teaspoon ginger
¾ cup pecans, coarsely chopped
3 tablespoons white corn syrup

Into cooked squash blend 3 tablespoons margarine, cream, and a mixture of 2 tablespoons brown sugar, salt, ginger, and ½ cup pecans. Turn into lightly greased 1-quart casserole and drizzle over top a mixture of ¼ cup pecans, corn syrup, 2 tablespoons brown sugar, and 1 tablespoon melted margarine. Bake in a 350° F. oven for about 20 minutes or until a crust is formed.

SERVES 4

BAKED STUFFED ACORN SQUASH

2 large acorn squash
1 small minced onion
2 tablespoons butter
3 cups soft bread crumbs
1 cup sausage
Paprika

Cut and seed acorn squash. Turn upside down on a greased pan and bake at 375° F. until almost tender.

Fry onion in melted butter, cooking until soft. Stir in soft bread crumbs; add cooked, crumbled, and drained sausage. Fill squash with stuffing. Dust with paprika. Bake until squash is tender, about 30 minutes.

SERVES 4 to 6

STUFFED HUBBARD SQUASH

1 small Hubbard squash
3 tablespoons butter
1 medium-sized onion, chopped
½ pound leanest ground round
½ pound chopped pork
1 tablespoon chopped parsley
Marjoram
1 cup cooked rice
Salt and pepper
2 to 3 tablespoons butter
2 egg yolks
2 tablespoons cream
Chopped parsley

Halve squash and remove seeds. Put the halves on a rack skin side down, cover with buttered paper to prevent drying, and bake in a moderate oven (350° F.) for 1 hour, or until tender. Hubbard squash may be baked whole.

Prepare stuffing. In a skillet in 3 tablespoons butter, lightly sauté onion, ground round, and pork, stirring constantly. Add 1 tablespoon parsley and a pinch of marjoram. Cover pan tightly and cook the mixture over very low heat, stirring from time to time to prevent scorching. If the mixture is too dry and tends to stick to the bottom of the pan, add a few drops of water. When the meat is tender, remove pan from heat, stir in rice, and season to taste with salt and pepper.

Scoop out the pulp from the squash halves, mash it, and thoroughly beat in 2 to 3 tablespoons butter and slightly beaten egg yolks. Season to taste with salt and pepper and add cream. Spoon the mashed pulp into the squash shells, pressing it against the sides to make an even lining, reserving a little for garnishing. Fill the hollows with meat stuffing. Garnish the edges with the remaining squash pulp forced through a pastry bag fitted with a star-shaped tube. Bake the stuffed squash in a hot oven (400° F.) for 15 minutes. Sprinkle with chopped parsley.

SERVES 4

Main Dishes

MEAT LOAF–STUFFED ACORN RINGS

2 acorn squash (about 1½ pounds each)
Salt
Ground cinnamon
1 pound leanest ground beef
¼ pound mushrooms (1 small can of stems and pieces will do)
1 medium-sized onion, finely chopped
2 eggs, beaten
¾ cup soft bread crumbs (1½ slices)
1½ teaspoons salt
½ teaspoon ground cinnamon
½ teaspoon nutmeg
½ teaspoon oregano leaves
½ teaspoon thyme leaves
¼ teaspoon pepper

Cut squash crosswise into 2-inch rings; discard ends and remove seeds. Place rings on a greased, rimmed baking sheet and sprinkle each lightly with salt and cinnamon.

In a bowl, mix together ground beef, mushrooms, onion, eggs, bread crumbs, salt, cinnamon, nutmeg, oregano, thyme, and pepper. Divide meat mixture equally among the squash rings, mounding meat portions in centers of rings. Bake uncovered in a 350° F. oven for 50 to 60 minutes or until squash is easily pierced.

SERVES 4

TURKEY-FILLED ACORN HALVES

A good choice for leftover Thanksgiving bird. You can use chicken, too!

2 acorn squash (1½ pounds each)
Butter or margarine
2 cups cubed cooked turkey or chicken
⅓ cup chopped green onion
1 2½-ounce can sliced black olives
1½ cups shredded Cheddar cheese
1 cup (4 ounces) diced green chilies
¾ teaspoon ground cumin
1 teaspoon garlic salt
¼ teaspoon paprika
Pepper
½ cup sour cream
¼ cup toasted sliced almonds

Cut squash in half crosswise; remove seeds. Cut a thin slice off stem and blossom ends so halves stand level and upright.

Spread 1 teaspoon soft butter or margarine over each cavity and turn squash, cavity sides down, on a rimmed baking sheet. Bake in a 350° F. oven for about 45 minutes, or until tender when pierced.

Meanwhile, combine turkey or chicken, green onion, olives, cheese, green chilies, cumin, garlic salt, paprika, pepper, and sour cream. Mix until blended.

Remove squash from oven, turn over, and fill each cavity with an equal amount of turkey mixture; sprinkle with almonds. Bake squash 15 to 20 minutes longer, or until heated through.

SERVES 4

SQUASH SOUFFLÉ

Mushroom sauce makes this delightful!

2 pounds squash
1½ tablespoons butter
½ teaspoon onion juice or chopped onion (optional)
½ teaspoon Worcestershire sauce
1 tablespoon flour
Salt and pepper to taste
2 eggs, separated

MUSHROOM SAUCE

2 tablespoons butter or margarine
2 tablespoons flour
1 cup milk
¼ teaspoon salt
Dash white pepper
1 small can sliced mushrooms

Cook squash and run through ricer. Melt butter in skillet, add onion juice or chopped onion and Worcestershire sauce, blending in flour, salt, and pepper. Beat egg yolks; add to squash, mixing well. Fold in stiffly beaten egg whites and put into casserole dish. Cook in 375° F. oven for 30 to 40 minutes.

To make Mushroom Sauce, melt butter over low heat in saucepan. Add flour; blend. Add milk, stirring constantly. Cook over medium heat until thick and smooth, stirring constantly. Add salt and pepper. Cover and cook 5 to 7 minutes. Add mushrooms from can with about ½ of liquid therein. Season to taste. This makes approximately 1 cup, an ample amount to serve over the soufflé.

SERVES 4

Pies

HONEY SQUASH PIE

½ cup honey
1 tablespoon flour
Dash salt
1 cup mashed cooked squash
2 eggs
1¼ cups milk
1 teaspoon mace
1 tablespoon margarine
1 unbaked 9-inch pastry shell

Mix honey, flour, and salt with squash. Beat eggs, and stir them into mixture. Heat milk and thoroughly mix with squash mixture; add mace and margarine. Pour into pie crust and bake in moderate oven until set, approximately 30 minutes.

SERVES 6 to 8

CROOKNECK PIE WITH SESAME SEED CRUST

4 small crookneck squash (about 1 pound)
¾ cup flaked coconut
3 tablespoons all-purpose flour
1½ cups sugar
¾ teaspoon ground nutmeg
¼ teaspoon salt
¼ cup lemon juice
¼ cup orange juice
5 eggs, slightly beaten

SESAME SEED CRUST

1¼ cups all-purpose flour, unsifted
¼ cup sesame seed
¼ teaspoon salt
½ cup solid shortening
3½ tablespoons ice water

Cut squash in half lengthwise, discard seeds, then finely shred squash; it will make about 2½ cups. Mix with coconut, flour, sugar, ½ teaspoon nutmeg, salt, lemon juice, and orange juice; let stand while you prepare the crust.

To make Sesame Seed Crust, combine flour, sesame seed, and salt. Cut in shortening until particles are the size of peas. Work in ice water. Roll out on a floured board and fit into a 9-inch pie pan.

To finish filling, blend eggs into squash mixture; pour into crust and sprinkle remaining nutmeg on top. Bake in a 350° F. oven for 55 minutes, or until a knife inserted in the center comes out clean.

SERVES 6

Pickles

SQUASH PICKLES

2 pounds yellow squash, thinly sliced
2 medium onions, sliced
¼ cup salt in water
2 cups white vinegar
2 cups sugar
1 teaspoon celery seed
1 teaspoon turmeric
2 teaspoons mustard seed

Soak squash and onions in salted water to cover for 2 hours. Drain.

Bring remaining ingredients to a boil and pour over vegetables. Let stand for 2 hours; then bring to a boil for 5 minutes. Pack in sterilized jars and seal.

MAKES 3 PINTS

Tomatoes

1 pound = 2 4-inch tomatoes = 1½ cups sliced
1 large raw tomato = 39 calories, 1.9 grams protein, 8.3 grams carbohydrates, 429 milligrams potassium, 1,580 units vitamin A, 40 milligrams vitamin C

Tomatoes—what's a garden without them? Plant several varieties, keep pinching back suckers that spring up in the junctions where leaves and stems meet, and stand back! Support the vines with stakes or chicken wire cages to keep tomatoes from rotting on the ground. Pick them when they are red and firm. Harvest frequently. If the weather turns cold, pick your green tomatoes. We've included many ways to use them green. You can ripen them by laying them stem down in a cool place (not in direct sunlight). They will store in the refrigerator up to 10 days before turning mushy.

To freeze: High water content makes freezing tomatoes tough. You can, however, freeze whole firm tomatoes for cooking just by wrapping in foil and freezing. You need to use these frozen tomatoes within 2 months. The best way to rid yourself of an abundant tomato crop is to freeze tomato sauce. It's great and convenient for cooking all kinds of dishes.

Soups

VEGETABLE JUICE COCKTAIL

Homemade cocktail is fresh and delicious.

⅝ bushel tomatoes
6 medium onions
2 stalks celery
2 large green peppers
20 parsley sprigs (not bunches)
5 bay leaves
½ cup salt
1 cup sugar
1 teaspoon pepper

Wash and chop vegetables. Place all ingredients in a large kettle and cook until vegetables are tender. Put through a colander. Bring juice to a boil, then pour into hot, sterile jars. Clean rims and seal. To be sure of sealing, put jars in a canning pot and boil water around jars for 15 minutes (10 minutes at sea level).

MAKES 12 QUARTS

CHILLED TOMATO-AVOCADO SOUP

6 tomatoes, chopped *or* 4 cups canned tomatoes
6 green onions, minced
1 clove garlic, minced
1 bay leaf
¼ teaspoon salt
1 cup water
2 1.5-ounce packages instant beef broth
2 cups hot water
1 avocado, diced
Lemon wedges
Whipped or sour cream

Combine chopped tomatoes, onion, garlic, bay leaf, salt, and 1 cup water. Simmer 20 to 30 minutes. Add broth packages dissolved in 2 cups hot water and simmer 15 minutes longer. Strain mixture through a fine sieve or cloth. Chill thoroughly. Spoon into bowls and add diced avocado. Serve with lemon wedges and whipped or sour cream for topping.

SERVES 6

ICED TOMATO SOUP

6 large ripe tomatoes, coarsely chopped
1 onion, finely chopped
¼ cup water
½ teaspoon salt
Sprinkling pepper
2 tablespoons tomato paste
2 tablespoons flour
Cold water
2 cups hot chicken broth or bouillon
1 cup heavy cream
Thin slices peeled tomato
Dill, finely chopped

In a saucepan put tomatoes, onion, ¼ cup water, salt, and pepper. Bring the liquid to a boil and cook briskly 5 minutes. Stir in tomato paste and flour mixed to a paste with a little cold water. Stir in broth or bouillon and continue to stir until the soup comes to a boil. Press the soup through a fine sieve, forcing through as much of the vegetable pulp as possible. Stir the soup over ice until cold. Stir in cream and correct seasoning with salt. Garnish each portion with thin slices peeled tomato sprinkled with finely chopped dill.

SERVES 4 to 6

TOMATO SOUP PARMENTIER

1 tablespoon butter
3 large carrots, coarsely chopped
3 medium-sized potatoes, coarsely chopped
4 tomatoes, peeled and quartered
8 cups boiling water
Salt and pepper
Pinch tarragon
Pinch marjoram
Croutons sautéed in butter
Sour cream

Melt butter in a soup kettle. Add carrots, potatoes, and tomatoes. Sauté the mixture for about 3 minutes, stirring constantly; then add 8 cups boiling water, and salt and pepper to taste. Season with a pinch each dried tarragon and marjoram. Simmer soup gently, covered, for about 1 hour or until vegetables are tender. Rub the mixture through a strainer. Heat the soup and serve with croutons sautéed in butter or with a topping of sour cream.

SERVES 14 to 16

Salads

TOMATO AND ONION MARINADE

2 medium tomatoes, sliced
1 medium cucumber, peeled, thinly sliced
½ medium onion, thinly sliced, separated into rings
Iceberg lettuce, shredded
2 tablespoons chopped parsley

DRESSING

½ cup salad oil
¼ cup wine vinegar
⅛ teaspoon black pepper
1 teaspoon whole oregano
1 teaspoon garlic powder
1 teaspoon salt

Alternate layers of tomato, cucumber, and onion in a shallow glass dish. Beat dressing ingredients together with a rotary beater; pour over vegetables and chill, covered, for 6 to 8 hours. Drain and serve on shredded lettuce. Sprinkle with chopped parsley.

SERVES 6

FRESH TOMATO ASPIC

Cream cheese makes this one of the best aspics.

6 to 8 fresh tomatoes
1 cup chopped celery
1 green pepper, chopped
Few drops garlic juice (if and as desired)
½ 2-ounce package cream cheese
½ tablespoon unflavored gelatin
¼ cup cold water
¼ cup hot water
¼ cup mayonnaise
Salt and pepper to taste
Marinated cucumbers (optional)

Cut tomatoes into small pieces over a bowl, conserving and using all liquid. Add celery, green pepper, garlic juice, and cream cheese broken into pieces.

Soften gelatin in cold water and add to it sufficient hot water (about ¼ cup) to dissolve gelatin. Add to tomato mixture; add mayonnaise, season to taste with salt and pepper, and pour into an oiled 1-quart ring mold.

Marinated cucumbers in the center make a tasty and pretty salad plate.

SERVES 8 to 10

FROSTED TOMATOES

2 peeled small onions
8 peeled large tomatoes
2 teaspoons salt
Pepper to taste
6 tablespoons mayonnaise
2 tablespoons minced parsley
1 teaspoon curry powder

Chop onion and tomatoes in wooden bowl. Add salt and pepper. Mix with chopper. Turn into freezing tray. Freeze until crystals start to form.

Mix mayonnaise and parsley, then add curry powder. Arrange frosty tomato mixture in chilled bouillon cups. Top with mound of curry mayonnaise.

SERVES 8

SWISS CHEESE AND CHERRY TOMATO SALAD

Great looking, great tasting.

Juice of 1 lemon
3 cloves garlic, crushed
1 teaspoon salt
½ teaspoon pepper
¾ cup vegetable oil
¼ pound bacon, diced
2 heads romaine lettuce, torn into small pieces
2 cups cherry tomatoes, halves
1 cup coarsely grated Swiss cheese
⅔ cup slivered almonds, toasted
⅓ cup grated Parmesan cheese
Salt and pepper to taste
1 cup croutons

To make dressing, combine lemon juice, garlic, salt, and pepper. Slowly add vegetable oil in a stream, beating continuously with a fork. Let stand 3 hours.

Sauté diced bacon until crisp. Drain on paper towels. In a salad bowl, combine romaine lettuce, tomatoes, Swiss cheese, almonds, and bacon. Toss with dressing, Parmesan cheese, salt, and pepper. Garnish with croutons.

SERVES 8

ITALIAN TOMATO SALAD

Italian tomatoes have a strange shape but taste great.

4 large tomatoes, sliced
4 red onions, sliced

¾ cup olive oil
¼ cup wine vinegar
2 teaspoons capers
2 teaspoons basil
1 teaspoon salt
¼ teaspoon pepper
Parsley sprigs

Alternate tomato and onion slices in overlapping circles on a platter. Blend oil, vinegar, capers, basil, salt, and pepper and pour about half of dressing over tomatoes and onions. Cover with plastic wrap and chill. Serve with remaining dressing and garnish with parsley.

SERVES 6 to 8

FIRE AND ICE TOMATO SALAD

6 large, firm tomatoes, peeled and quartered
1 large green pepper, cut into strips
1 large red onion, sliced and separated into rings
1 cucumber, peeled and sliced

DRESSING

¾ cup vinegar
4½ teaspoons sugar
1½ teaspoons celery salt
1½ teaspoons mustard seed
½ teaspoon salt
⅛ teaspoon red pepper
⅛ teaspoon black pepper
¼ cup cold water

Put tomatoes, green pepper, and onion into a large bowl. Mix dressing ingredients and boil hard for 1 minute. Pour dressing immediately over vegetables. Cool, stirring occasionally. When cooled, cover and chill. Before serving, add cucumber, peeled and sliced. Keeps several days without cucumber.

SERVES 8

CHERRY TOMATOES WITH CREAM CHEESE

24 cherry tomatoes
1 8-ounce package cream cheese
2 tablespoons catsup
1 tablespoon lemon juice
1 tablespoon horseradish
1 teaspoon light cream
¼ teaspoon red pepper
Parsley
Watercress
Juice of ½ lemon

Wash tomatoes and dry. Remove a slice from each at stem end. Soften cream cheese. In a medium bowl, combine cheese, catsup, 1 tablespoon lemon juice, horseradish, cream, and pepper. Mix well with fork. Press cheese mixture through pastry bag with star top, making rosettes on each tomato. Decorate each with parsley. Arrange on a bed of watercress sprinkled with lemon juice. Refrigerate at least 30 minutes before serving.

SERVES 12

TOMATOES WITH HEARTS OF PALM

6 large tomatoes
1 cup cooked green beans
French dressing
6 large hearts of palm
Parsley
Lettuce

Peel tomatoes and scoop out pulp. Stuff tomatoes with cooked green beans cut into small pieces. Pour 1 tablespoon well seasoned French dressing over the beans in each tomato. Cut hearts of palm into inch-long pieces and garnish each stuffed tomato. Sprinkle with chopped parsley and serve very cold on crisp lettuce.

SERVES 6

Main Dish

TOMATOES STUFFED WITH SMOKED SALMON

½ cup ground smoked salmon (canned salmon may be used)
1 tablespoon butter
1 tablespoon grated onion or instant onion flakes
1 tablespoon lemon juice
1 tablespoon finely minced parsley
12 Italian plum tomatoes
Salt and pepper to taste
Salad greens

Combine salmon with butter, grated onion, lemon juice, and finely minced parsley. Remove the center part of the tops of the Italian plum tomatoes and carefully scoop out pulp, seeds, and juice. Season the hollowed-out tomatoes with salt and pepper. Stuff tomatoes with the salmon mixture, and serve cold on a bed of salad greens.

SERVES 12

Side Dishes

MARY'S STUFFED TOMATOES

6 medium tomatoes
1 beaten egg
2 tablespoons parsley
1 medium onion
¼ cup bread crumbs
Salt and pepper to taste
1 tablespoon paprika
2 tablespoons butter
½ cup grated American cheese

Cut the tops from tomatoes. Scoop out pulp and chop; add egg to pulp. Then add parsley, onion, bread crumbs, salt, pepper, paprika, and butter. Mix well; fill each tomato with mixture. Bake at 350° F. in greased 9-inch square baking dish filled with ⅜ cup water. Cook ½ hour, or until tender. During last 5 minutes, put grated cheese on top.

SERVES 6

CHERRY TOMATOES IN CHIVE CREAM

You can serve them with just the cooking butter and snipped green onions or fresh herbs, you can sprinkle them with Parmesan cheese, or you can give them this sauce of chives and cream.

2 pints cherry tomatoes
4 tablespoons butter
1 teaspoon salt
Freshly ground pepper to taste
1 cup heavy cream
2 tablespoons minced chives

Wash tomatoes and remove stems. Melt butter in a large skillet; add tomatoes, salt, and pepper and cook 2 minutes, shaking the pan frequently to coat tomatoes with butter. Add cream and chives and continue cooking 2 minutes more. With a slotted spoon, remove tomatoes to a serving dish. Cook cream over higher heat until it is reduced by half. Pour sauce over tomatoes and serve immediately.

SERVES 4 to 6

Pie

SMITH'S GREEN TOMATO PIE

Green tomatoes turned into apple pie!

1 pastry shell and top crust
Approximately 6 thinly sliced green tomatoes (enough to fill pie)
⅛ cup brown sugar
⅔ cup white sugar

2 tablespoons flour
Sprinkle cinnamon
Pinch nutmeg

Fill a pastry-lined pie pan with thinly sliced green tomatoes. Sprinkle generously with sugar which has been mixed with flour. Sprinkle with cinnamon and a pinch of nutmeg. Cover with top crust. Bake at 400° F. for 15 minutes; reduce heat and continue baking at 350° F. for 45 minutes.

SERVES 6 to 8

Chili Sauces and Catsups

SHAUNA'S CHILI SAUCE

24 ripe tomatoes, skinned
8 onions
4 green peppers
2 cups vinegar
2 cups sugar
¼ cup salt
1 tablespoon celery salt
1½ teaspoons cinnamon
1½ teaspoons allspice
1 teaspoon cloves, whole or powdered

Coarsely chop clean tomatoes. Finely chop clean onions and green peppers. Put into a large kettle. Stir in vinegar, sugar, salt, celery salt, cinnamon, allspice, and cloves. Boil slowly 3 hours, stirring occasionally. Pour into hot, sterilized jars. Wipe rims clean. Seal.

MAKES 8 PINTS

ANOTHER CHILI SAUCE

Mild—like a salsa.

1 quart tomatoes, skinned
2 large onions, chopped
1 cup chopped green peppers
1 cup sugar
1 cup vinegar
1 cup water
3 teaspoons salt
½ teaspoon cayenne pepper
1 teaspoon ground cloves
1 teaspoon ground cinnamon

Mix tomatoes, onions, green peppers, sugar, vinegar, water, and salt together in suitable-sized kettle. Put cayenne, cloves, and cinnamon in kettle with other ingredients. Boil until mixture is the desired consistency. Stir occasionally as it will stick easily. Place in jars and seal while hot.

Six times the recipe fills a large pressure cooker with an average yield of 12 to 14 pints, depending on how long it is allowed to cook down.

MAKES ABOUT 2 PINTS

HOMEMADE CATSUP

This catsup will clear your sinuses. Great on veal, pot roast, pork, all beef cuts.

10 pounds tomatoes
1 quart vinegar
3 cups sugar
3½ teaspoons dry mustard
2 teaspoons cinnamon
2 teaspoons salt
1½ teaspoons ginger
1 teaspoon black pepper
½ teaspoon nutmeg
½ teaspoon allspice
½ teaspoon cloves, ground
½ teaspoon mace
½ teaspoon turmeric
¼ teaspoon cayenne pepper

Scald tomatoes in boiling water 1 minute and peel. Set aside. Mix all other ingredients in a large kettle. Stir in tomatoes. Bring to a boil. Simmer to desired consistency (3 to 10 hours).

Pour into hot sterilized quart jars. Wipe rims clean. Seal immediately. Age 1 month before using.

For a bushel of tomatoes, multiply all other ingredients by 8 to get 32 quarts.

MAKES 4 QUARTS

GOURMET TOMATO CATSUP

20 pounds ripe tomatoes
4 sweet red peppers
6 medium onions
2 cups cider vinegar
1½ cups sugar
2 tablespoons salt
4 teaspoons paprika
2 teaspoons celery seeds
2 teaspoons dry mustard
2 teaspoons whole allspice
2 teaspoons whole cloves
4 sticks cinnamon

Wash tomatoes and peppers carefully. Steep tomatoes in rapidly boiling water for about 1 minute, or until the skins rub off easily. Drain them immediately. Remove skins, cut off stem ends, and quarter tomatoes. Remove stem ends and seeds from peppers and quarter. Peel and quarter onions. Put the vegetables through the finest blade of a food chopper and place in a large enameled kettle.

Cook mixture over low heat for about 30 minutes, stirring frequently. When vegetables are soft, rub them through a fine sieve, return the pulp to the kettle, and boil rapidly until it thickens slightly. Add to the kettle vinegar, sugar, salt, paprika, celery seeds, dry mustard, and a cheesecloth bag containing allspice, cloves, and cinnamon sticks. Stir the mixture until sugar is entirely dissolved and cook over low heat until it is very thick, stirring frequently. Remove spice bag and pour catsup into hot sterilized jars; seal them and store in a cool place.

MAKES 15 to 20 PINTS

Pickles and Relishes

RIPE TOMATO RELISH

This is not only delicious, but the kitchen smells so good while it is cooking.

8 quarts ripe tomatoes
2 to 3 onions
1 quart vinegar
2 teaspoons cinnamon
Small amount allspice
8 chili peppers
2½ cups sugar
2 teaspoons cloves
2 teaspoons nutmeg
Salt to taste

Combine; boil until thick.

MAKES 6 PINTS

GREEN TOMATO PICKLE

Sure to give you character.

1 gallon green tomatoes, sliced
6 sliced onions
6 sliced green peppers
1 tablespoon ground black pepper
1 tablespoon whole cloves
1 tablespoon powdered cinnamon
1 tablespoon white celery seed
1 tablespoon white mustard seed
1 tablespoon (scant) ground mace
1 tablespoon dry mustard
2 cups brown sugar
1 tablespoon (scant) ground horseradish
Vinegar (enough to cover)

Let tomatoes, onions, and green peppers soak overnight in salt water. Next morning squeeze dry. Place vegetables and all remaining ingredients in a pot on stove and let come to a boil. Seal in sterile jars while hot.

MAKES 4 QUARTS

DILL GREEN TOMATOES

Thanks, Nana—they are tart and our very favorites.

Green tomatoes to fill 4 1-quart jars
4 cloves garlic
4 sticks celery
4 sweet green peppers, quartered
Onions and cauliflower (optional)
2 quarts water
1 quart vinegar
1 cup salt
Dill to taste

Use small firm green tomatoes. Pack into sterilized 1-quart jars. Add to each quart jar 1 garlic clove, 1 stick celery, and 1 green pepper cut in quarters. Add onion and cauliflower if desired.

Make a brine of the water, vinegar, and salt, and boil with the dill 5 minutes. Put some dill in top of each jar. Pour hot brine over the tomato mixture and seal at once. Ready for use in 4 to 6 weeks.

MAKES 4 QUARTS

GREEN TOMATO REFRIGERATOR PICKLES

3 large cloves garlic
3 small dried hot chili peppers
3 teaspoons mixed pickling spice
10 to 12 medium-sized green tomatoes
2 medium-sized onions
1 or 2 red or green bell peppers
3 or 4 large carrots
2 or 3 stalks celery
7½ cups water
2½ cups white vinegar
4 tablespoons salt

Quarter garlic cloves and divide between 3 jars, each about 1-quart size. Break chili peppers in half and drop 2 halves into each jar. Place 1 teaspoon pickling spice in each jar.

Core tomatoes; cut each into 6 to 8 wedges. Cut onions and bell peppers into 1-inch squares. Cut carrots in half lengthwise, then cut carrots and celery into 1½-inch lengths. Distribute vegetables in jars.

Heat water, vinegar, and salt to boiling; pour into jars. Cool, cover, and chill at least 3 weeks before sampling. Pickles keep up to 3 months.

MAKES 3 QUARTS

GREEN TOMATO RELISH

2 teaspoons salt
12 large onions
1½ quarts vinegar
10 quarts green tomatoes
8 cups sugar
2 cups water
3 tablespoons flour
1 teaspoon cloves
1 teaspoon pepper
2 teaspoons turmeric

Mix salt, onions, vinegar, tomatoes, sugar, and water. Cook 1 hour. Add flour, cloves, pepper, and turmeric. Cook 5 more minutes. Bottle hot.

MAKES 8 to 10 PINTS

WASHINGTON GREEN TOMATO MINCEMEAT

They say this recipe came to America on the Mayflower!

1 lemon
2½ pounds green tomatoes (about 6 cups)
Cold water
4 pounds Jonathan apples, coarsely chopped
3 cups sugar
1 15-ounce package seedless raisins
¼ cup beef suet, ground
½ cup vinegar
2 teaspoons allspice

1 teaspoon nutmeg
1 teaspoon salt
1 teaspoon vanilla or almond flavoring
½ teaspoon cloves
Candied peel or dates (optional)

Grind lemon. Set aside.

Grind tomatoes. Put in a large kettle. Pour in cold water to cover. Bring to a boil. Pour off liquid. Add fresh cold water to cover. Bring to a boil, then pour off liquid. Repeat once more.

Stir in lemon and remaining ingredients. Simmer 30 minutes. Pour into hot, sterilized pint jars to within 1 inch of top. Wipe rims clean. Seal; screw on bands tightly by hand. Process in a boiling water bath 39 minutes (30 minutes at sea level).

To make a mincemeat pie, pour 1 pint jar mincemeat into an unbaked pie crust. Put on top crust. Bake at 450° F. for 30 minutes.

MAKES 6 to 8 PINTS

GREEN TOMATO MINCEMEAT

This is a meatless mincemeat.

3 pounds green tomatoes (about 10 medium-sized)
2 pounds medium-sized apples
2 whole lemons
1 cup butter or margarine
4 cups seedless raisins
1 pound brown sugar
3 teaspoons salt
4 teaspoons ground cinnamon
¾ teaspoon ground cloves
¾ teaspoon nutmeg
¼ teaspoon ground allspice

Wash and quarter tomatoes and unpeeled apples; remove apple cores. Chop tomatoes and apples with a food processor or by hand. Cut off and discard ends of lemons, then quarter or slice and remove seeds. Chop lemons in a food processor or by hand.

In a 6- to 8-quart kettle, combine tomatoes, apples, lemons, butter, raisins, and sugar. Bring to a boil over medium heat, stirring. Add salt, cinnamon, cloves, nutmeg, and allspice. Simmer gently, uncovered, for about 1 hour or until thick and liquid is absorbed. Stir often; reduce heat if necessary to prevent sticking.

To can, ladle hot mincemeat into 3 hot sterilized quart canning jars to within ½ inch of rim. Wipe rim and set on hot canning lid; screw on ring band. Stand jars on a rack in a kettle and add enough hot water to cover jars by 1 to 2 inches. Keep at a gentle boil for 15 minutes. Remove from water, cool, then test for a good seal.

To freeze, let cool, then spoon into freezer containers and freeze.

MAKES ABOUT 3 QUARTS

GREEN TOMATO MINCEMEAT PIE

4 cups green tomato mincemeat (see recipe above)
½ cup chopped walnuts
3 tablespoons brandy (optional)
1 9-inch pastry shell and top crust
1 to 2 tablespoons butter or margarine

Combine green tomato mincemeat with chopped walnuts and brandy (optional). Spoon into pastry-lined pan; dot with 1 to 2 tablespoons butter or margarine; add top crust and flute edges. Bake in a 425° F. oven until golden and bubbly, about 35 minutes.

SERVES 6 to 8

Turnips

1 pound = 4 2-inch turnips = 2 cups sliced
1 cup sliced = 36 calories, 1.2 grams protein, 7.6 grams carbohydrates, 291 milligrams potassium, some vitamin C

Turnips—that edible root that most of us have tried to avoid since childhood. Take another look; all those rabbits (who love the stuff) can't be wrong! The turnip is a cool-season crop, stores well, and requires little care. Turnips should be about 2 inches across when harvested, moist and crisp. Pull the turnip out by the base of the leaves. Use the greens immediately or discard. You can store turnips up to 2 weeks in the crisper drawer of the refrigerator.

To freeze: You can freeze turnips, but they lose some of their crispness, so you'll need to use them in casseroles or stews. Peel and slice or dice. Scald 2½ to 3 minutes. Chill in cold water, drain, and package.

Soup

TURNIP SOUP

This is the mainstay of French home cooking.

Stew meat (soup bones, chicken pieces, or other meat)
Cold water to cover
½ teaspoon salt
2 or 3 potatoes
2 or 3 onions
Several carrots
½ small head cabbage cut in quarters
2 or 3 turnips
2 or 3 stalks celery, including leaves
Grated cheese (optional)

BOUQUET GARNI (A packet of spices tied together for easy removal before serving)

3 or 4 sprigs parsley
1 bay leaf
2 sprigs thyme
1 garlic clove (optional)

In a pan of cold water, place several soup bones, pieces of chicken, or other favorite stew meat. The water should cover the meat. Add salt. When the water is boiling, add potatoes, onions, carrots, cabbage, turnips, celery, and *bouquet garni.* When the mixture starts to boil again, put heat on simmer and let soup cook 3 hours. Serve with bread and Swiss cheese; grated cheese may be spooned into the broth.

SERVES 6 to 8

Salads

TURNIPS WITH A DIP

They have a crunchy texture when eaten raw.

2 cups sour cream
8 ounces cream cheese
1 tablespoon grated onion
¼ teaspoon Worcestershire sauce
3 ounces chipped beef, shredded
Raw turnips, peeled and thinly sliced

Mix together sour cream, cream cheese, onion, Worcestershire sauce, and chipped beef. Let stand 1 hour. Use as a dip for raw turnip slices.

MAKES 4 CUPS

TURNIP AND CARROT SLAW

4 cups grated turnips
2 cups grated carrots
1 Bermuda onion, chopped

DRESSING

¾ cup sugar
1 cup cider vinegar
½ cup oil
1 teaspoon celery seed
1 teaspoon dry mustard
1 teaspoon salt

Toss turnips, carrots, and onion in a bowl. Combine all dressing ingredients in a saucepan. Bring dressing to a boil. Pour over vegetables. Chill.

SERVES 6 to 8

Side Dishes

MASHED TURNIPS

6 to 8 small young turnips, peeled and sliced
2 slices bacon
2 tablespoons butter
Salt and pepper to taste
Dashes cayenne pepper (optional)

Boil turnips and bacon uncovered about 30 minutes. Discard bacon and drain turnips.

Puree turnips, adding butter and seasonings.

SERVES 6 to 8

TURNIPS AU GRATIN

2 cups turnips
1 tablespoon flour
1 tablespoon butter
1 cup milk, scalded
¾ cup Cheddar cheese, grated
½ teaspoon salt
¼ teaspoon pepper
½ cup dry bread crumbs
3 tablespoons butter, melted
Paprika

Peel turnips and cut into ½-inch cubes. Cook in boiling salted water until just tender. Drain and put in a buttered casserole.

Make a sauce of flour, butter, and scalded milk. Cook until thickened. Add cheese, salt, and pepper. Cook sauce until cheese is melted and pour over turnips. Top with bread crumbs mixed with melted butter. Sprinkle with paprika. Bake uncovered at 350° F. for 15 minutes.

SERVES 4

LUCERNE WHITE TURNIPS

Especially good with boiled beef.

12 small or 6 medium white turnips
¼ cup cubed bacon
1 large onion, chopped
½ teaspoon salt

Peel the turnips and slice into julienne strips; cook them in boiling, salted water until barely tender. Fry bacon in a skillet; add onion and cook until golden brown. Drain turnips, salt them, and sauté with the bacon and onions over low heat for about 20 minutes, or until golden brown.

SERVES 6

Zucchini

1 pound = 3 to 4 medium zucchini = 2 cups sliced
1 cup cooked = 22 calories, 1.8 grams protein, 4.5 grams carbohydrates, 254 milligrams potassium, 540 units vitamin A, 16 milligrams vitamin C

The zucchini crop is probably what motivated you to buy this book. This member of the squash family doesn't know when to quit! You need to harvest the stuff daily (it's a great job for bored children in the summer). If you turn your back, they will double in size! A zucchini 1 yard long is not unusual in a garden left alone for a week. We like zucchini picked about 5 or 6 inches long. It's nice to have a few large ones for stuffed zucchini and to impress the neighbors (who probably turned out the lights and hid in the bathroom when they saw you coming with another generous armload of zucchini). If you let 1 zucchini on the plant grow to maturity it will stop the rest of the plant from producing, which can be a great relief!

To freeze: Zucchini does well frozen in casseroles that can go from freezer to oven. Zucchini bread also freezes well for up to two months. Some people parboil and then freeze zucchini slices. We haven't had much luck doing that—the zucchini becomes soggy.

Soups

ZUCCHINI SOUP

6 tablespoons butter
3 large onions, thinly sliced
¼ cup water
6 pounds zucchini squash washed and thinly sliced (5 quarts)
2 large green peppers, cleaned and cut in thin slices
3 cloves garlic
2¼ teaspoons salt
½ teaspoon pepper
1 cup lightly packed parsley sprigs
1 cup lightly packed fresh basil leaves and/or ¼ cup lightly packed fresh tarragon leaves, if desired
1 can regular strength chicken broth, *or* 2 cups water and 2 chicken bouillon cubes
1 bay leaf

Melt butter in an 8-quart or larger pan. Put in onions and cook, stirring until soft. Add water and then stir in squash and green peppers, garlic, salt, and pepper. Cover and cook 3 minutes; then turn down heat, cover, and simmer, stirring often until squash is very tender (12 to 15 minutes). Remove from heat; stir in parsley sprigs, basil leaves, and/or tarragon leaves. Puree about 1 cup at a time in a blender until there are 3 cups; then empty the blender and start over. Makes 6 pints. Can be frozen until used.

Heat to simmering chicken broth (or water and chicken bouillon) and bay leaf. Add 1 pint of the puree. Heat, stirring, until piping hot. Season to taste with salt. Remove bay leaf. Serve.

SERVES 6 to 8

ZUCCHINI GAZPACHO

Best if made the day before and allowed to marinate.

1 cup bell pepper, finely chopped
2 cups zucchini, sliced thin and quartered
1 cup grated carrots
1 cup celery, finely diced
1 cup cucumbers, finely diced
½ cup chopped onions
2 tablespoons olive oil
1¼ cups beef bouillon (strong)
3 tablespoons lemon juice
6 tomatoes, skinned and chopped, *or* large can stewed tomatoes
Basil, salt, and pepper to taste

GARNISH

Croutons
Sour cream

Combine all ingredients except garnish and chill. Serve chilled in small bowls before or with your meal. Serve with croutons and dab of sour cream.

SERVES 6 to 8

CHILLED ZUCCHINI BUTTERMILK SOUP

½ cup sliced onion
1 tablespoon vegetable oil
2 cups sliced zucchini
1 teaspoon chicken bouillon
½ teaspoon salt
2 cups buttermilk

Sauté onion in oil (do not brown). Add sliced zucchini; steam until zucchini is tender. Sprinkle on chicken bouillon and salt; turn a time or two to distribute seasonings. Chill slightly.

When ready to serve soup, place 2 cups chilled buttermilk in blender; add 1 cup chilled zucchini-onion mixture. Whiz until well blended. Taste for seasoning. Add more salt and chicken bouillon if desired.

SERVES 4

PRETEND SPLIT PEA SOUP

3 cups sliced zucchini
½ cup water
2 tablespoons instant minced onion
1 teaspoon parsley flakes
1 cube chicken bouillon
½ teaspoon salt
2 tablespoons margarine
2 tablespoons flour
⅛ teaspoon pepper
Dash cayenne
1 cup milk
½ cup light cream
Sour cream and paprika (optional)

Combine zucchini, water, onion, parsley, chicken cube, and salt in a saucepan. Cook until zucchini is tender with only a small amount of water left. Put in blender and puree.

In another pan, melt margarine, add flour, pepper, salt, and cayenne. Blend well. Add milk and cream. Simmer, stirring until thickened. Stir in puree, mixing well. If soup is too thick, add milk.

Serve with a spoonful of sour cream on each bowl, topped with paprika.

SERVES 4

Salads

ZUCCHINI ASPIC

1 3-ounce package lemon gelatin
1 cup hot water
¾ cup sauterne wine
2 tablespoons lemon juice
2 tablespoons sugar
¼ teaspoon salt
1 cup zucchini, sliced thin (1 small)
½ cup finely diced celery
2 tablespoons grated onion
½ teaspoon celery seed

Dissolve gelatin in hot water; add wine, lemon juice, sugar, and salt. Stir well. Chill. When mixture begins to thicken, stir in remaining ingredients. Spoon into 6 individual oiled molds. Chill until firm.

SERVES 6

ZUCCHINI SALAD DRESSING

Keeps well in refrigerator.

8 ounces cream cheese
1 cup mayonnaise
½ teaspoon salt
1 tablespoon sugar
1 teaspoon lemon juice
1 cup zucchini, ground
1 tablespoon Worcestershire sauce
1 teaspoon dill seed

Put all ingredients except dill seed in a blender and blend until almost smooth. Remove from blender, stir in dill seed, and chill. If dressing is too thick, add milk.

MAKES 3 CUPS

ZUCCHINI BEAN SALAD

½ head lettuce, torn into small pieces
½ head romaine, torn into small pieces
2 cups zucchini, grated
1 15-ounce can kidney beans
1 cup French-style green beans
1 15-ounce can garbanzo beans
½ cup grated Monterey Jack cheese
3 green onions, minced
3 tablespoons bacon bits
Salt to taste

Toss all ingredients (except salt) lightly. Cover with your favorite salad dressing. Salt to taste.

SERVES 4 to 6

MARINATED ZUCCHINI SALAD

DRESSING

⅔ cup cider vinegar
2 tablespoons wine vinegar
⅓ cup oil
½ cup sugar
1 teaspoon salt
½ teaspoon pepper

SALAD

½ cup diced onion
½ cup chopped green pepper
½ cup diced celery
10 small zucchini, sliced thin
1 2-ounce jar diced pimiento

Combine dressing ingredients. Add onion, green pepper, celery, zucchini, and pimiento; mix. Marinate in refrigerator at least 6 hours or overnight.

SERVES 10

Side Dishes

ELLIE'S FRESH ZUCCHINI

Simple and good—lets you taste the vegetables.

1 large or 8 small zucchini
2 tablespoons butter
3 tablespoons cooking oil
1 clove garlic
¼ teaspoon sweet basil
1 tomato, cut into wedges

Slice zucchini and sauté in butter and cooking oil. Mince garlic clove, add basil to it, and sprinkle on squash. Add tomato wedges and cover. Cook slowly until tender, about 20 minutes.

SERVES 4

ZUCCHINI WITH SOUR CREAM TOPPING

8 small zucchini
Salt and pepper to taste
¾ cup sour cream
½ cup grated Cheddar cheese

Cook whole zucchini until tender, about 10 minutes. Slice cooked squash lengthwise in half and place in a baking dish. Blend salt and pepper into sour cream and spread over zucchini. Sprinkle with cheese. Broil just until cheese melts and begins to brown. Serve immediately.

SERVES 4 to 6

ZUCCHINI AND CHEESE

3 medium zucchini
1 medium onion, thinly sliced
1 tablespoon salad oil
Salt and pepper to taste
1 teaspoon crushed oregano
1 8-ounce can tomato sauce
1 8-ounce package mozzarella cheese
Parmesan cheese

Cut zucchini into 1½-inch spears lengthwise. Cook onion in oil and add zucchini halves, cut side up. Sprinkle with salt, pepper, and oregano. Pour tomato sauce over all. Cook until tender. Melt mozzarella cheese over and sprinkle Parmesan on top. Serve.

SERVES 6 to 8

FRIED ZUCCHINI

Can be an appetizer also.

2 pounds zucchini
3 eggs, beaten
3 tablespoons honey
1 teaspoon water
½ cup flour
¾ teaspoon salt
2 tablespoons celery seed
Oil

Slice zucchini about ½ inch thick. Dip in batter made from eggs, honey, water, flour, salt, and celery seed blended well. Fry zucchini slices in deep oil on medium heat just so it bubbles gently. Turn several times, piercing with a fork occasionally until it is tender. Drain and serve.

SERVES 4

FROSTED ZUCCHINI

3 medium-sized zucchini
½ cup mayonnaise
¼ cup minced green onion
3 tablespoons grated Parmesan cheese
½ teaspoon oregano leaves
⅛ teaspoon garlic powder
Dash pepper
About ¼ cup fine dry cracker crumbs

Cut zucchini crosswise into ¾-inch slices. Arrange slices in a single layer in a vegetable steamer. Cover and steam over boiling water until barely tender, about 5 minutes. Drain, cool, and blot dry.

Mix mayonnaise, green onion, Parmesan cheese, oregano, garlic powder, and pepper. Frost 1 side of each zucchini slice with the mayonnaise mixture, then dip top in cracker crumbs. Place on a cookie sheet, top side up; cover and chill, if made ahead. Let warm to room temperature, if chilled.

Broil slices about 4 inches from heat until lightly browned, about 3 to 6 minutes.

MAKES ABOUT 24 ZUCCHINI PIECES

BAKED ZUCCHINI AND PEAS WITH PUMPKIN SEEDS

Don't throw away those pumpkin seeds—they taste great with zucchini.

½ pound fresh mushrooms, sliced
2 tablespoons butter
5 medium zucchini, sliced
1 10½-ounce can mushroom soup
1 10-ounce package frozen peas, partially defrosted
1 4-ounce jar salted pumpkin seeds

Cook mushrooms in butter until slightly brown. Arrange layer of mushrooms in buttered casserole, add layer of zucchini; spread with some soup. Add a layer of peas. Repeat until all vegetables are used. Spread remaining soup on top. Cover and bake at 375° F. for 30 minutes. Remove from oven and cover with pumpkin seeds. Bake uncovered 15 minutes.

SERVES 8 to 10

SCALLOPED ZUCCHINI

2 pounds zucchini (about 6 medium)
¼ pound pork sausage (optional)
¼ cup chopped onion
½ cup (about 14) finely crushed saltines
2 slightly beaten eggs
1 teaspoon salt
½ teaspoon monosodium glutamate
⅛ teaspoon dried thyme, crushed
Dash garlic salt
½ cup grated Parmesan cheese

Scrub squash; trim ends off. Cook whole squash, covered, in boiling salted water for 15 minutes, or until just tender. Drain thoroughly, reserving ½ cup liquid; chop zucchini coarsely (you should have about 5 cups).

If using sausage, cook sausage and onion together in a 10-inch skillet over medium heat until sausage is browned and onion is tender; drain. Add squash, reserved liquid, and remaining ingredients, except 2 tablespoons of the cheese. Mix well. Turn into an ungreased 1½-quart casserole; sprinkle with the reserved cheese. Bake in a 350° F. oven 40 to 45 minutes or until set and delicately browned.

SERVES 8

ZUCCHINI SUPREME

The best name for it—it's wonderful.

6 slices bacon
4 zucchini, sliced
2 eggs, separated
1 cup sour cream
2 tablespoons flour
½ teaspoon salt
½ cup grated sharp Cheddar cheese
½ cup bread crumbs

Fry bacon until crisp. Drain; crumble. Set aside. Simmer zucchini in salted water for 10 minutes or until just tender. Drain and set aside. Beat egg whites until stiff. Set aside. Combine sour cream, egg yolks, flour, and salt. Fold into beaten egg whites.

In a 9-inch-square casserole, layer half the zucchini, half the sour cream mixture, half the cheese, and all the bacon; repeat layers of zucchini, sour cream mixture, and cheese. Sprinkle with bread crumbs. Bake at 350° F. for 20 to 25 minutes.

SERVES 6

ZUCCHINI AND CORN CASSEROLE

Can be prepared the day before.

1 pound zucchini
½ green pepper, minced

1 small onion, minced
Oil
1 tablespoon flour, rounded
1 cup milk
2 egg yolks
1 3-ounce can cream-style corn
Salt and pepper
Cracker crumbs from 3 to 4 crackers, buttered

Cook zucchini whole for 5 minutes. Slice zucchini thin.

Sauté green pepper and onion in a little oil. To this add the flour and the milk blended with egg yolks. Cook sauce until thick.

Mix the corn and zucchini and put into a greased baking dish. Pour sauce over it. Salt and pepper to taste. Spread buttered cracker crumbs on top. Bake at 350° F. for 30 to 40 minutes.

SERVES 8

NANA'S TOMATO-ZUCCHINI CASSEROLE

3 medium zucchini, sliced
1 large onion, diced
3 medium tomatoes, sliced
4 anchovy filets, cut up
1 tablespoon capers
1 clove garlic, minced
1 teaspoon salt
2 tablespoons basil
Pepper to taste
½ cup Parmesan cheese
Butter

In a greased dish, layer half of the zucchini, onions, and tomatoes. Top with half of the anchovies; sprinkle half of the remaining ingredients over all. Repeat layers. Bake uncovered at 375° F. for 35 to 45 minutes.

SERVES 6 to 8

ZUCCHINI CASSEROLE

The mozzarella and spaghetti sauce mix give this a wonderful Italian flavor.

2½ pounds zucchini cut into ⅜-inch slices (8 cups)
½ cup chopped onion
½ cup chopped green pepper
4 tablespoons butter
1 3-ounce can sliced mushrooms, drained
1 package dry spaghetti sauce mix
1 cup water
1 6-ounce can tomato paste
1 4-ounce package shredded mozzarella cheese
2 tablespoons grated Parmesan cheese

Cook zucchini 4 to 5 minutes in boiling, salted water; remove from pan and drain well. In the same pan cook onion and green pepper in butter until tender, but not brown. Remove from heat and stir in mushrooms, dry spaghetti sauce mix, water, and tomato paste. Mix. Stir in zucchini and mozzarella cheese. Put into a 10″ × 6″ × 2″ baking dish or a 1½-quart casserole. Sprinkle with Parmesan cheese. Bake at 350° F. for 30 to 35 minutes.

SERVES 6 to 8

MIXED VEGETABLE-ZUCCHINI SAUTÉ

Goes well with beef.

2 tablespoons butter or margarine
1 teaspoon chili powder
1 pound zucchini, cut into ¼-inch slices
¼ pound mushrooms, sliced
1 medium-sized green pepper, seeded and sliced
2 tablespoons water
Garlic salt and pepper
½ cup thinly sliced green onion
12 to 16 cherry tomatoes, halved
1 cup shredded Swiss cheese
1 firm ripe avocado

Melt butter in a wide stove-to-table frying pan or casserole dish over medium heat. Stir in chili powder, then add zucchini, mushrooms, and green pepper. Add the water, cover, and steam 3 to 4 minutes or until vegetables are just tender when pierced; stir several times. Season to taste with garlic salt and pepper, then gently stir in the green onions and tomatoes.

Sprinkle cheese over vegetable mixture, cover pan, and steam for about 1 minute or until cheese is melted. Meanwhile, quickly peel, pit, and slice avocado, arrange over top, and serve at once.

SERVES 6

MERINGUE-TOPPED VEGETABLE CUSTARD

You can substitute other squash for the zucchini if you wish.

2 tablespoons butter or margarine
6 medium-sized (2 pounds) zucchini, shredded
1 large green pepper, chopped
1 large onion, chopped
1 teaspoon salt
1 teaspoon dried basil
¼ teaspoon ground nutmeg
¼ teaspoon pepper
2 tablespoons flour
1 cup sour cream
6 eggs, separated
4 cups shredded Cheddar cheese
2 tablespoons sesame seed

In a wide frying pan, melt butter over medium-high heat. Add squash, green pepper, onion, salt, basil, nutmeg, and pepper. Cook, stirring often, until liquid evaporates, 20 to 25 minutes. Add flour and cook 1 minute. Cool.

Beat together sour cream and egg yolks. Mix into the vegetable mixture, and add 2 cups of the Cheddar cheese. Spread into a well-buttered shallow 1½-quart casserole. Beat egg whites until stiff moist peaks form. Fold in remaining 2 cups Cheddar cheese and spread over top. Sprinkle with sesame seed. Bake in a 350° F. oven until custard is set in center, 60 to 70 minutes. Let stand 10 minutes.

SERVES 6

STUFFED ZUCCHINI

6 zucchini
3 cups soft bread crumbs
1 small onion, diced
3 tablespoons parsley
1 teaspoon salt
⅛ teaspoon pepper
2 eggs, beaten
½ cup Parmesan cheese
¾ cup butter

Boil zucchini in salted water for 5 minutes. Cut each zucchini in half lengthwise. Mix bread crumbs, onion, parsley, salt, pepper, and eggs; fill squash halves. Dot each half with 1 tablespoon butter and sprinkle with Parmesan cheese. Bake at 350° F. for 30 minutes.

SERVES 8 to 10

Main Dishes

ZUCCHINI FRITTATAS

A frittata is an Italian omelet. They are thin and yummy.

7 small zucchini
3 tablespoons olive oil
2 tablespoons butter
8 eggs
1 teaspoon salt
½ teaspoon pepper, freshly ground
½ cup grated Parmesan cheese
3 ounces prosciutto (Italian ham) in small pieces (optional)

Cut zucchini into ¼-inch slices. Sauté in oil and butter until tender. Beat eggs with salt and pepper. Pour over zucchini. Cook until almost set. Sprinkle cheese and prosciutto on top. Put under broiler until cheese melts and browns slightly. To serve, cut into wedges.

SERVES 6

BUTTERFIELD'S ZUCCHINI

A vegetarian main dish served with homemade bread.

3 large zucchini
Salt
2½ cups grated Monterey Jack cheese
6 tablespoons diced green chilies
¼ cup chopped pine nuts
3 tablespoons chopped green onions
1 2½-ounce can sliced black olives
Seasoned salt

Parboil the zucchini in salted water for 3 minutes. Remove and cool, then chop off ends and slice in half lengthwise. Partially hollow out the zucchini halves and salt them. Mix together the cheese, chilies, pine nuts, green onions, and olives; heat into zucchini shells. Sprinkle with seasoned salt and place on a greased baking sheet. They may be set aside at this point. When you're ready, bake at 350°F. for 20 minutes.

SERVES 6

ZUCCHINI-CORN SOUFFLÉ

¼ cup butter or margarine
1 minced onion
3 cups shredded zucchini (about 3 small)
¼ cup flour
½ cup milk
1 9-ounce can cream-style corn
½ teaspoon salt
⅛ teaspoon pepper
1 cup shredded Swiss cheese
¼ cup grated Parmesan cheese
8 eggs, separated

In a 3-quart pan, melt butter or margarine over medium heat. Add minced onion; sauté until soft. Stir in zucchini and cook over high heat until limp, about 5 minutes. Drain off liquid.

Stir in flour until well mixed. Gradually stir in milk and cook, stirring constantly, until mixture boils and thickens. Add corn, salt, pepper, Swiss cheese, and Parmesan cheese; stir until cheeses melt. Remove from heat and beat in 8 egg yolks with a wooden spoon.

Beat 8 egg whites until moist, soft peaks form; carefully fold into sauce. Pour into a 2- or 2½-quart dish that has been well greased and dusted with grated Parmesan cheese. Bake in a 375°F. oven for 45 to 50 minutes or until a wooden pick inserted comes out clean.

SERVES 4 to 5

ZUCCHINI TOSTADAS

Oil
8 6-inch tortillas
1½ cups cooked kidney or pinto beans
½ pound grated Monterey Jack or Cheddar cheese
2 cups cooked, diced potatoes
½ small onion, thinly sliced
3 tablespoons oil
2 tablespoons red wine vinegar
Salt and pepper
1½ cups diced zucchini
6 cups shredded lettuce or cabbage
1 cup sliced radishes

GARNISHES

Guacamole
Fresh tomato sauce
Sour cream
Lemon or lime wedges

Heat ¼-inch oil in small frying pan until very hot. Fry 1 tortilla at a time and turn so that it fries crisp and puffs slightly. Blot with paper towels.

Heat beans and divide among fried tortillas. Sprinkle beans with cheese and put under the broiler until cheese melts.

Toss together potatoes and onions with oil and vinegar; salt and pepper lightly. Divide among tortillas and top with zucchini, lettuce or cabbage, and radishes.

Serve with guacamole, fresh tomato sauce, sour cream, and lemon or lime wedges.

MAKES 8 TOSTADAS

ZUCCHINI QUICHE

2 tablespoons butter or margarine
1 pound zucchini, trimmed and coarsely chopped
½ cup sliced onion
¾ teaspoon salt, divided
½ teaspoon oregano
¼ teaspoon basil
¾ cup shredded Swiss cheese
1 baked 9-inch pie shell
1½ cups half-and-half
1½ teaspoons cornstarch
3 eggs
Pinch nutmeg
Dash liquid hot pepper sauce

Melt butter or margarine in a large skillet over medium heat. Add zucchini, onion, ½ teaspoon salt, oregano, and basil. Cook and stir until zucchini is tender, about 5 minutes. Increase heat and continue to cook until moisture is completely evaporated, stirring occasionally. Remove from heat. Toss with cheese and immediately distribute evenly on bottom of pie shell.

In a bowl, mix half-and-half with cornstarch. Beat in eggs, nutmeg, hot pepper sauce, and remaining salt. Pour into pie shell. Bake at 400° F. until set and lightly browned on top, about 25 minutes. Serve hot or at room temperature.

SERVES 6

IMPOSSIBLE RATATOUILLE PIE

Vegetarian main dish.

1 cup chopped zucchini
1 cup chopped pared eggplant
½ cup chopped tomato
½ cup chopped green pepper
¼ cup chopped onion
1 medium clove garlic, crushed
¼ cup margarine or butter
¾ teaspoon salt
⅛ teaspoon pepper
½ teaspoon dried thyme leaves
½ teaspoon dried basil leaves
1 cup shredded Monterey Jack cheese
1¼ cups milk
¼ cup dairy sour cream
¾ cup Bisquick baking mix
3 eggs

Heat oven to 400° F. Lightly grease a 10″ × 1½″ pie plate.

Cook zucchini, eggplant, tomato, green pepper, onion, and garlic in margarine in a 10-inch skillet over medium heat, stirring occasionally, until vegetables are crisp-tender, 5 to 10 minutes. Stir in salt, pepper, thyme, and basil. Spread in pie plate; sprinkle with cheese.

Beat remaining ingredients until smooth, 15 seconds in blender on high speed or 1 minute with hand beater. Pour into pie plate. Bake until knife inserted halfway between center and edge comes out clean, 30 to 35 minutes. Let stand 5 minutes. Refrigerate any remaining pie.

SERVES 4 to 6

SPAGHETTI FOR SUMMER

A quick-to-fix vegetable pasta dish, for a summer dinner party.

1 cup sliced zucchini
1½ cups broken broccoli
1½ cups snow peas

1 cup baby peas
6 sliced asparagus spears
1 pound spaghetti
12 cherry tomatoes, cut in half
3 tablespoons olive oil
2 teaspoons minced garlic, divided
¼ cup Italian parsley
Salt and pepper
10 sliced mushrooms
⅓ cup pine nuts
⅓ cup butter
½ cup fresh grated Parmesan cheese
1 cup heavy cream
⅓ cup chopped fresh basil
⅓ cup chicken consommé (optional)

Blanch zucchini, broccoli, peas, and asparagus. Drain and refresh under cold water. Cook spaghetti until al dente (firm to the bite), 8 to 10 minutes. Sauté tomatoes in 1 tablespoon olive oil with 1 teaspoon garlic and chopped parsley. Add salt, pepper, and mushrooms.

In another large skillet sauté pine nuts. Add the rest of the garlic and the parboiled vegetables. Simmer until hot.

In a pan large enough to hold all ingredients melt butter, add cheese, cream, and basil. Stir and melt cheese. Add pasta and toss. If sauce is too thick, add the consommé. Add about ⅓ of the vegetables. Toss again. Divide among 6 soup bowls and top with the remaining vegetables and tomatoes.

SERVES 6

BECKY'S ZUCCHINI LASAGNE

May be frozen after preparation.

2 cloves garlic, minced
½ cup chopped onion
2 tablespoons olive oil
½ pound ground beef
1 1-pound can tomatoes
1 6-ounce can tomato paste
1 4-ounce can sliced mushrooms
¾ cup dry red wine
1½ teaspoons oregano
¼ teaspoon thyme
½ teaspoon basil
Salt and pepper to taste
4 large zucchini
8 ounces mozzarella cheese, thinly sliced
8 ounces ricotta cheese, crumbled
½ cup grated Parmesan cheese

Sauté garlic and onion in oil until vegetables are tender but not brown. Add meat and stir to keep crumbly until browned. Add tomatoes, tomato paste, mushrooms, wine, oregano, thyme, basil, salt, and pepper. Simmer, uncovered, for 1½ hours.

Oil a shallow casserole. Cut zucchini into strips ¼ inch thick and place half in bottom of casserole. Top with half the mozzarella and ricotta. Add half of the meat sauce. Repeat layers. Top with Parmesan cheese. Bake uncovered at 350°F. for 30 minutes.

SERVES 6

DEEP-DISH ZUCCHINI PIZZA

One of the best pizzas you'll ever eat.

1 pound zucchini, thinly sliced
1 clove garlic, minced
3 tablespoons oil
½ teaspoon basil
½ teaspoon oregano
½ teaspoon salt
2 teaspoons fresh parsley, minced
1 8-ounce can crescent rolls
2 eggs, beaten
1 8-ounce can tomato paste
1 cup grated Mozzarella cheese
½ pound hot Italian sausage, *or* ¼ pound pepperoni, thinly sliced

Sauté zucchini and garlic in oil. Add basil, oregano, salt, and parsley. Place triangles of crescent roll dough in a deep, ungreased, pyrex

9-inch pie pan. Press pieces together to form a crust. Spread on zucchini and spice mixture evenly. Pour on beaten eggs. Bake for 15 minutes at 325° F. Then pour on tomato sauce and sprinkle with cheese. If using Italian sausage, brown first, then sprinkle over top of pizza. With pepperoni, place slices evenly over top of pizza.

Bake another 25 minutes at 325° F.

SERVES 4

MEXICAN LENTIL-ZUCCHINI BURGERS

You can freeze these up to a month.

1 cup water
1¼ teaspoons salt, divided
⅓ cup lentils
1 pound ground beef
½ cup finely chopped onions
½ cup nonfat dry milk
½ cup shredded zucchini
¼ teaspoon pepper
1 tablespoon Worcestershire sauce
1 teaspoon ground cumin

In a pan, bring water with ¼ teaspoon salt to a boil. Add lentils and simmer, covered, until tender enough to mash easily, about 30 minutes. Drain, then mash with a fork. Combine with ground beef, onion, dry milk, zucchini, remaining 1 teaspoon salt, pepper, Worcestershire, and cumin. Mix with your hands to thoroughly blend. Form meat mixture into 6 equal portions and shape into patties about ¾ inch thick.

Broil patties 2 to 3 inches from heat source (or on a greased grill about 6 inches above glowing coals) about 6 minutes on each side for medium rare. Or cook in a greased frying pan over medium-high heat, about 4 to 5 minutes on each side.

MAKES 6 PATTIES

STUFFED ZUCCHINI MEAT LOAF

1 large zucchini (about 12 inches long)
1 pound lean ground beef
½ pound sausage
½ cup chopped onion
½ cup chopped celery
¼ cup chopped bell pepper
1 small can tomato sauce
1 egg
1 cup bread crumbs, *or* 1 cup cooked rice (brown is best)
1½ teaspoons salt

Cut zucchini in half lengthwise. Clean out seeds and puncture pulp with a fork several times.

Brown meats. Sauté onion, celery, and bell pepper. Combine tomato sauce, egg, bread crumbs, and salt. Mix meats, onion mixture, and sauce together. Fill each half of zucchini with meat mixture, mounding to outer edge. Place in a 9″ × 12″ pan with 1 inch of water in bottom of pan. Bake at 350° F. until tender, about 45 minutes. Slice and serve.

SERVES 6 to 8

STUFFED ZUCCHINI FOR THE BARBECUE

A good way to use that giant zucchini hidden in your garden. You can tell if it is still tender—the skin can be easily pierced.

1 giant zucchini (6 to 7 pounds—about 18 inches)
2 tablespoons melted butter
Garlic salt
2 pounds lean ground lamb (or lean beef ground round)
2 cups cooked brown rice
2 eggs
1 large onion
½ cup tomato-based chili sauce (see "Tomatoes" for some great recipes)

2 cloves garlic, minced
2 teaspoons dried basil
2 teaspoons dried oregano
2 teaspoons Worcestershire sauce
½ teaspoon salt
½ teaspoon pepper
½ cup grated Parmesan cheese

About 2 hours before you plan to eat, ignite 30 to 40 briquets in a barbecue that has a lid. When covered with gray ash (30 to 45 minutes), bank the coals on either side of the fire grate and place a drip pan in the center.

Cut zucchini in half lengthwise. Scoop out and discard seeds and fibrous material. Then score flesh in 1-inch squares, cutting only halfway through to outer skin. Brush flesh with melted butter or margarine and sprinkle lightly with garlic salt; set aside.

Combine lean ground lamb, rice, eggs, onion, tomato-based chili sauce, garlic, basil, oregano, Worcestershire, salt, and pepper. Mound meat mixture in zucchini halves.

Place zucchini on grill directly above drip pan and sprinkle evenly with Parmesan cheese. Cover barbecue, and adjust dampers according to manufacturer's directions. Cook 1¼ to 1½ hours, or until meat is no longer pink when slashed.

SERVES 8 to 10

Breads and Pancakes

SPICY ZUCCHINI BREAD

Stays very moist.

3 eggs
1 cup vegetable oil
2 cups sugar
2 teaspoons vanilla
2 cups fresh, grated zucchini
1 8-ounce can drained, crushed pineapple
3 cups unsifted flour
2 teaspoons soda
1 teaspoon salt
½ teaspoon cinnamon
¾ teaspoon nutmeg
1 cup chopped nuts (optional)

Mix eggs to blend; add oil, sugar, and vanilla. Continue beating until thick and foamy. With a spoon, stir in zucchini and pineapple. Combine flour, soda, salt, cinnamon, and nutmeg; stir until blended. Add nuts, if desired. Blend. Put batter in 2 greased loaf pans. Bake at 350°F. for 1 hour.

If you prefer, you may delete the pineapple and increase the zucchini. However, the pineapple gives a more moist bread.

MAKES 2 LOAVES

NANA'S ZUCCHINI BREAD

This great recipe of Nana's never fails to be moist and delicious.

2 eggs
⅔ cup vegetable oil
1⅓ cups sugar
2 teaspoons vanilla
1⅓ cups grated, peeled zucchini
2 cups flour
½ teaspoon baking powder
2 teaspoons soda
¼ teaspoon salt
½ teaspoon nutmeg
½ to 1 cup nuts, if desired

Mix eggs to blend; add oil, sugar, and vanilla. Beat until thickened. Stir in zucchini; then add flour, baking powder, soda, salt, and nutmeg. Add nuts if desired. Bake at 350°F. in a well-greased tube pan until bread tests done.

Variation: Exclude spices and add 4 squares bitter chocolate—makes a moist chocolate cake. Bake in a tube pan.

MAKES 1 10-INCH TUBE PAN LOAF

ZUCCHINI CORN BREAD

You can use white flour for a lighter bread.

¾ cup whole wheat flour (or white flour)
¾ cup cornmeal
1½ teaspoons baking powder
½ teaspoon salt
1 egg, beaten
2 tablespoons oil
1 tablespoon honey
¾ cup milk
¾ cup zucchini, ground

Combine flour, cornmeal, baking powder, and salt. Beat egg, oil, honey, and milk together. Add zucchini and liquid mixture to dry ingredients; stir well. Pour batter into an oiled 9″ × 9″ pan. Bake 25 minutes in a 400°F. oven.

SERVES 9

ZUCCHINI PANCAKES

2 eggs, beaten
1 cup milk
1 tablespoon honey
3 tablespoons oil
1 cup ground zucchini
1½ cups whole wheat flour
1 tablespoon baking powder
¾ teaspoon salt
Butter and honey for syrup

Combine eggs with milk, honey, and oil. Add zucchini, then sifted flour, baking powder, and salt, stirring very little. Spoon batter onto lightly greased griddle at medium heat. Melt together equal amounts of butter and honey to use as syrup. Serve warm.

MAKES 4 4-INCH PANCAKES

Desserts

GOOD FOR YOU ZUCCHINI COOKIES

The best cookies you'll find—kids love them, adults delight in the flavor and ingredients.

1½ cups flour
½ teaspoon salt
1 teaspoon baking soda
½ teaspoon nutmeg
½ teaspoon cinnamon
¼ teaspoon cloves
½ cup margarine
1 cup ground zucchini
⅔ cup honey
1 egg, beaten
½ cup rolled oats
1 cup dates, finely chopped
1 cup walnuts, chopped
½ cup shredded coconut (optional)

Stir together flour, salt, baking soda, nutmeg, cinnamon, and cloves. In another bowl, combine margarine, zucchini, honey, and egg. Combine zucchini mixture with dry ingredients. Add rolled oats, dates, walnuts, and coconut. Drop by heaping spoonfuls onto an oiled cookie sheet. Bake at 325°F. for 15 minutes or until cookies are golden.

MAKES 2 DOZEN

CHOCOLATE ZUCCHINI CAKE

Rich, elegant, and good.

½ cup soft shortening
½ cup oil
1¾ cups sugar
2 eggs
1 teaspoon vanilla
½ cup sour milk
2½ cups flour

2 tablespoons cocoa
1 teaspoon soda
½ teaspoon baking powder
½ teaspoon cinnamon
½ teaspoon cloves
4 tablespoons Nestle's Quik
2 cups zucchini, shredded
½ cup chocolate chips

GLAZE

1 cup powdered sugar
1 teaspoon cinnamon
Water

Cream together shortening, oil, and sugar. Then add eggs, vanilla, and sour milk, beating them together well. Combine flour, cocoa, soda, baking powder, cinnamon, cloves, and Nestle's Quik, and add in, beating well. Stir in zucchini. Pour into a greased 9″ × 13″ pan and sprinkle the top with-chocolate chips. Bake at 325° F. for 50 to 60 minutes.

Prepare glaze. Combine powdered sugar and cinnamon and add enough water to make a runny glaze. Spread over warm cake.

SERVES 6 to 8

ZUCCHINI DATE TORTE

2 eggs, beaten
1 cup brown sugar
1 tablespoon oil
1 teaspoon vanilla
½ teaspoon salt
1 teaspoon cinnamon
¾ cup flour
2½ teaspoons baking powder
2 cups zucchini, grated
1 cup dates, diced
½ cup chopped walnuts
Whipped cream

Beat eggs, brown sugar, oil, vanilla, salt, and cinnamon in a bowl. Slowly stir in flour and baking powder, which have been combined. Stir in zucchini, dates, and walnuts. Pour into a greased 9″ × 9″ pan. Bake at 350° F. for 60 minutes. Let sit for 1 hour before serving. Cut into squares. Serve with whipped cream.

SERVES 9

ZUCCHINI SPICE PIE

Like a pumpkin pie.

¾ cup brown sugar
1½ cups ground zucchini, well drained
1½ cups evaporated milk
2 tablespoons molasses
¼ teaspoon nutmeg
1 tablespoon flour
½ teaspoon salt
1 teaspoon ginger
1½ teaspoons cinnamon
½ teaspoon cloves
2 eggs
1 9-inch pastry shell, unbaked

Put all filling ingredients in a blender. Blend at high speed for at least 1 minute. Pour into an unbaked pastry-lined 9-inch pie pan. Bake at 450° F. for 10 minutes; then lower oven to 350° F. and bake for an additional 45 minutes.

SERVES 6 to 8

Pickles and Relishes

ZUCCHINI PICKLES

4 to 5 quarts cut zucchini, peeled
3 large green bell peppers, sliced
5 large yellow onions, sliced or chopped
3 red peppers, *or* 2 4-ounce jars pimientos
½ cup salt
2 to 3 trays ice cubes
5 cups sugar
5 cups white vinegar
3 teaspoons mustard seed
3 teaspoons celery seed
1 teaspoon turmeric

Cover zucchini, green peppers, onions, and red peppers with salt and ice. Let sit 3 hours. Pour off brine. Combine sugar, white vinegar, mustard seed, celery seed, and turmeric; boil pickles in this solution for 2 minutes. Pack in sterilized jars and seal.

If pimiento is used, add to hot pickling solution instead of to zucchini mixture.

MAKES 10 to 12 PINTS

DILL PICKLED ZUCCHINI

These are not as firm as cucumber pickles, but delicious.

3 quarts water
¾ cup pickling salt
1 quart cider vinegar
24 to 30 small zucchini (each 4 inches long)
¾ teaspoon dill weed
1 clove garlic
½ teaspoon alum
¼ teaspoon crushed red pepper
¾ teaspoon dill seed

Heat water, pickling salt, and vinegar to boiling. Meanwhile, fit quart jars with as many small zucchini as possible. To each jar add dill weed, garlic, alum, red pepper, and dill seed. Pour hot liquid into jars. Seal with lids. Put in canning pot with lids immersed in water, simmering for 15 minutes. Take out. Best to let sit for at least 2 weeks before serving.

MAKES 6 to 7 PINTS

ZUCCHINI BREAD 'N' BUTTER PICKLES

Let these age a while for the best flavor.

1 quart apple cider vinegar
3½ cups sugar
3 tablespoons pickling salt
2 teaspooons celery seed
1 teaspoon turmeric
2 teaspoons mustard seed
4 quarts zucchini, sliced ¼ inch thick
1 quart onions, sliced ¼ inch thick

Bring vinegar, sugar, salt, celery seed, turmeric, and mustard seed to a boil. Pour over freshly sliced zucchini and onion and let stand 1 hour. Bring mixture to a boil and boil 10 minutes. Pack hot into hot sterilized jars. Seal at once.

MAKES 8 to 10 PINTS

NANA'S ZUCCHINI RELISH

10 cups zucchini, ground
4 large onions, ground (4 cups)
5 tablespoons noniodized salt
2¼ cups vinegar
6 cups sugar
1 tablespoon cornstarch
2 red peppers, chopped
2 green peppers, chopped
1 tablespoon nutmeg
1 tablespoon dry mustard
1 tablespoon turmeric
1 teaspoon celery seeds
½ teaspoon pepper

Combine zucchini, onions, and salt and let stand overnight. Next day rinse with cold water and drain. Mix vinegar, sugar, cornstarch, red and green peppers, and remaining spices with zucchini-onion mixture. Cook 30 minutes. Seal in sterilized jars.

MAKES 6 to 8 PINTS

SPICY ZUCCHINI HAMBURGER RELISH

10 cups zucchini, ground
3 cups onions, ground
10 small red peppers, ground
4 green peppers, ground

5 tablespoons salt
3 cups brown sugar
1 tablespoon cornstarch
3 cups vinegar
1 teaspoon coarse black pepper
1 teaspoon turmeric
1 teaspoon dry mustard
1 teaspoon nutmeg

Combine zucchini, onions, and red and green peppers with salt and let sit overnight. Next morning rinse thoroughly and mix well with sugar, cornstarch, vinegar, and remaining spices. Boil 30 minutes. Seal in hot jars.

MAKES 6 PINTS

HOT SALSA MADE WITH ZUCCHINI

10 cups zucchini, ground
3 cups onions, ground
10 small hot red peppers, ground or finely grated
2 green peppers, ground or finely grated
5 tablespoons salt
1 cup brown sugar
1 tablespoon cornstarch
2 cups vinegar
5 cups tomatoes, ground
1 teaspoon garlic powder
1 tablespoon cumin
2 teaspoons dry mustard
1 teaspoon crushed red pepper
1 teaspoon nutmeg
1 teaspoon coarse black pepper
1 teaspoon turmeric

Combine zucchini, onions, red and green peppers, and salt; let sit overnight. Next morning rinse thoroughly, using colander or large strainer. Mix together with sugar, cornstarch, vinegar, tomatoes, and remaining spices. Mix well and boil 30 minutes. Seal in hot jars.

MAKES 8 PINTS

ZUCCHINI MARMALADE

3 pounds zucchini
4 oranges
1 lemon
¼ teaspoon soda
10 cups sugar, *or* 8 cups honey
1 6-ounce bottle fruit pectin (if you use honey, make this a 6-ounce package of dry pectin)
Paraffin

Grind zucchini, oranges, and lemon. Combine in a pan with soda and sugar. Let sit 30 minutes. Bring to a rolling boil, while stirring; then simmer 60 minutes, occasionally skimming off the foam that forms on top. Remove from heat and add pectin, stirring well. Ladle into hot jars and cover at once with ½ inch hot paraffin, or seal with canning lids.

If you use honey, follow directions above, but after adding the dry pectin, boil hard 4 minutes; then ladle into jars.

MAKES 6 PINTS

Index